More praise for *Documentary Storytelling*

Sheila Curran Bernard's *Documentary Storytelling* is an essential, pragmatic, common-sense approach to making nonfiction films for the student and/or first-time filmmaker, based on the author's deep awareness of documentary film history and theory, and her intimate knowledge of how today's most important documentarians formulate their works.
—Gerald Peary, film critic, *The Boston Phoenix*

While documentaries are nonfiction, they are certainly not objective, and even the smallest choices in writing, filming, interviewing, narrating, or scoring can drastically alter the perspective of the film, and in turn, the audience. Bernard is keenly aware of the power of persuasive images, and her insistence on complexity and integrity is a consistent theme throughout the book.
—Alyssa Worsham, *The Independent*

If you fancy yourself as a documentary film-maker, or simply want to improve your understanding of observational storytelling, buy this book, read it, and apply the ideas contained within.
—Quentin Budworth, *Focus Magazine*

Even if you consider yourself pro, it is a good read and worth the time. For the beginner it should be a required read. We can make it look great, but without a story it is nothing.
—Dan Shellenbarger, dvartdan.com

Documentary *Storytelling*. That's what this book is about. It's about the story, how to convey that story eloquently, effectively, and ethically . . . This book is absolutely brilliant . . . . packed full of interviews with award-winning documentary filmmakers offering up information, advice, and wisdom you'll find interesting and useful.
—Krista Galyen, *AAUG Reviews*

What a valuable aid to documentary filmmakers. The importance of a topic won't cut it if the story isn't told well and Bernard's book cuts right to the chase.
—Paul Stekler, producer/director, *Last Man Standing*

Documentary Storytelling

Second Edition

Documentary Storytelling

Making Stronger and More Dramatic Nonfiction Films

Second Edition

Sheila Curran Bernard

AMSTERDAM • BOSTON • HEIDELBERG • LONDON
NEW YORK • OXFORD • PARIS • SAN DIEGO
SAN FRANCISCO • SINGAPORE • SYDNEY • TOKYO

ELSEVIER

Focal Press is an imprint of Elsevier

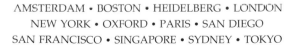

Focal
Press

Acquisitions Editor: Elinor Actipis
Project Manager: Dawnmarie Simpson
Assistant Editor: Robin Weston
Marketing Manager: Christine Degon Veroulis
Cover Design: Eric DeCicco
Cover Photograph: istockphotos.com, Philip Sigin-Lavdanski

Focal Press is an imprint of Elsevier
30 Corporate Drive, Suite 400, Burlington, MA 01803, USA
Linacre House, Jordan Hill, Oxford OX2 8DP, UK

∞ Recognizing the importance of preserving what has been written, Elsevier prints its books on acid-free paper whenever possible.

Library of Congress Cataloging-in-Publication Data
Bernard, Sheila Curran.
  Documentary storytelling: making stronger and more dramatic nonfiction films/Sheila Curran Bernard.
    p. cm.
  Rev. ed. of: Documentary storytelling for film and videomakers. 2004.
  Includes bibliographical references and index.
  ISBN-13: 978-0-240-80875-8 (pbk. : alk. paper)
  ISBN-10: 0-240-80875-4 (pbk. : alk. paper)   1.   Documentary films—Production and direction.   2.   Documentary films—Authorship.   I.   Bernard, Sheila Curran. Documentary storytelling for film and videomakers.   II.   Title.
PN1995.9.D6B394 2007
070.1′8—dc22

                                                                        2006030461

British Library Cataloguing-in-Publication Data
A catalogue record for this book is available from the British Library.

ISBN 13: 978-0-240-80875-8
ISBN 10: 0-240-80875-4

For information on all Focal Press publications
visit our website at www.books.elsevier.com

Printed in the United States of America

07   08   09   10   10   9   8   7   6   5   4   3   2   1

Working together to grow
libraries in developing countries

www.elsevier.com | www.bookaid.org | www.sabre.org

ELSEVIER   **BOOK AID**
                  International   **Sabre Foundation**

In memory of Henry Hampton

Table of Contents

Preface to the Second Edition

Documentaries are many things to many people, often simultaneously. They are a form of self expression, like novels, songs, or paintings. They are a form of journalism, independent and unmediated. They are tools for bridging the divide between cultures or exposing the harsh realities of a volatile world. They inspire, motivate, educate, exacerbate, and entertain. Documentaries reflect all that is great, challenging, disturbing, and humorous about the human condition. But first, they must reach an audience. Within these pages, you'll find strategies for accomplishing this through storytelling, the crafting of a unique narrative that conveys not only the film's subject but also its themes and authorship, and does so honestly.

This new edition contains about 20 percent new material, with some previous content revised or removed to keep the book at an affordable length. Updated content includes an examination of new films, more discussion of independent, lower-budget work, an expanded look at international approaches to storytelling, and additional filmmaker interviews.

ACKNOWLEDGMENTS

Since the first edition was published, I had the opportunity to serve as the Anschutz Distinguished Fellow at Princeton University. The semester was valuable in shaping many of the ideas contained in this new edition, and I am grateful to my students and to Sean Wilentz and Judith Ferszt of Princeton's American Studies program. Special thanks also go to those whose interviews appear in these pages (listed in Sources and Notes in Part V), and to Paula Apsell, Barbara Decharo, Martha Fowlkes,

Peter Frumkin, Jim Gilmore, Robert Lavelle, Xan Parker, Terry Rockefeller, Kate Roth, Susanne Simpson, Bennett Singer, Eric Stange, and Melanie Wallace. Thanks to Deborah Schneider and Cathy Gleason at Gelfman-Schneider, and to manuscript reviewers including Debbie Brodsky, Valerie Brown, Jennifer Lawson, Peter Lutze, Michael Ogden, Geoff Poister, and Linda Sever. Special thanks to the team at Focal Press, especially Elinor Actipis, senior acquisitions editor, for their guidance and support through both editions. For everything else, I need to thank my parents, David and Kathleen Bernard; my sisters, brother, and their families; and Joel D. Scheraga.

Sheila Curran Bernard
October 2006

Introduction

1

These are exciting times for documentary films and filmmakers. Changes in technology and the way media is produced and consumed are creating new opportunities, and documentary stories are finding new audiences both locally and globally. Not just documentary films, documentary *stories*. Look at the films that have been winning acclaim recently at Cannes, at the Academy Awards, in Banff and Berlin and Bergen. *Born into Brothels. Grizzly Man. March of the Penguins. Super Size Me.* These films succeed not because they're important or inspiring or because they motivate action and activism. They succeed—and they often *are* important, inspirational, and motivational—because they grab audiences and take them on an unforgettable journey. They do this through story.

Documentary storytelling involves a range of creative choices about a film's structure, point of view, balance, style, casting, and more. No matter what your specific role—producer, director, writer, editor, cinematographer, researcher, commissioning editor, or executive producer—decisions about storytelling will confront you throughout your career. Storytelling lies at the heart of most good documentaries: strong characters, compelling tension, a credible resolution. It's a must for many, if not most, programmers and financiers, especially those seeking to reach national or international audiences. But even local and specialized productions, which may have built-in audiences (students, museum-goers, employees), can be made stronger through better storytelling, usually at no extra expense and sometimes at lower cost.

Yet how do documentary filmmakers learn to tell strong and competitive stories? Bookstore shelves are crowded with guides

1

to story and structure in dramatic filmmaking, many of which are excellent. But documentarians work with fact, not fiction; we're not free to invent plot points or character arcs and instead must find them in the raw material of real life. Our stories depend not on creative invention but on creative *arrangement*, and our storytelling must be done without sacrificing journalistic integrity. It's a tall order.

To that end, this book offers some basics of documentary storytelling—what it is, how it's done, and what mistakes to look out for. It also offers a range of examples to demonstrate that good storytelling is a strategy, not a blueprint. *Grizzly Man* is a very different film, for example, than *The Boys of Baraka*, and yet both tell strong, memorable stories. Understanding what story is and how it works to your advantage is a step toward finding your own creative voice as a filmmaker.

DEFINING DOCUMENTARY

Documentaries bring viewers into new worlds and experiences through the presentation of factual information about real people, places, and events, generally portrayed through the use of actual images and artifacts. A presidential candidate in Colombia is kidnapped (*The Kidnapping of Ingrid Betancourt*); children in Calcutta are given cameras and inspired to move beyond their limited circumstances *(Born into Brothels)*; executives and traders at Enron play fast and loose with ethics and the law (*Enron: The Smartest Guys in the Room*). But factuality alone does not define documentary films; it's what the filmmaker does with those factual elements, weaving them into an overall narrative that strives to be as compelling as it is truthful and is often greater than the sum of its parts. "The documentarist has a passion for what he finds in images and sounds—which always seem to him more meaningful than anything he can invent," wrote Erik Barnouw in his 1974 book, *Documentary*. "Unlike the fiction artist, he is dedicated to *not* inventing. It is in selecting and arranging his findings that he expresses himself."

Story is the device that enables this arrangement. A story may begin as an idea, hypothesis, or series of questions. It becomes more focused throughout the filmmaking process, until the finished film has a compelling beginning, an unexpected middle, and a satisfying end. Along the way, the better you understand your story, even as it's evolving, the more prepared you'll be to tell it creatively and well. The visuals you shoot will be stronger. You're likely to cast and scout locations more carefully and waste less time filming scenes that aren't necessary. And perhaps surprisingly, you'll be better prepared to follow the unexpected—to take advantage of the twists and turns that are an inevitable part of documentary production, and recognize those elements that will make your film even stronger.

DOCUMENTARY AS A SUBSET OF NONFICTION FILM AND VIDEO

Think of the range of nonfiction material available in a bookstore. There are magazines aimed at special interests and ages. There are manuals with instructions for building furniture or running software. Some nonfiction books are created quickly to meet time-sensitive market interest. Others take years to research and craft. One book on a topic might be heavily illustrated and superficial; another, on the same topic, might be a Pulitzer Prize–winner with a gripping narrative that appeals to even the general reader.

This same kind of variety exists in the world of nonfiction media. The crowded schedule of televised "reality" programs includes how-to shows, game shows, and shows involving manufactured social experiments (such as contestants living in isolation or temporarily swapping homes or even spouses). Camera crews travel with bounty hunters, police officers, and animal rescue personnel. Stories of predators and prey, autopsies, haunted houses, deadly weather, and celebrities may intrigue viewers, but often offer little in the way of substance. And certainly, there are programs interspersed in these schedules that satisfy Barnouw's definition of documentary, although they vary widely when it comes to artistry, depth, or import.

At their best, documentaries should do more than help viewers pass the time; they should demand their active engagement, challenging them to think about what they know, how they know it, and what more they might want to learn. A good documentary confounds our expectations, pushes boundaries, and takes us into worlds—both literal worlds and worlds of ideas—that we did not anticipate entering. To do this, they generally must grab us first by playing on our very basic desire for a good story well told. When the audience is caught up in a life-and-death struggle for a union (*Harlan County, U.S.A.*), in Mick Jagger's futile efforts to calm the crowd at a free Rolling Stones concert (*Gimme Shelter*), or in the story of a family's rift over whether or not a deaf child should be given a chance to hear (*Sound and Fury*), there is nothing as powerful as a documentary. Some documentaries have surprising impact. Jeanne Jordan and Steven Ascher learned that their film, *Troublesome Creek*, about the efforts of Jordan's parents to save their Iowa farm from foreclosure, had influenced farming policy in Australia; Jon Else's *Cadillac Desert*, the story of water and the transformation of nature in the American West, was screened to inform policy makers on Capitol Hill.

Whether they entertain, inform, or both, documentaries matter. Nick Fraser, commissioning editor for the BBC's *Storyville*, compares the best of today's documentaries to the New Journalism that emerged in the United States in the 1960s. "As a journalistic premise, the idea that someone did the reporting took root in these years," he wrote in an article published in *Critical Quarterly* (and discusses further in Chapter 20 of this book). "By making it possible for individual voices to exist, the New Journalism countered the growing power of corporate expression."

SUBJECTIVITY

The power of documentary films comes from the fact that they are grounded in fact, not fiction. This is not to say that they're "objective." Like *any* form of communication, whether spoken, written, painted, or photographed, documentary filmmaking involves the communicator in making choices. It's therefore unavoidably subjective, no matter how balanced or neutral the presentation seeks to be. Which stories are being told, why, and by whom? What information or material is included or excluded? What choices are made concerning style, tone, point of view, and format? "To be sure, some documentarists claim to be 'objective,'" noted Barnouw, "a term that seems to renounce an interpretive role. The claim may be strategic but is surely meaningless."

Within that subjectivity, however, there are some basic ethical guidelines for documentary filmmaking. Audiences trust documentaries—and that trust is key to the film's power and relevance. Betray that trust by implying that important events happened in a way that they did not, selecting only those facts that support your argument, or bending the facts in service of a more "dramatic" story, and you've undermined the form and your film. This doesn't mean that you can't have and present a very strong and overt point of view, or, for that matter, that you can't create work that is determinedly neutral. It does means that your argument or neutrality needs to be grounded in accuracy.

WHO WANTS DOCUMENTARY STORIES?

In today's documentary marketplace, nearly everyone is looking for strong stories. A small sampling:

- From the website for the Sundance Documentary Fund: "In supporting independent vision and creative, compelling stories, the Sundance Documentary Fund hopes to give voice to the diverse exchange of ideas crucial to developing an open society" (www.Sundance.org)
- From the Discovery Channel website for producers, a list of "Required Materials" includes: "One- to two-page treatment that describes the proposed program, story line, visual approach, acts, and production team" (http://discovery.com/utilities/about/submissions/faq.html)
- From Channel 4's "Documentary Briefing" (May 2006), Commissioning Editor Meredith Chambers: *"Cutting Edge* can take the form of a present-tense adventure story . . . a single-narrative story where people go abroad, in the wider sense, to do something extraordinary, and where we do not know the outcome at the start of filming. This is where the risk is, and it should be clear we have taken that. Something inherent in the situation is going to unfold in a way that cannot help but be interesting." (www.channel4.com/corporate/4producers/commissioning/documents/Docs2006.pdf)
- From the website for the National Endowment for the Humanities, which funds American public media: "NEH

... seeks to fund those films that will best bring the issues, approaches, and materials of the humanities to broad public audiences. Producers should have a well-thought-out story outline, define the target audience, and have a strong commitment to the project" (www.neh.gov)

WHO TELLS DOCUMENTARY STORIES?

The range and breadth of documentary filmmaking worldwide is actually quite astonishing. Some documentary filmmakers work within production houses or stations. In the United States, many work independently, with varying degrees of financial and technical support from national or local governments, commissioning stations or broadcast venues, and/or foundations and corporations. Some filmmakers work to reach regional or local audiences, including community groups; others strive for national theatrical or broadcast release and acclaim at prestigious film festivals worldwide.

A common element at all levels of production is story. In 1992, for example, musician Peter Gabriel cofounded a group called Witness, which provides video equipment and training to people worldwide who want to document injustice as part of a struggle for human rights. The first chapter of the group's *Practical Guide for Activists*, available on the web (www.witness.org), is titled "How to Tell a Story." Filmmaker and writer Onyekachi Wambu, interviewed in Chapter 25, describes the important role of media storytelling in raising awareness of African involvement in that continent's development. At the other end of the production spectrum, some of the longest running and most influential documentary series on American public television today, including the science series *Nova* (modeled after the BBC's *Horizon*), are founded on the notion that complex ideas can best be conveyed through powerful storytelling.

STORYTELLING, NOT WRITING

Documentary storytelling does not refer specifically or exclusively to writing. Instead, it describes the conceptual process that begins at the moment an idea is raised and continues through production and postproduction. A film's author is the person (or people) with primary responsibility for the film's story and structure, which often means that person is the producer and/or director, working as or in tandem with a writer and editor. (It's unfortunate that many documentary festivals have adopted the practice, more common to dramatic features, of attributing a film to its director. Unless a film is produced, written, and directed by a single person, it is misleading to credit the director as the author. Films are invariably collaborative, and they begin with ideas and stories that often originate with producers and/or writers.) In any case, whether the film is formally written out in a progression from treatment to final script or whether it's merely outlined for the convenience of the production team, the filmmakers routinely address story issues that are familiar to other types of authors, from playwrights to novelists. "Who are your characters? What do they want? What are the stakes if they don't get it? Where is the tension? Where is the story going? Why does it matter?" And so on.

When a writer is credited on a documentary film, the job performed may vary. At times, it refers to someone integrally involved in the film's development and production; at other times, it's a credit for scripted narration. But note that there is no documentary counterpart to the lone screenwriter writing the Great American Screenplay "on spec" (unpaid), hoping to sell it to Hollywood. Documentary filmmakers may toil (unpaid) for months or years on a project, but they're pushing the entire project along, not just a script, and often the script is the last element to take shape. What people generally pitch and sell are documentary concepts, usually presented at some stage of preproduction or production as an outline, treatment, or rough cut.

ABOUT THE BOOK

The idea for this book emerged from my experiences as a documentary filmmaker, writer, and consultant on a range of projects, large and small. I've worked with established as well as emerging filmmakers on productions intended not only for broadcast and theatrical release but also for museum and classroom use.

It became clear to me that underlying issues of story and structure can generally be applied regardless of a project's style or length. It also became clear that despite the growing popularity of documentary films and filmmaking, discussion of the form was still too often clouded by misinformation and misconceptions, particularly the notion that it's better and more "real" to shoot a documentary first and find the story later.

As Susan Froemke, formerly principal filmmaker at Maysles Films, makes clear in Chapter 21, even the most committed vérité filmmakers plan for story. There may be exceptions, but in general, filmmakers who shoot first and try to figure the story out later risk missing a story entirely or realizing in the editing room that they didn't shoot the elements they need to tell the story they now want to tell. The result is likely to be a cobbled-together film in which many of the elements don't work or aren't as powerful as they might have been with a little preparation and forethought. Last-minute narration can't compensate for a flawed structure. And gimmicks and hype—whether pumped-up music, flashy editing, or hints of danger around every corner—won't be distracting enough to keep the audience from realizing that the story is weak or missing altogether.

INTENDED READERSHIP

This book is for anyone working in documentary filmmaking (and across the spectrum of nonfiction programming) who has an interest in understanding how story and structure work. It's written with both the experienced and novice filmmaker in mind, as well as people who enjoy documentaries or use them in their work. It's my hope that by understanding the storytelling choices filmmakers make, viewers will become better and more critical consumers of nonfiction programming in general. They'll have a clearer understanding of why something does or does not ring "true," why some films seem to carry greater emotional or intellectual weight, why some programs leave them feeling manipulated or bored, and how shifts in point of view or tone can change the nature of the presentation. In today's media-saturated world, media literacy is more important than ever.

FORMAT AND METHODOLOGY

The sections of this book are intended only as a guide. For instance, there may be information throughout the book—not just in the section on editing—that will prove useful to someone editing a film. Generally speaking, Part I introduces the concepts of story and structure and applies them to the initial stages of a film's conception. Part II looks further at the development of a story from idea to treatment. Part III looks at storytelling in the field and in the editing room. Part IV includes conversations about documentary storytelling with professionals whose work is diverse in both content and style, from direct cinema to archival filmmaking, and whose involvement includes creating and commissioning documentary work as well as using it to advance organizational goals. Many of those interviewed have enjoyed lengthy and distinguished careers, while others are just starting out. Additional material from these interviews and from conversations with several other filmmakers is interspersed throughout the book.

The stages of filmmaking generally described in this book are research, development, outline, treatment, shooting treatment, assembly, and assembly script, further revised as rough cut, fine cut, picture lock, and script lock. Not all films follow this path, however, and throughout the book I've tried to acknowledge the variants that exist, whether for reasons of budget, schedule, or production style. Documentaries involving extensive dramatic recreations or those driven by an underlying essay are sometimes scripted (or at least a preliminary script is drafted) prior to production. Some treatments are long documents, while others consist of a few pages submitted for the approval of an executive producer. There are also times when an event demands an immediate response from filmmakers, in which case shooting sooner rather than later is the only way to go. I trust that filmmakers can pick and choose from this information as needed to suit their circumstances.

Examples in this book that are drawn from actual films are identified as such. Otherwise, the examples were created by me for illustration purposes, and any resemblance to actual films, whether produced or proposed, is purely coincidental. At the back of the book, I've included some information on films cited, many of which are now available for purchase or rental through online vendors.

OBSERVATIONS

In preparing both editions of this book, I screened a wide variety of films and spoke with a range of filmmakers, many of whom raised the same basic points:

- The availability of lower-cost digital video technology in many ways increases the need for filmmakers to shoot smarter. It's very possible to shoot everything and end up in the editing room with nothing.
- Time is an increasingly rare commodity for filmmakers, especially during preproduction and editing. Yet time is often what enables a film to have depth, in terms of research, themes, and layers of storytelling; it can enhance creativity. As a group, we need to resist the push to turn out documentary *products*, rather than documentary films. While some excellent documentary programming is produced quickly and/or inexpensively, not all stories lend themselves to rapid or low-cost turnaround.
- Story does not have to mean three-act drama, and it definitely does not mean artificial tension that is imposed from without. Story comes organically from *within* the material and the ways in which you, the filmmaker, structure it.
- Documentary filmmakers, increasingly, offer a powerful addition to or contradiction of mainstream media. Trust your audience and give them the appropriate evidence, even—or perhaps especially—when it allows room for doubt.
- Share the humor. No matter how grim the situation or subject, audiences cannot take a program that is unrelieved misery. Watch any of the top documentaries of the past few years, and notice not only how often you're on the verge of tears, but also, even within the same film, how often you're laughing.

There are many ways to tell a quality documentary story, many stories to be told, an increasing number of filmmakers to tell them, and high-quality, lower-cost technology with which to tell them. So tell an honest story and a good one. Contribute to our understanding of who we are, where we've been, and what we might become. Be open-minded. Be rigorous. Have fun. And whether you call them "docs" or "documentaries," know that you're referring not to some old and ill-fitting stereotype of films that are dry, dull, and dutiful, but to a form of creative expression that is exciting, challenging, and dynamic.

Part I

STORY DESIGN

2

Story Basics

A *story* is the narrative, or telling, of an event or series of events, crafted in a way to interest the audience, whether they are readers, listeners, or viewers. At its most basic, a story has a beginning, middle, and end. It has compelling characters, rising tension, and conflict that reaches some sort of resolution. It engages the audience on an emotional and intellectual level, motivating viewers to want to know what happens next.

Strategies for good storytelling are not new. The Greek philosopher Aristotle first set out guidelines for what he called a "well-constructed plot" in 350 BCE, and those basics have been applied to storytelling—on stage, on the page, and on screen—ever since. Expectations about how storytelling works seem hardwired in audiences, and meeting, confounding, and challenging those expectations is no less important to the documentarian than it is to the dramatist.

Don't be confused by the fact that festivals and film schools commonly use the term *narrative* to describe only works of dramatic fiction. Most documentaries are also narrative, which simply means that they tell stories (whether or not those stories are also *narrated* is an entirely different issue). How they tell those stories and what stories they tell separates the films into subcategories of genre or style, from cinéma vérité to film noir.

A few storytelling terms:

EXPOSITION

Exposition is the information that grounds you in a story: who, what, where, when, and why. It gives audience members the tools they need to follow the story that's unfolding and, more importantly, it allows them inside the story. It doesn't mean giving away everything, just giving away what the audience needs, when the audience needs it. Exposition is occasionally discussed as something to be avoided, but it's necessary to an audience's understanding of the film, and its presentation, usually in the first act, doesn't have to be heavy-handed.

Exposition in theater used to be handled by the maid who bustled onstage at the start of a play and said, to no one in particular, or perhaps to a nearby butler, "Oh, me, I'm so very worried about the mistress, now that the master has gone off hunting with that ne'er-do-well brother of his, and without even telling her that his father, the Lord of Pembrokeshire, has arranged to sell this very house and all of its belongings before a fortnight is up!" In documentary films, the corollary might be those programs that are entirely front-loaded with narration that tells you information you're unprepared for or don't really need to know—and when you do need the information, you generally can't remember it. Front-loading also frequently occurs when filmmakers decide to put the entire backstory—all of the history leading up to the point of their story's attack—at the beginning of the film.

Exposition can be woven into a film in many ways. Sometimes expository information comes out when the people you're filming argue: "Yeah? Well, we wouldn't even be in this mess if you hadn't decided to take your paycheck to Vegas!" Sometimes it's revealed through headlines or other printed material, as some exposition is conveyed in *The Thin Blue Line*. Good narration can deftly weave exposition into a story, offering viewers just enough information to know where they are. (Voice-over material drawn from interviews can sometimes do the same thing.) Exposition can also be handled through visuals: an establishing shot of a place or sign; footage of a sheriff nailing an eviction notice on a door (*Roger & Me*); the opening moments of an auction (*Troublesome Creek*). Toys littered on a suburban lawn say "Children live here." Black bunting and a homemade shrine of flowers and cards outside a fire station say "Tragedy has occurred." A long shot of an elegantly dressed woman in a large, spare office high up in a modern building says "This woman is powerful." A man on a subway car reading an issue of *The Boston Globe* tells us where we are, as would a highway sign or a famous landmark—the Eiffel

Tower, for example. Time-lapse photography, title cards, and animation can all be used to convey exposition, sometimes with the added element of humor or surprise—think of the cartoons in *Super Size Me*.

THE NARRATIVE SPINE, OR *TRAIN*

Films move forward in time, taking audiences with them. You want the storytelling to move forward, too, and to motivate the presentation of exposition. In other words, you want the audience to be curious about the information you're giving them. When exposition involves backstory—how we got to where we are now—it's often a good idea to get a present-day story moving forward (even if the story is in the past) before looking back. This overall story—your film's narrative spine—has been described by producers Ronald Blumer and Muffie Meyer of Middlemarch Films (*Benjamin Franklin, Liberty! The American Revolution*) as the film's *train*.

The train is the element of story that drives your film forward, from the beginning to the end. Get a good train going, and you can make detours as needed for exposition, complex theory, additional characters—whatever you need. Sometimes, these detours let you seed in information that will pay off later in the film; sometimes, the detours are motivated by the train, and the audience *wants* to take a side track to learn more. Look at the case studies in Chapter 7, and you'll see how much of a documentary can be "off track" and, if the train is powerful enough, never feel like it's doing anything but moving steadily forward. The trick is to get the train going and to remember to get back on "on track" in a reasonable period of time. If you don't have a train going, those detours will seem unfocused and, more than likely, dull. Your train will be derailed.

Here's an example: You're thinking of telling a story in chronological order about this guy named Jim Jones who becomes a Pentecostal minister in Indiana and has an interracial church and it's the 1950s and—it's not very interesting. But if you pick up this same story much later in time, as a congressman goes to Guyana to rescue some Americans from what their relatives fear is a dangerous cult, and the congressman is killed while members of this cult line up to drink cyanide-spiked juice, chances are the audience will stay with you as you break away from this train to explore the decades of social, political, cultural, and even personal change that created Jim Jones and the tragedy of Jonestown. The drama is already there; it's a matter of finding the "creative arrangement," the strongest way to tell it.

In considering the train, it helps to think about drawing in an audience that doesn't know or care one way or another about the topic you're following. Some people are deeply curious about space exploration, for example, but many people aren't. If you're creating a film that you hope will reach a general audience, whether at a museum, on television, or in theaters, you need to think about how to get a story under way that will grab that audience. Then—and this is what makes you a good documentary filmmaker, not a mediocre one—you want to see how much information that story will allow you to convey even to the disinterested, because you're going to *get* them interested.

In other words, rather than pandering to the lowest common denominator—creating a breathless film about space exploration that's filled with platitudes and exciting music, but little else—your goal is to create a film that's driven by a story, one that will motivate even general viewers to *want* to know more of those details that thrill you. They'll grow to care because those details will matter to the story unfolding on screen. The train of *Super Size Me* is a 30-day McDiet, for example, but look at how much information the film conveys about nutrition and obesity. The train in *Daughter from Danang* is a reunion between an Amerasian woman and the Vietnamese mother who gave her up for adoption 22 years earlier, but in the telling you learn about social and political history during the last years of the Vietnam War.

An interesting example of a film with a less apparent train is *An Inconvenient Truth*. The film is reportedly built around a PowerPoint presentation developed by former Vice President Al Gore and presented by him to a range of audiences. We see him on a lecture tour, and these speeches (and voice-overs) are intercut with sync and voice-over from a more introspective conversation Gore had with filmmaker Davis Guggenheim about his life, career, and family. The train of this film doesn't come from the subject of global climate change, nor did the filmmakers build a train around any particular lecture tour itinerary. The train builds from Gore's first words, "I used to be the next president of the United States." The personal, introspective essay about Gore drives this film, although in terms of screen time and import, it takes a backseat to the warnings about global warming.

A good exercise is to watch a number of successful documentaries that are very different in subject and style and see if you can identify the train. You also might want to see if, given the same subject and story, you could find another train. How might it change the film's look? Length? Effectiveness?

THEME

In literary terms, *theme* is the general underlying subject of a specific story, a recurring idea that often illuminates an aspect of the human condition. *Eyes on the Prize*, in 14 hours, tells an overarching story of America's civil rights struggle. The underlying themes include race, poverty, and the power of ordinary people to accomplish extraordinary change. Themes in *The Day after Trinity*, the story of J. Robert Oppenheimer's development of the atomic bomb, include scientific ambition, the quest for power, and efforts to ensure peace and disarmament when both may be too late.

The best documentary stories, like memorable literary novels or thought-provoking dramatic features, not only engage the audience with an immediate story—one grounded in plot and character—but with themes that resonate beyond the particulars of the event being told. *Sound and Fury*, for example, is not only about a little girl and her family trying to decide if she should have an operation that might enable her to hear, it's also about universal issues of identity, belonging, and family.

"Theme is the most basic lifeblood of a film," says filmmaker Ric Burns (see also Chapter 18). "Theme tells you the tenor of your story. *This* is what this thing is about." Burns chose to tell the story of the ill-fated Donner Party and their attempt to take a shortcut to California in 1846, not because the cannibalism they resorted to would appeal to prurient viewers but because their story illuminated themes and vulnerabilities in the American character. These themes are foreshadowed in the film's opening quote from Alexis de Tocqueville, a French author who toured the United States in 1831. He wrote of the "feverish ardor" with which Americans pursue prosperity, the "shadowy suspicion that they may not have chosen the shortest route to get it," and the way in which they "cleave to the things of this world," even though death steps in, in the end. These words presage the fate of the Donner Party, whose ambitious pursuit of a new life in California will have tragic consequences.

Themes may emerge from the questions that initially drove the filmmaking. On one level, *My Architect* is about a middle-aged filmmaker's quest to know the father he lost at the age of 11, some 30 years before. But among the film's themes are impermanence and legacy. "You sort of wonder, 'After we're gone, what's left?' " Kahn says in bonus material on the film's DVD. "How much would I really find of my father out there? . . . I know there are buildings. But how much emotion, how much is really left? And I think what really kind of shocked me is how many people are still actively engaged in a relationship with him. They talk to him as if he's still here. They think of him every day. In a way I find that very heartening."

ARC

The *arc* refers to the way or ways in which the events of the story transform your characters. An overworked executive learns that his family should come first; a mousy secretary stands up for himself and takes over the company; a rag-tag group of kids that nobody ever notices wins the national chess tournament. In pursuing a goal, the protagonists learn something about themselves and their place in the world, and those lessons change them—and may, in fact, change their desire for the goal.

In documentary films, story arcs can be hard to find. Never, simply in the interest of a good story, presume to know what a character is thinking or feeling. Only present evidence of an arc if it can be substantiated by factual evidence. For example, in *The Day after Trinity*, physicist J. Robert Oppenheimer, a left-leaning intellectual, successfully develops the world's first nuclear weapons and is then horrified by the destructive powers he's helped to unleash. He spends the rest of his life trying to stop the spread of nuclear weapons and in the process falls victim to the Cold War he helped to launch; once hailed as an American hero, he is accused of being a Soviet spy.

In *The Thin Blue Line*, we hear and see multiple versions of a story that begins when Randall Adams's car breaks down on a

Saturday night and a teenager named David Harris offers him a ride. Later that night, a police officer is shot and killed by someone driving Harris's car, and Adams is charged with the murder. The deeper we become immersed in the case, the more clearly we see that Adams's imprisonment and subsequent conviction are about politics, not justice. He is transformed from a free man to a convicted felon, and that transformation challenges the viewer's assumptions about justice and the basic notion that individuals are innocent until proven guilty.

In *Murderball*, a documentary about quadriplegic athletes who compete internationally in wheelchair rugby, a few characters undergo transformations that together complement the overall film. There's Joe Soares, a hard-driving American champion now coaching for Canada, whose relationship with his son changes noticeably after he suffers a heart attack. Player Mark Zupan comes to terms with the friend who was at the wheel during the accident in which he was injured. And Keith Cavill, recently injured, adjusts to his new life and even explores wheelchair rugby. All of these transformations occurred over the course of filming, and the filmmakers made sure they had the visual material they needed to *show* them in a way that felt organic and unforced.

PLOT AND CHARACTER

Films are often described as either plot or character driven. A *character-driven* film is one in which the action of the film emerges from the wants and needs of the characters. In a *plot-driven* film, the characters are secondary to the events that make up the plot. (Many thrillers and action movies are plot driven.) In documentary, both types of films exist, and there is much gray area between them. Errol Morris's *The Thin Blue Line* imitates a plot-driven *noir* thriller in its exploration of the casual encounter that leaves Randall Adams facing the death penalty. Circumstances act *upon* Adams; he doesn't set the plot in motion except inadvertently, when his car breaks down and he accepts a ride from David Harris. In fact, part of the film's power comes from Adams's inability to alter events, even as it becomes apparent that Harris, not Adams, is likely to be the killer.

In contrast, *Daughter from Danang* is driven by the wants of its main character, Heidi Bub, who was born in Vietnam and given up for adoption. Raised in Tennessee and taught to deny her Asian heritage, Bub is now estranged from her adoptive mother. She sets the events of the film in motion when she decides to reunite with her birth mother.

As in these two examples, the difference between plot- and character-driven films can be subtle, and one often has strong elements of the other. The characters in *The Thin Blue Line* are distinct and memorable; the plot in *Daughter from Danang* is strong and takes unexpected turns. It's also true that plenty of memorable documentaries are not "driven" at all in the Hollywood sense. *When the Levees Broke*, a four-hour documentary about New Orleans during and after Hurricane Katrina, generally follows the chronology of events that devastated a city and its people. As described by supervising editor and coproducer Sam Pollard in Chapter 22, there is a narrative arc to each hour and to the series. But the complexity of the four-hour film and its interweaving of dozens of individual stories, rather than a select few, differentiate it from a more traditional form of narrative.

Some films present a "slice of life" portrait of people or places. With shorter films, this may be enough, particularly if there is humor involved. *Where Did You Get That Woman?*, for example, offers a portrait of a Chicago washroom attendant, and in the light-hearted *Gefilte Fish*, three generations of women explain how they prepare a traditional holiday dish. (The third generation, the filmmaker, unscrews a jar.) With longer films of this type, there still needs to be some overarching structure. Frederick Wiseman's documentaries are elegantly structured but not "plotted" in the sense that each sequence makes the next one inevitable, but there is usually an organizing principle behind his work, such as a "year in the life" of an institution. Still other films are driven not by characters or plot but by questions, following an essay-like structure (employed, for example, by Michael Moore in *Fahrenheit 9/11*). Some films merge styles: *Super Size Me* is built around the film-maker's 30-day McDonald's diet, but to a large extent the film is actually driven by a series of questions, making it an essay. This combination of journey and essay can also be found in Nathaniel Kahn's *My Architect* and Per Saari's *Why He Skied*, which he discusses in Chapter 24.

DRAMATIC STORYTELLING

Because *dramatic* storytelling often refers more specifically to character-driven stories, it's worth looking at some of the basic elements that make these stories work. As set out by authors David Howard and Edward Mabley in their book, *The Tools of Screenwriting*, these are:

- The story is about *somebody* with whom we have some empathy.
- This somebody wants *something* very badly.
- This something is *difficult*—but possible—to do, get, or achieve.
- The story is told for maximum *emotional impact* and *audience participation* in the proceedings.
- The story must come to a *satisfactory ending* (which does not necessarily mean a happy ending).

Although Howard and Mabley's book is directed at dramatic screenwriters, the list is useful for documentary storytellers as well. Your particular film subject or situation might not fit neatly within these parameters, so further explanation follows.

Who (or What) the Story Is About

The *somebody* is your protagonist, your hero, the entity whose story is being told. Note that your hero can, in fact, be very "unheroic," and the audience might struggle to empathize with him or her. But the character and/or character's mission should be compelling enough that the audience cares about the outcome. In *The Execution of Wanda Jean*, for example, Liz Garbus offers a sympathetic but unsparing portrait of a woman on death row for murder.

The central character doesn't need to be a person. In Ric Burns's *New York*, a seven-episode history, for example, the city itself is the protagonist, whose fortunes rise and fall and rise over the course of the series. But often, finding a central character through which to tell your story can make an otherwise complex topic more manageable and accessible to viewers. We see this strategy used in *I'll Make Me a World*, a six-hour history of African-American arts in the 20th century. For example, producer Denise Green explores the Black Arts Movement of the 1960s by viewing it through the eyes and experience of Pulitzer Prize–winning poet Gwendolyn Brooks, an established, middle-aged author whose life and work were transformed by her interactions with younger artists who'd been influenced by the call for Black Power.

What the Protagonist Wants

The *something* that somebody wants is also referred to as a goal or an objective. In *Blue Vinyl*, filmmaker Judith Helfand sets out, on camera, to convince her parents to remove the new siding from their home. Note that a filmmaker's on-screen presence doesn't necessarily make him or her the protagonist. In Steven Ascher and Jeanne Jordan's *Troublesome Creek: A Midwestern*, the filmmakers travel to Iowa, where Jeanne's family is working to save their farm from foreclosure. Jeanne is the film's narrator, but the protagonists are her parents, Russel and Mary Jane Jordan. It's their goal—to pay off their debt by auctioning off their belongings—that drives the film's story.

Active versus Passive

Storytellers speak of active versus passive goals and active versus passive heroes. In general, you want a story's goals and heroes to be active, which means that you want your story's protagonist to be in charge of his or her own life: To set a goal and then to go about doing what needs to be done to achieve it. A passive goal is something like this: A secretary wants a raise in order to pay for breast enhancement surgery. She is passively waiting for the raise, hoping someone will notice that her work merits reward. To be active, she would have to do something to ensure that she gets that raise, or she would have to wage a campaign to raise the extra money she needs for the surgery, such as taking a second job. Not all passivity is bad: Randall Adams, locked up on death row, is a passive protagonist because he can't do anything, which is part of what makes the story so compelling. In general, though, you want your protagonist to be active, and you want him or her to have a goal that's worthy. In the example of the secretary, will an audience really care whether or not she gets larger breasts? Probably not. If we had a reason to be sympathetic—she had been disfigured in an accident, for example—maybe we would care, but it's not a very strong goal. Worthy does not mean a goal has to be noble—it doesn't all have to be about ending world hunger or ensuring world peace. It does have to matter enough to be worth committing significant time and resources to. If you only care a little about your protagonists and what they want, your financiers and audience are likely to care not at all.

Difficulty and Tangibility

The something that is wanted—the goal—must be *difficult* to do or achieve. If something is easy, there's no tension, and without tension, there's little incentive for an audience to keep watching. Tension is the feeling we get when issues or events are unresolved, especially when we want them to be resolved. It's what motivates us to demand, "And then what happens? And what happens after *that*?" We need to know, because it makes us uncomfortable *not* to know. Think of a movie thriller in which you're aware, but the heroine is not, that danger lurks in the cellar. As she heads toward the steps, you feel escalating tension because she is walking *toward* danger. If you didn't know that the bad guy was in the basement, she would just be a girl heading down some stairs. Without tension, a story feels flat; you don't care one way or the other about the outcome.

So where do you find the tension? One solution is through conflict, defined as a struggle between opposing forces. In other words, your protagonist is up against someone (often referred to as the *antagonist* or *opponent*) or something (the *opposition*). In Barbara Kopple's *Harlan County, U.S.A.*, for example, striking miners are in conflict with mine owners. In Heidi Ewing and Rachel Grady's *The Boys of Baraka*, the tension comes from knowing that the odds of an education, or even a future that doesn't involve prison or death, are stacked against a group of African-American boys from inner-city Baltimore. When a small group of boys is given an opportunity to attend school in Kenya as a means of getting fast-tracked to better high schools in Baltimore, we want them to succeed and are devastated when things seem to fall apart.

Note that conflict can mean a direct argument between two sides, pro and con (or "he said, she said"). But such an argument can also weaken tension, especially if each side is talking past the other or if individuals in conflict have not been properly established. If the audience goes into an argument caring about the individuals involved, though, it can lead to powerful emotional storytelling. Near the end of *Daughter from Danang*, the joyful reunion between the American adoptee and her Vietnamese family gives way to feelings of anger and betrayal brought on by the family's request for money. The palpable tension the audience feels stems not from taking one side or another in the argument, but from empathy for both sides.

Weather, illness, war, self-doubt, inexperience, hubris—all of these can pose obstacles as your protagonist strives to achieve his or her goal. And just as it can be useful to find an individual (or individuals) through whom to tell a complex story, it can be useful to personify the opposition. Television viewers in the 1960s, for example, at times seemed better able to understand the injustices of southern segregation when reporters focused on the actions of individuals like Birmingham (Alabama) Police Chief Bull Connor, who turned police dogs and fire hoses on young African Americans as they engaged in peaceful protest.

Worthy Opponent

Just as you want your protagonist to have a worthy goal, you want him or her to have a worthy opponent. A common problem for many filmmakers is that they portray opponents as one-dimensional; if their hero is good, the opponent must be bad. In fact, the most memorable opponent is often not the opposite of the hero, but a complement to him or her. In the film *Sound and Fury*, young Heather's parents oppose her wishes for a cochlear implant not out of malice but out of their deep love for her and their strong commitment to the Deaf culture into which they and their daughter were born. Chicago Mayor Richard Daley was a challenging opponent for Dr. Martin Luther King, Jr., in *Eyes on the Prize* specifically because he *wasn't* Bull Connor; Daley was a savvy northern politician with close ties to the national Democratic Party and a supporter of the southern-based civil rights movement. The story of his efforts to impede Dr. King's campaign for open housing in Chicago in 1966 proved effective at underscoring the significant differences between using nonviolence as a strategy against *de jure* segregation in the South and using it against *de facto* segregation in the North.

Note here, and throughout, that you are not in any way *fictionalizing* characters who are real human beings. You are evaluating a situation from the perspective of a storyteller, and working with what is there. If there is no opponent, you can't manufacture one. Mayor Daley, historically speaking, *was* an effective opponent. Had he welcomed King with open arms and been little more than an inconvenience to the movement, it would have been dishonest to portray him as a significant obstacle.

Remember that the opposition does not have to have a human face. In *The Boys of Baraka*, the goals of the boys, their families, and their supporters are threatened by societal pressures in Baltimore and by political instability in Kenya, which ultimately puts the Baraka program in jeopardy. In *Born into Brothels*, similarly, efforts to save a handful of children are threatened by societal pressures (including not only economic hardship but also the wishes of family members who don't share the filmmakers' commitment to removing children from their unstable homes), and by the fact that the ultimate decision makers, in a few cases, are the children themselves. The audience experiences frustration—and perhaps recognition—as some of these children make choices that in the long run are likely to have significant consequences.

Tangible Goal

Although difficult, the goal should be *possible* to do or achieve, which means that it's best if it's both concrete and realistic. "Fighting racism" or "curing cancer" or "raising awareness of a disease" may all be worthwhile, but none is specific enough to serve as a story objective. Follow your interests, but seek out a specific story that will illuminate it. *The Boys of Baraka* is clearly an indictment of racism and inequality, but it is more specifically the story of a handful of boys and their enrollment in a two-year program at a tiny school in Kenya. *Born into Brothels* illuminates the difficult circumstances facing the children of impoverished sex workers in Calcutta, but the story's goals are more tangible. Initially, we learn that filmmaker Zana Briski, in Calcutta to photograph sex workers, has been drawn to their children. "They wanted to learn how to use the camera," she says in voice-over. "That's when I thought it would be really great to teach them, and to see this world through their eyes." Several minutes later, a larger but still tangible goal emerges: "They have absolutely no opportunity without education," she says. "The question is, can I find a school—a good school—that will take kids that are children of prostitutes?" This, then, becomes the real goal of the film, one enriched by the children's photography and exposure to broader horizons.

Note also that the goal is not necessarily the most "dramatic" or obvious one. In Kate Davis's *Southern Comfort*, a film about a transgendered male dying of ovarian cancer, Robert Eads's goal is not to find a cure; it's to survive long enough to attend the Southern Comfort Conference in Atlanta, a national gathering of transgendered people, with his girlfriend, Lola, who is also transgendered.

Emotional Impact and Audience Participation

The concept of telling a story for greatest *emotional impact* and *audience participation* is perhaps the most difficult. It's often described as "show, don't tell," which means that you want to present the evidence or information that allows viewers to experience the story for themselves, anticipating twists and turns and following the story line in a way that's active rather than passive. Too often, films tell us what we're supposed to think through the use of heavy-handed narration, loaded graphics, or a stacked deck of interviews.

Think about the experience of being completely held by a film. You aren't *watching* characters on screen; you're right there with them, bringing the clues you've seen so far to the story as it unfolds. You lose track of time as you try to anticipate what happens next, who will do what, and what will be learned. It's human nature to try to make sense of the events we're confronted with, and it's human nature to enjoy being stumped or surprised. In *Enron: The Smartest Guys in the Room*, you think Enron's hit bottom, that all of the price manipulation has finally caught up with them and they'll be buried in debt—until someone at Enron realizes that there's gold in California's power grid.

Telling a story for emotional impact means that the filmmaker is structuring the story so that the moments of conflict, climax, and resolution—moments of achievement, loss, reversal, etc.—adhere as well as possible to the internal rhythms of storytelling. Audiences expect that the tension in a story will escalate as the story moves toward its conclusion; scenes tend to get shorter, action tighter, the stakes higher. As we get to know the characters and understand their wants and needs, we care more about what happens to them; we become invested in their stories. Much of this structuring takes place in the editing room. But to some extent, it also takes place as you film, and planning for it can make a difference. Knowing that as Heidi Bub got off the airplane in Danang she'd be greeted by a birth mother she hadn't seen in 20 years, what preparations did the filmmakers need to make to be sure they got that moment on film? What might they shoot if they wanted to build up to that moment, either before or after it actually occurred? (They shot an interview with Heidi and filmed her, a "fish out of water," as she spent a bit of time in Vietnam before meeting with her mother.) In the edited film, by the time Heidi sees her mother, we realize (before she does) how fully Americanized she's become and how foreign her family will seem. We also know that the expectations both she and her birth mother have for this meeting are very high.

You want to avoid creating unnecessary drama—turning a perfectly good story into a soap opera. There's no reason to pull in additional details, however sad or frightening, when they aren't relevant. If you're telling the story of a scientist unlocking the genetic code to a certain mental illness, for example, it's not necessarily important that she's also engaged in a custody battle with her former husband, even if this detail seems to spice up the drama or, you hope, make the character more "sympathetic." If the custody battle is influenced by her husband's mental illness and her concerns that the children may have inherited the disease, there is a link that could serve the film well. Otherwise, you risk adding a layer of detail that detracts, rather than adds.

False emotion—hyped-up music and sound effects and narration that warns of danger around every corner—is a common problem, especially on television. As in the story of the boy who cried wolf, at some point it all washes over the viewer like so much noise. If the danger is real, it will have the greatest storytelling impact if it emerges organically from the material.

Raising the Stakes

Another tool of emotional storytelling is to have something at stake and to raise the stakes until the very end. Look at the beginning of *Control Room*. The film intercuts story cards (text on screen) with images of everyday life. The cards read: *March 2003/The United States and Iraq are on the brink of war./Al Jazeera Satellite Channel will broadcast the war . . . /to forty million Arab viewers./The Arab world watches . . . /and waits./CONTROL ROOM.* Clearly, these stakes are high.

The stakes may also be very personal. In both *My Architect* and *Why He Skied*, for example, the filmmaker sets out to understand the death and life of a close relative. Or the stakes may affect the audience directly: This was the argument driving *An Inconvenient Truth*, Al Gore's presentation about the threat of global climate change. In the hands of a good storyteller, even small stakes can be made large when their importance to those in the story is conveyed. For example, how many people in America—or beyond, for that matter—really care who wins or loses the National Spelling Bee, held each year in Washington, D.C.? But to the handful of children competing in *Spellbound*, and to their families and communities, the contest is all-important. Through skillful storytelling, the filmmakers make us care not only about these kids but about the competition, and as the field narrows, we can't turn away.

Stakes may rise because (genuine) danger is increasing, or time is running out. In *Sound and Fury*, for example, the stakes rise as time passes, because for a child born deaf, a cochlear implant is most effective if implanted while language skills are being developed. How do the filmmakers convey this? We see Heather's much younger cousin get the implant and begin to acquire spoken language skills; we also learn that Heather's mother, born deaf, would now get little benefit from the device. As Heather enrolls in a school for the deaf without getting an implant, we understand that the decision has lifelong implications.

A Satisfactory Ending

A satisfactory ending, or resolution, is often one that feels both unexpected and inevitable. It must resolve the one story you set out to tell. Say you start the film with a problem: A little girl has a life-threatening heart condition for which there is no known surgical treatment. Your film then goes into the world of experimental surgery, where you find a charismatic doctor whose efforts to solve a very different medical problem have led him to create a surgical solution that might work in the little girl's situation. To end on this surgical breakthrough, however, won't be satisfactory.

Audiences were drawn into the story of the little girl, and this surgeon's work must ultimately be related to that story. Can his work make a difference in her case? You need to complete the story with which the film began.

Note that there is never just one correct ending. Suppose, for example, that your film is due to be aired months before the approval is granted that will allow doctors to try the experimental surgery on the girl. Make *that* your ending, and leave the audience with the knowledge that everyone is praying and hoping that she will survive until then. Or perhaps the surgery is possible, but at the last minute the parents decide it's too risky. Or they take that risk, and the outcome is positive. Or negative. Or perhaps the doctor's breakthrough simply comes too late for this one child but may make a difference for hundreds of others. Any of these would be a satisfactory ending, provided it is factual. It would be unethical to manipulate the facts to imply a "stronger" or more emotional ending that misrepresents what you know the outcome to be. Suppose, for example, that the parents have already decided that no matter how much success the experimental work is having, they will not allow their daughter to undergo any further operations. You cannot imply that this remains an open question (e.g., with a teaser such as "Whether the operation will save the life of little Candy is yet to be seen.").

Ending a film in a way that's satisfying does not necessitate wrapping up all loose ends or resolving things in a way that's upbeat. The end of *Daughter from Danang* is powerful precisely because things remain unsettled; Heidi Bub has achieved the goal of meeting her birth mother, but even two years after her visit, she remains deeply ambivalent about continued contact. At the end of *The Thin Blue Line*, Randall Adams remains a convicted murderer on death row, even as filmmaker Errol Morris erases any lingering doubts the audience might have as to his innocence.

Documentary Storytelling 3

Armed with an understanding of story, how do you apply it to an idea you have for a documentary? Suppose, for example, that you're thinking of doing a film about Elvis Presley, a diner in your home town, or images of Islam in American popular culture. Something about the topic has caught your interest, and you think you want to take it to the next level.

First, ask yourself what it is about the topic that grabs you. As the initial audience for your film, your gut reaction to the subject is important. Chances are it wasn't a sweeping notion of Elvis Presley that caught your attention, but an account, perhaps, of his time in the military. It's not the fact that there's a diner in your hometown, but that rising taxes and a dwindling customer base have left the owners open to offers from developers looking to build a mall despite significant local opposition. You hadn't thought much about images of Islam in America until you watched a couple of newly-arrived students from Iraq and the Sudan trying to make their way through a pep rally at your son's school, and you found yourself seeing American culture—high school culture—through their eyes.

We're surrounded by subjects that offer potential for documentary storytelling. Current events or an afternoon spent browsing the shelves at a local library or bookstore may trigger ideas. Some filmmakers find stories within their own families. Alan Berliner made *Nobody's Business* about his father, Oscar; Deborah Hoffman made *Confessions of a Dutiful Daughter* about her mother's battle with Alzheimer's. Even when you're very close to a subject, however, you'll need to take an impartial view to determine whether or not it would make a film that audiences will want to see.

This is also true when you adapt documentaries from printed sources; a story may read well on paper, but not play as well on screen. In making the series *Cadillac Desert*, drawn from Marc Reisner's book of the same name, producer Jon Else (Chapter 19) chose three of the roughly 40 stories in Reisner's book; Else and his team then conducted their own research and determined the best way to tell those stories on film.

Alex Gibney, the producer and writer of *Enron: The Smartest Guys in the Room*, began the film after his sister-in-law urged him to read the book by Peter Elkind and Bethany McLean. "My first step was to wonder if I should have my head examined for doing a film about accounting," he says in bonus material on the DVD. But the book, he said, "floored me, because it was so rich, in terms of characters . . . . That was the aspect of the story that really got me, this whole idea of these all-American characters, who are not to-the-manor born, inventing themselves and a company out of whole cloth." Still, he "had to make a film out of it," he says, and "find my own way into the story."

STORY RIGHTS

In general, if you're using books and magazines solely for research purposes, you don't need to obtain any of the underlying rights. When the film is indelibly linked to a book, however, as was the case with *Enron, Cadillac Desert, A Brief History of Time* (Errol Morris's film built on Stephen Hawking's book), or *A Midwife's Tale* (Laurie Kahn-Leavitt's film built on Laurel Thatcher Ulrich's book), you will need to come to a legal arrangement with the author or copyright holder. Consult with a good entertainment lawyer if you have questions about legality, or if you need or want exclusive access to material (or an event). Better to be safe than to waste precious time and money on a subject you can't legally pursue.

Note that when you are negotiating for the rights to a story, you will want to retain creative control over your film. The author may be an expert on the subject, but you are an expert on translating it on film to a general audience. You don't need a degree in science to make an extraordinary science documentary or a degree in social work to create a compelling portrait of runaway teens. What you need are intelligence, curiosity, an ability to learn fast, and a readiness to consult with people who *are* experts in those fields. Ideally, there is a positive collaboration between expert and filmmaker that serves to enrich the film.

"FINDING" THE STORY DURING PRODUCTION

One of the biggest misconceptions about documentary filmmaking is that it happens spontaneously. In fact, it's fairly common to hear filmmakers talk about the story revealing itself over the course of the production or even in the editing room. While this may be true, with experienced filmmakers this tends to mean *not* that a filmmaker has simply shot material without any story in mind, but that he or she alters the story's focus or, more likely, its *structure* during production and postproduction. Even vérité projects, which are significantly crafted in the editing room, are generally begun with a sense of the story and its potential development. You can't know where real life will take you, but you can certainly anticipate a range of outcomes and determine whether or not the story holds

Puja running, from *Born into Brothels*. Photo by Gour, courtesy of Kids with Cameras.

sufficient promise. Filmmaker Susan Froemke, when she was the principal filmmaker at Maysles Films, spent months conducting research before she was confident that she had the right characters and story through which to explore the issue of poverty in *Lalee's Kin* (Chapter 21).

Sometimes an opportunity comes along that precludes extensive planning. Filmmakers Gail Dolgin and Vicente Franco had just days to decide whether or not to travel to Vietnam after they learned about an upcoming reunion between Heidi Bub and the birth mother who'd given her up during "Operation Babylift" in 1975. "We all really believed that we were going into a happy reunion, and we had no idea whether we would come back with anything more than that," Dolgin says. "It just grabbed us with the possibilities of raw emotion and passion, and those are great elements for a documentary. And we're also drawn to films where we don't know what's going to happen—we have a concept and we go with it." At a minimum, the filmmakers had a basic, straightforward narrative of an adoptee returning to her homeland, although whether or not that could be turned into a documentary remained to be seen. "Maybe there would be a film that would explore what happens when you lose your birthplace identity," Dolgin says. "Heidi grew up in southern Tennessee, and we imagined going back with her and having her rediscover her roots in some way. But we had no idea, truly. We just went. And of course as soon as we got there it became clear that what we had anticipated was going to go in a different direction." In Vietnam, the filmmakers found themselves immersed in the complex story they told in *Daughter from Danang*.

Frederick Wiseman, renowned for his exploration of American institutions (*Hospital, Basic Training, Welfare, Public Housing, Domestic Violence*) has told interviewers that once he is given permission to film, he moves quickly, spending weeks shooting and then finding his themes and point of view over the course of several months of editing. But note that there is an inherent structure to Wiseman's work—the rhythms of daily life and of the individual stories he picks up over the course of filming—and a distinctive style that he brings to his films. For a

1998 interview (published in *The Boston Phoenix*) about the film *Public Housing*, writer and filmmaker Gerald Peary asked Wiseman if he looked for "drama" while shooting. "The first thought: I'm trying to make a movie," Wiseman responded. "A movie has to have dramatic sequences and structure. . . . So yes, I am looking for drama, though I'm not necessarily looking for people beating each other up, shooting each other. There's a lot of drama in ordinary experiences." It's also worth noting that Wiseman's style of shooting almost invariably necessitates a high shooting ratio (footage filmed versus footage that ends up on screen) and a lengthy editing period.

SERENDIPITY

It's not unusual for filmmakers to begin one project, only to be drawn by the characters and situations they encounter toward a film that is both different and stronger than they anticipated. In publicity material for the film *Sound and Fury*, director Josh Aronson says that he initially intended to film five deaf individuals whose experiences covered a range of viewpoints on deafness. But in his research, he discovered the Artinians, a family in which two brothers—one hearing, one not—each had a deaf child. This created an opportunity to explore conflict within an extended family over how to raise deaf children. In another example, filmmaker Andrew Jarecki was making a film about birthday party clowns when he discovered, through one of his characters, the story that he eventually told in his documentary, *Capturing the Friedmans*—that of a family caught up in a devastating child abuse case.

Knowing that this may happen, or is even *likely* to happen, doesn't mean that you shouldn't approach a general idea by looking first for the best story you can, given the subject as you then understand it. Knowing at least your baseline story helps you to anticipate, at a minimum, what you'll need to make the film, including characters and location setups. In his work with emerging filmmakers at the University of California, Berkeley, Jon Else requires that they head out "with some bomb-proof fallback plan," so that even if everything on the shoot goes wrong, they still come back with something.

EVALUATING STORY IDEAS

Beyond the conviction that a story you're developing will work well on film, the following important practical considerations may be helpful to consider.

Access and Feasibility

Does your film provide entré into new or interesting worlds, and can you obtain access to those worlds? Whether it's the worlds of Cuban immigrants, both before and after they arrive in the United States (*Balseros*) or the lives of would-be basketball stars (*Hoop Dreams*), a film that takes viewers inside experiences beyond their own is often well received. Aside from exclusive or extraordinary access, any film, even one shot in your grandmother's kitchen, depends on some kind of access being granted, whether it is personal (your grandmother), location (permission to bring your equipment into her home), or archival (access to her photo album or those poems she's been writing all these years). Sometimes, *lack* of access may become part of the story, as with Michael Moore's pursuit of General Motors chairman Roger Smith, in *Roger & Me.*

In some cases, exclusive access to well-known figures raises the interest level. News producer Alexandra Pelosi was allowed to shadow George W. Bush as he campaigned for the presidency in *Journeys with George*, for example. In other cases, it's not the fame of the subject but the intimate access the filmmakers gain, often over a period of years, that makes the resulting films exceptional.

As you develop your idea, you need to determine if what you need for production is really possible. Can you get inside a cyclotron to film? Will that Pulitzer Prize–winning author grant you an interview? Will you be allowed to follow a third-grade student during that spelling bee? Several years ago, I worked on a science documentary for which we wanted to film cyclists in the Tour de France to illustrate the conservation of mass and energy. The success of a good portion of that film depended on access to the tour and to exclusive CBS Sports coverage of it. Had we not been able to arrange these, we would have had to find a different illustration.

As an additional note, gaining access usually means establishing a relationship and building trust with the people who can grant it. This is a professional relationship, although filmmakers often grow very close to their subjects. It's important to respect that trust, so be truthful about yourself and your project from the start. You can generally get people to talk to you even if they know that you don't agree with their position, as long as you make it very clear that they will be given a fair hearing and that you value their point of view. (Again, there are exceptions. Filmmakers such as Nick Broomfield [*Kurt & Courtney*] and Michael Moore may push the boundaries of access as a matter of style; they may show up with the cameras rolling deliberately to put their subjects on edge.)

Affordability

In terms of budget and schedule, is it realistic to think that you can afford to tell the story you want to tell, in the way you want to tell it? Even if digital technology can put a relatively inexpensive camera in your hands, getting your film shot, edited, and technically ready for broadcast or theatrical release will still be very expensive. Even celebrated filmmakers have trouble raising money these days. Have you set your sights too high? Don't think small, just realistically. Know that some types of documentaries are costlier to produce than others, and that "extras," such as the rights to use a single clip of archival film from a private collection or a short piece of music from your favorite album, could set you back thousands of dollars.

Passion and Curiosity

Do you care deeply about the subject? Passion is going to be your best weapon against discouragement, boredom, frustration, and confusion. Passion is not the unwavering conviction that you are right and the whole world must be made to agree with you. Instead, it is the commitment to the notion that this idea is exciting, relevant, and meaningful, and perhaps more importantly, that it's something you can look forward to exploring in the months or even years to come.

Passion is also an ingredient that commissioning editors and funders want to see when filmmakers approach them for support. Filmmaker Hans Otto Nicolayssen, currently senior consultant at the Norwegian Film Commission in Bergen, used to review proposals for short and documentary films on behalf of Filmkontakt Nord (FkN), which he helped to found. His first criteria for making a grant? "Passion," he says. "I always start with the question, 'Why are you telling me this story now?'" Nicolayssen says a proposal should convey not only the filmmaker's skill but also his or her connection to the material.

Audience

Who is your intended audience? Many documentaries, whether produced independently or in-house, are created with an audience in mind. It's always possible that the film you thought would only reach your immediate geographic region will be a breakout hit, but in general, you should have some idea whom you *want* it to reach: age, geographic area, educational level, etc. This doesn't mean that you shouldn't try to also reach a wider audience, just that you're likely to approach MTV's audience differently, for example, than Discovery's, or that you hope to reach public television not only in the United States but also in the United Kingdom and Germany. Is your film not intended for broadcast, but for use by community or educational groups? Do you want to try to release your film theatrically? Does it have the potential to be the next *Super Size Me* or *March of the Penguins*? These questions are worth thinking about early on in the process.

On the other hand, plenty of filmmakers simply begin to develop their films without worrying, at first, about audiences or even funding, as was the case with *The Kidnapping of Ingrid Betancourt* (Chapter 17) and *Why He Skied* (Chapter 24). Sometimes, events necessitate working quickly—an opportunity will pass if no action is taken. The subject may seem too obscure or too personal to seek sponsorship early on, and a more convincing case for the film's appeal may be made when there is footage to show. In some cases, filmmakers nearly complete their films before submitting them to "open calls" for program slots or festival competition, and in that way they gradually find an audience and possibly funds for completion. If there's a story in you that has to get made, and you have the resources to go ahead and make it, this route gives you freedom that others don't. Keep in mind, though, that in the end, you still want to reach people with a subject and story that grab them, hold them, and—ideally—stay with them long after the lights are back on.

Relevance

Will anybody care about your film, or can you make them care? This can be a tough one. You may be passionate about 14th-century Chinese art or the use of mushrooms in gourmet cuisine, but can you really find a compelling story that will be worth others not only funding but watching? It's possible to make people care about all sorts of things, but it usually takes the right approach.

By rising beyond its specifics, a story may gain greater relevance for a wider audience. According to information on his website, Alan Berliner's *The Sweetest Sound* started out as a documentary about names and gradually became a documentary about the filmmaker's name, one that he discovered he shared with about a dozen other people worldwide. In Berliner's hands, the film becomes a humorous and thought-provoking essay about identity and the perception of self, both internal and external—a film that has appeal far beyond people named Alan Berliner. *Daughter from Danang* has layers of story that each adds relevance: the reunion of an adopted daughter and her birth mother, the cultural dissonance felt by an American woman returning to the Vietnamese homeland she barely remembers, the changes that have occurred in both countries in the years since 1975, and questions about expectation and need, both emotional and material, that are made all the more difficult by barriers of language and culture.

Timeliness

One aspect of relevance, though not always the most important one, is timeliness. Television executives may plan documentary programming to coincide with major events, anniversaries, or even high-profile motion picture releases—anything to capitalize on public and press interest. In other cases, filmmakers may argue for audience interest in a subject because it expands on current topics in the news or on television, or it's a story from the past that has particular relevance in the present time. The fact that a subject is topical, however, is not by itself a reason to pursue it, because by the time you finish the film, interest in that issue may have passed. In fact, the quality of being "evergreen," meaning the film will have a shelf-life of many years as opposed to many months, can be a positive selling point. A film on elephant behavior or the American electoral process in general may be evergreen, whereas a film that specifically explores a particular environmental campaign or issues in the American presidential campaign of 2004 probably will not be.

Visualization

Is the story visual, and if not, can you make it visual? This is an important question whether you're telling a modern-day story that involves a lot of technology or bureaucracy, or you're drawn to a historical story that predates the invention of still or motion picture photography. A film subject that doesn't have obvious visuals requires additional foresight on the part of the filmmaker; you'll need to anticipate exactly *how* you plan to tell the story on film. The opposite may also be true: A subject can be inherently visual—it takes place in a spectacular location or involves state-of-the-art microscopic photography, for example—without containing an obvious narrative thread.

One trend in nature and wildlife programming is to tell stories about the natural world by focusing on human subjects, as when the PBS series *In the Wild* sent celebrities on journeys of discovery. The actress Goldie Hawn, for example, traveled through India in search of a partially blind female elephant she'd encountered seven years earlier (*The Elephants of India*, with Goldie Hawn). But some films put animals center stage, as Luc Jacquet demonstrated with his blockbuster hit, *March of the Penguins*. A powerful story of love, loss, and survival, the film's protagonists are emperor penguins, who face opposition from nature itself, and the forces that drive them forward in the harsh and unforgiving climate of Antarctica.

Hook

Another question to ask as you evaluate the story is, does it have a hook? In its simplest form, the hook is what got you interested in the subject in the first place. It's that bit of information that reveals the essence of the story and its characters, encapsulating the drama that's about to unfold. *Sound and Fury*, for example, is the story of the little girl who wants a cochlear implant. The hook is not that she wants this operation, nor that the implant is a major feat of medical technology. The hook is that the little girl's parents, contrary to what many in the audience might expect, aren't sure they want her to have the operation. It's the part of the story that makes people want to know more.

Existing Projects

What else has been done on the topic? It's useful, before you get too far, to explore what other films have been made on a subject and when. In part, this may simply inform your own storytelling. What worked or didn't work about what a previous filmmaker did? How will your project be different and/or add to the subject? It's not that you can't tackle a subject that's been covered; look at the range of projects on the American civil rights movement, the threat of nuclear war, or dinosaurs. Just because HBO broadcast a film on the 1963 church bombing in Birmingham (*4 Little Girls*) doesn't mean there isn't a different angle you could take in telling the story for the History Channel or for theatrical release. But knowing as much as you can about your subject also means knowing how else it's been treated on film.

DEVELOPING THE STORY

Once you've decided that your idea is worth pursuing, you'll need to start refining the story and planning how you'll tell it. There's no single way to do this, and furthermore, it's a process that tends to continue from the moment an idea strikes you until the final moments of postproduction. In general, depending on the needs of the project, the budget, and the schedule, you are likely to write some form of outline, treatment, and script, and/or several drafts of one or all of them. Many producers create what's known as a "shooting treatment" or a "shooting script" prior to filming that is used as a blueprint for the work ahead (for examples, see Chapter 11). A small minority of projects are fully scripted in advance, with material shot to accompany narration or scripted "scenarios" (as in recreation docudramas). Some projects are never scripted. The direct cinema film, *Lalee's Kin*, existed on the page only in terms of a basic description for the commissioning network (HBO) and an outline from which the editor could work.

IF YOU ALREADY KNOW YOUR STORY, WON'T YOUR PRESENTATION BE BIASED?

Knowing your story (or at least the germ of it) at the start of a project is not the same thing as knowing exactly what you want to say and how. It simply means having an idea of the narrative spine on which you could hang your subject and having at least some idea of themes you want to explore. From there, you need to research, develop, and shoot your story with questions and an open mind. Give the "opposition" a fair hearing. Building on an earlier example, as sympathetic to the diner owners as you may feel at the start of your project, you might come to find yourself sympathizing with the developers, or discovering that a third solution, while meaning the end of the diner, is best for the town.

Suppose you've decided to explore the story of Thomas Jefferson and his relationship with a slave, Sally Hemings. That's a complex story that can be tackled from many points of view, past and present. If you start that project having already decided to paint Jefferson solely as exploiter and Hemings as victim, you probably shouldn't make the film. Having an ax to grind or a point to make is not the same thing as having the germ of a story to explore. The film that ensues is almost guaranteed to be a one-sided rant that is neither engaging nor informative. Besides, if you already know everything, why make the film? It's a long, hard, and often thankless process, and if there's nothing in it for you as the filmmaker—nothing to learn, to discover, to be surprised or confused or challenged by—why expend the energy?

Films that end up advocating a position or idea—that these chemicals shouldn't have been dumped, that law enforcement used too much force, that laws are being broken—can be as hard-hitting or irreverent or personal as you want. But as you make them, you want to remain open to new and even conflicting information, whether or not it ends up on screen. The more effectively you can present your case, the better the film will stand up to scrutiny.

TELLING AN ACTIVE STORY

A significant percentage of the documentaries on television these days are about events that are over and done with. You still need a narrative to unfold over the course of the film; one solution is to keep the storytelling (and interviews) in the moment. You build the story and tell it in ways that leave the outcome uncertain. Witnesses, for example, do not say: "I found out later he was fine but at this point I got a call from somebody, Andy I think it was, he later became mayor, and Andy told me that my boy Jimmy was down the well." Instead, ask your storytellers to stick to what is known at this point in your narrative, such as, "I got a call that Jimmy was in the well. I ran screaming for help." By doing this, you build tension. Starting with, "I found out later he was fine," lets all of the suspense out of your story. Surprisingly, this is a common mistake, not only in interviews but in scripted narration, such as, "Although he wasn't badly hurt, Jimmy had fallen down a deep well." Note that your adherence to present tense does not mean that you can't offer interpretations of the past. For example, an expert witness might be interviewed saying, "People complain about overregulation, that there's too much of it. But there are laws that should have made the contractors responsible for sealing that well up. Instead, they left it open, and a little boy fell in." The expert hasn't yet said when or how—or if—the boy got out.

When considering a topic or story that's in the past, whether recent or distant, you'll also need to consider how you're going to bring that story to life on screen. For example, suppose that members of the local historical society want you to make a film about their town's founding in 1727, and they want to include some material about the origins of some of the wonderful old architecture that still survives. They're excited by the fact that many of the local families are descended from early residents, and they have access to a decent collection of old oil portraits as well as photographs and even some letters. What does it add up to? Not much that will interest anyone who's not a direct relative of the folks on camera, because there's no story being told on screen—yet. When Ken Burns, Ric Burns, and Geoffrey Ward used artifacts and images from the 19th century in *The Civil War*, they used them in the service of a powerful story—the North against the South. What's the *story* of this town's history? Or if there is none, can a present-day story be told that would motivate a look back?

In the search for narrative, some filmmakers find a "guide" to the past—for example, the town's mayor says, "Let's set out to see where this great city came from," and off he or she goes. But there are often more creative devices. What if students from the local middle school are researching the town's history in order to write a play that they will perform later that year? That's a possible framework. What if a local builder is trying to restore the town's oldest house, which has been renovated repeatedly over the years? In order to do so he's got to peel back the layers one by one, offering a reason to explore the town's architectural history while also giving us a chance to follow the kind of building renovation that audiences enjoy. These aren't earth-shattering ideas, but they demonstrate ways to consider a subject that might not seem, at first glance, to have much potential as a film. A more detailed discussion about approaching subjects and about moving film stories forward in time can be found in later chapters.

Approach 4

If you gave any group of filmmakers some gear and the same general story, you'd end up with films that were very different in style, tone, point of view, focus, and more. These differences describe the *approach*: how you present a story on screen. Do you intend to create a half-hour special or a 10-hour series? Is your tone humorous? What production elements will you use, such as live shooting, recreations, a narrator, time-lapse photography, or animation?

It's helpful to begin thinking about your approach almost as soon as you come up with a subject or story that interests you. If you've become passionately interested in an 18th century battle, for example, you'll need to think about how to visualize the story, which occurred before the invention of photography. (Peter Watkins's *Culloden*, for example, used the style of a 1950s black-and-white television documentary to recreate and report on the 1746 Battle of Culloden.) If you want to film a local day-care center, it would be good to know early on what kind of access you'll want and what sort of filming schedule you'll need. Following the residents of a group home on a week-long trip to Jerusalem is very different than filming those same residents over the course of a year as neighbors seek their eviction. Your approach will evolve as your knowledge of the material increases and you have a better sense of what's practical, but it's good to start off with some ideas.

One way to begin the process is to screen many films and talk with your collaborators about which elements you like or don't like, and which might best serve the project at hand. Do you want to create an intimate portrait or a stylized whodunit? A historical film that uses archival footage, or one that uses recreations

Scene from "Doctor Atomic" in *Wonders Are Many*. Photo courtesy of Jon Else.

(or both)? Watching several films by the same filmmaker can also help you to get a sense of how style and approach change depending on the project. Conversely, you'll notice how some filmmakers bring a fairly established style to subjects chosen, in part, because they are *suited* to that style.

Approach involves the essence of the film itself. Suppose, for example, that you're drawn to the issue of abused, abandoned, and stray pets and what happens to them in shelters. You might decide to:

- Create a journalistic piece on animal welfare that uses experts and news-style footage to explore controversial issues such as unethical breeding, the culture of "fight dogs," and the issue of euthanasia;
- Create a vérité portrait of one shelter and its staff for whom these issues are part of a day-to-day struggle, as Cynthia Wade and Heidi Reinberg did in the feature-length documentary, *Shelter Dogs*;
- Script and narrate a film that involves a family reenacting its search in local shelters for a dog to bring into their home, and then film the process by which experts can rebuild trust and calm aggression in dogs that have been abused; or
- Put yourself in the picture, with the "train" being your search in local shelters for the perfect dog, a journey that

allows you to take side trips and find out more about how the dogs came to be there, how many are in shelters nationwide, and what fate they face if they *aren't* adopted. In the end, you either find or don't find the dog of your dreams.

As another example, suppose you know what elements you want to use for an historical film, but not how to use them. You have a collection of diaries, letters, and newspaper clips pertaining to your story, which is set in the past. You might do the following:

- Have actors read this material in voice-over as you present archival stills or footage, perhaps complemented with evocative modern-day footage;
- Have actors in period costume embody the authors of this archival material, speaking the words on camera. This was the approach Middlemarch Films took in producing the series *Liberty! The American Revolution*, which was featurelike in its dramatization of the events surrounding the founding of the United States; or
- Have actors perform this archival material on camera but without costumes or makeup, as was done in the HBO film *Unchained Memories*, in which actors read the words of elderly former slaves, as documented by workers for the Works Progress Administration.

Another example: Who will tell the stories in your film? What will drive the narrative?

- In *Grizzly Man*, the narrative is driven by filmmaker Werner Herzog's quest to understand the life and work of naturalist Timothy Treadwell. In his voice-over narration and his appearances on camera, Herzog makes his presence known and at times argues against Treadwell's views about the natural world.
- In *Enron: The Smartest Guys in the Room*, the point of view is omniscient, although it's derived to some extent from the book of the same title by Peter Elkind and Bethany McLean, both of whom are interviewed on camera. The narration, read by actor Peter Coyote, is anonymous and informational. This style is the most "traditional" for television documentaries. But the use of an omniscient narrator in this

film makes a lot of sense: A few title cards could never have provided the kind of detail needed for audiences to follow the enormously complex story unfolding on screen. And while the filmmaker might have cast himself as a storyteller, there is no obvious reason to do so, and a number of reasons *not* to. (For one, the cast of characters is already quite large: three top Enron executives, the Enron traders, various whistle-blowers, and the two journalist/book authors.)

- In Nick Broomfield's *Kurt & Courtney*, a film about the death of rock star Kurt Cobain that paints an unflattering portrait of his widow, Courtney Love, Broomfield (like Herzog) makes himself and his quest to make the film the *story* of the film. But the style is noticeably different: Broomfield, much like Judith Helfand in *Blue Vinyl* and Michael Moore in *Bowling for Columbine*, is confrontational, in a style somewhat akin to televised investigative journalism.

- In the Academy Award–winning *Born into Brothels*, co-filmmaker Zana Briski appears on camera and speaks the voice-over narration, but she's also playing an active role in the story unfolding on screen, whose outcome she does not know when the filmmaking begins. In other words, the story of the film is not the story about making the film; it's the story of her work with children in Calcutta's red light district and her efforts to open doors to education and opportunity on their behalf.

- A strictly vérité film, such as *Lalee's Kin*, is driven by the events unfolding on screen; there is no "storyteller" as the term is being used here, although of course the storyteller is implied in the film's very existence, from planning to editing. Because there is no overt storyteller, these films are often described as "observational" or "fly-on-the-wall."

- *Murderball* is an example of a film that, like many documentaries, is a hybrid of vérité and other filmmaking styles. While there is no narrator, the film is "narrated" in a few ways, including interviews (seen on screen and heard in voice-over) and text on screen (e.g., *For the first time, Joe will face his former U.S.A. teammates.*). The filmmakers follow an ongoing rivalry between quadriplegic rugby teams representing the United States and Canada; they create intimate portraits of key players on the American team and of the American coach of the Canadian team;

they combine footage of these top athletes in action with everyday footage—dressing, driving, dating—that rounds out our sense of them as characters; and they contrast these athletes, who have already been through physical and emotional rehabilitation following devastating injury or illness, with a young man for whom the shock of disability is still new, so that we can appreciate the distance the players have come. There is a "no limits" sense to this film's style, including its soundtrack, and that carries through to participants' willingness to share private moments. The filmmakers play no observable role on screen.

- In some of the more popular biography series on television, the focus is less on storytelling and more on a sort of narrated "scrapbook" approach to a celebrity's life, telling the key events in chronological order and building to emotional highs and lows, such as illness, marriage, or scandal. That these films work is less a tribute to storytelling than to the audience's interest in the subject. Like family photos (which generally fascinate the immediate family but no one else), they're of interest mostly because viewers care about the celebrities on screen, not because there's a particularly strong story being told.

In discussing your approach, be aware that filmmakers, as mentioned, often combine approaches. Many documentaries contain at least some scenes that are observational. Some use narration (or text on screen, which plays the same role) but use it sparingly. Some combine voice-over with narration, or script voice-over in lieu of narration. Some films contrive situations that then unfold on screen, becoming observational; for example, Alan Berliner invited a dozen other people named "Alan Berliner" to dinner at his New York City apartment, and included footage of the event in his film, *The Sweetest Sound*. Perhaps you want to include a demonstration of some sort. For a science series called *The Ring of Truth*, I was involved in arranging a sequence in which we drove a yellow rental truck 183 miles due south and charted the path of Antares at the start and end of our journey, in order to do a modern-day version of an ancient measurement of the Earth's circumference. Erroll Morris filmed a teacup shattering for *A Brief History of Time*, so that he could play with the notion of it *un*shattering. (Morris also set up and filmed dominoes cascading to use as a recurring motif in *The Fog of War*. This stylized means of visualizing themes and concepts has become increasingly popular; it can be seen, for example, in the casino footage and magic act cut into *Enron*.) Some filmmakers have taken advantage of easy-to-use, relatively low cost digital technology and put video cameras in the hands of subjects, from soldiers to schoolchildren, and helped them to tell their own stories.

There is an approach to consider for almost every aspect of your filmmaking. Will you interview people alone, together, inside, outside, or informally? Will the interviewer be on camera or off screen? If off screen, will the questions be heard at all by the viewers? (More information about interviewing can be found in Chapter 12.) Not every detail needs to be considered right up front, but, for example, if you're telling the story of a particular military unit, rather than interview members separately, there might be value in bringing them together and filming their interaction. (What you want, however, is for this interaction to be genuine. You almost never want to ask nonactors to recreate the past, especially if it includes dialogue, and you don't want to set up scenes in which people tell each other information that they already know, as in "Well, Jim, wasn't it a good thing that we invented that breathing apparatus?" "Yes, Pete, without it, many more lives might have been lost.") In *Grizzly Man*, there's a somewhat stilted sequence in which the coroner gives Timothy Treadwell's former girlfriend the watch he was wearing when he was killed. To me, the scene feels set up and self-conscious (which may have been Herzog's intent); it begins to feel genuine toward the very end, after the obvious dialogue is over and the participants are waiting for the camera to stop running. If you're trying to film two people in a natural moment, they generally need to be *doing* something that focuses their attention on something other than each other or, more importantly, the camera.

DOCUMENTARY OR DIATRIBE?

Some people decide to make documentaries because they're very passionate about a subject and determined to bring others to their point of view. This can be a great place to start, but it's important to also step back and ask yourself if you can be open-minded as you explore the evidence and honest as you present it, warts and all, to viewers. To some extent, this is a version of "showing, not telling." Like a lawyer claiming a client's innocence or guilt, a filmmaker has no particular credibility *per se*. Instead, he or she must prove the case by weaving an honest argument out of compelling and factual evidence.

The temptation to make a film in order to support a prede-termined conclusion ("I want to show that animal testing is bad.") should be avoided. For one thing, illustrated lectures are rarely interesting. For another, you're likely to be as bored making a film whose conclusion is foregone as your audience will be while watching it. You can start from a hypothesis: "I can't imagine a single scenario in which animal testing is justified," but you should then be willing to really speak with people—scientists, patients, animal rights advocates, and others—who both share and strongly disagree with your initial premise. You may discover a new passion, or find greater complexity in a passion you already had. (Note that you don't necessarily need to put all or even most of these people on screen. You just need to do your homework, so that whatever story you tell contains the complexity it demands.)

There is a difference between starting with a foregone conclusion and having a strong point of view, either as a filmmaker or within your film. The producers of *Eyes on the Prize*, for example, would never have argued against the need for a civil rights movement. But we were continually reminded by the production executives that the strength of our storytelling lay in our willingness to let the evidence of history, and the experiences of those involved along the spectrum of viewpoints, speak for themselves. The audience would make up its own mind.

The opposite can also be effective. Look at Erroll Morris's Academy Award–winning *The Fog of War*. The film offers a platform to the uncontested and at times seemingly self-serving views of its subject, former U.S. Secretary of Defense Robert S. McNamara. That's the point of the film: Morris leaves it to the audience to decide whether they want to accept or discredit McNamara's words. The approach is solid, because the rules of the film are clear. Had Morris set out to create a history of American conflict in the 20th century, then McNamara's views alone would not have been enough.

Being open minded does not mean that your film has to be open-ended or all-inclusive. Once you've done your homework, you still need to find a story within your subject, and you only have 30, 60, or maybe 90 minutes in which to tell it. You don't have to include everything, give everyone's point of view, or even, necessarily, find an opposing point of view. *The Boys of Baraka* did not offer a menu of other alternative educational programs for at-risk Baltimore youth, nor were there critics arguing against programs like the Baraka School. *Born into Brothels* did not spend screen time telling you how or where Zana Briski learned photography or how she'd chosen the particular cameras the children in Calcutta were using, nor did the filmmakers include voices of people who thought, for example, that Briski shouldn't be interfering in a foreign culture. Even if such concerns exist, filmmaking always involves choices.

But if, in the approach you've taken, you uncover contradictory evidence, it will sometimes strengthen your argument to include it because the evidence raises the audience's trust that they're not being manipulated. Look at *Super Size Me*, which is explored in greater detail in Chapter 7. Starting his 30-day diet, director Morgan Spurlock is critical but also somewhat ambivalent about McDonald's and a lawsuit that blames fast food for the obesity of two teenaged girls. He lays out the basic construction of his experiment on camera and brings in three independent doctors to measure the results. (Some critics have argued that the artificiality of this experiment stacks the decks against McDonald's, but I don't agree. Knowing the setup, the audience can and should bring its own skepticism to the table; the experiment is obviously extreme.) Throughout the film, Spurlock also allows interviewees with whom he might be assumed to be sympathetic—doctors, lawyers, school personnel, people on the street—to paint themselves (at times) as mercenary, misinformed, or ignorant. How difficult is it to understand that 64 ounces of soda contains a lot of sugar? Or to look across a lunchroom and notice that the teens you're feeding are eating nothing but high-fat, high-salt junk food? By the film's end, Spurlock has learned and conveyed a great deal of unflattering evidence against the fast-food industry, but his call for change is directed at consumers.

ARCHIVAL FILMMAKING

Say "archival films" and most people think of Ken Burns and *The Civil War*. While this is a great example of archival filmmaking, there are plenty of other films that use archival (or simply *stock* or *third-party*) footage and stills. Used specifically, *archival* and *stock* both refer to material available from public or private archives and/or commercial vendors. Used more generally, however, these words (and the term *third-party*) describe any imagery the film-makers didn't create themselves. Home movies, amateur videos, surveillance tapes, and footage shot for public relations, education or training, for example, might generally be described as stock footage.

Third-party footage (and sound) shows up in a wide range of documentaries. *Grizzly Man* wouldn't have been possible without the footage created by Timothy Treadwell himself. *Enron* includes pivotal audio recordings of Enron traders manipulating the power grid in California, sound the filmmakers discovered in the archives of a power company in Washington State. Alan Berliner has been collecting others' family photos and home movies for years, the visual history of people whose identities are unknown to him, and he used these eloquently in films such as *Nobody's Business* and *The Sweetest Sound*. The archival imagery in Jay Rosenblatt's *Human Remains* was selected not to tell any particular story, but because the men it captures on screen—including Mao, Hitler, and Stalin, known to history for the atrocities they committed—are seen doing disturbingly ordinary things, such as eating or playing with dogs and children.

How you use the archival material is also important. *The Civil War*, mentioned earlier, used archival imagery (mostly still pho-tographs) to illustrate and advance a powerful and thematically rich narrative. That series has also spawned a wealth of knockoffs. Take two parts archival material, the thinking seems to go, add one part emotional music, a dash of brand-name actors in voice-over, and you've got a film. The missing element, too often, is story.

With archival films, the story is often driven by narration, with visuals playing a supporting role. In rare cases, however, where sufficient archival resources exist, the visuals may drive the storytelling. This was the case with two public television histo-ries, *Vietnam: A Television History* (about the Vietnam War) and *Eyes on the Prize* (about the American civil rights movement). Both series covered events for which extensive news footage existed, with stories covered in depth and over a significant period of time. In developing *Eyes*, executive producer Henry Hampton decided that rather than present a survey of the civil rights struggle between the 1950s and 1980s, he wanted to feature a selection of stories from within that period and let them unfold as dramas on screen. Editors on *Eyes* often had sufficient archival footage to craft complete scenes that could then be augmented with modern-day interviews (conducted by the *Eyes* producers). Narration occurred only where it was needed to seam together other elements.

Producers of *Vietnam* and *Eyes* also followed rigorous rules for the use of this archival material. An image could not "stand in" for something else, and the rules of chronology applied to footage just as it did to facts. This meant that if you were telling the story of rioting in Detroit in 1967, you couldn't use a great scene that you knew had been shot on a Thursday if your narrative was still discussing events on Tuesday. Care was also taken with sound effects and the layering of sound onto otherwise silent film footage. "We sent all our silent archival footage to the Imperial War Museum in London, and they matched sound effects," says Kenn Rabin, describing his work as an archivist on *Vietnam* (see Chapter 23). If the footage showed a particular helicopter or a particular weapon firing, the sound effect would be of that model helicopter or that model weapon. "We were very careful not to add anything that would editorialize," Rabin adds. "For example, we never added a scream or a baby crying," unless you could see that action on screen.

Many historical films and series cover events for which there isn't as significant a visual record, or there is none. Furthermore, the existence of historical visual material does not mandate its use; producers may decide to tell their stories using other means, such as recreations. But when historical stills and motion picture are used, how important is it that the images represent what they're being used to portray? This is a subject of some debate among filmmakers and historians. Producers of *The Civil War* grappled with this issue in making their series because the photographic record for their story was extremely limited. At a conference in 1993 ("Telling the Story: The Media, The Public, and American History"), Ken Burns presented a clip from *The Civil War* and then said that, with two exceptions, none of the "illustrative pictures" actually depicted what the narrative implied. "There is a street scene taken in the 1850s of a small Connecticut town, which is used to illustrate Horace Greeley's 1864 lament about the bloodshed of the Civil War," Burns offered. "There are Southern quotes over pictures of Northern soldiers. None of the hospitals specifically mentioned are actually shown, particularly Chimborazo in Richmond . . . . The picture of Walt Whitman is, in fact, several years too old, as is the illustration for Dix." Burns added, "There's not one photograph of action or battle during the Civil War, and yet nearly 40 percent of the series takes place while guns are actually going off. What do you do? What are the kind of licenses that you take?"

His question is an interesting one and not yet sufficiently explored by filmmakers or the public. In the skilled hands of filmmakers who have the resources and commitment to work with a stellar group of media and academic personnel, the storytelling may override the limited imagery (see Chapter 18 for more discussion of this with filmmaker Ric Burns). But too often, and increasingly, substitutions are made not for historical or storytelling reasons, but because schedules and budgets mandate shortcuts. Not every image needs to be specific to time and place, of course. But if you're using archival stills or motion picture footage as visual evidence of the past, the images you select matter.

Another problem filmmakers encounter is that the cost to use commercial archival images (and prerecorded music, especially popular music) is often extremely high. In some cases, music and images may be added by the filmmakers and featured in the soundtrack or on screen. But they can also be hard to avoid, even in the background. If you're filming a character as he's arrested and a radio in a nearby car is blaring the latest hit, you might have to pay large fees for that snippet of song—or present the arrest without its sync soundtrack. At what point are rights issues hampering a filmmaker's freedom to document real life, or to explore the past and use material from the historical record? These are important issues, and while they're beyond the scope of this book, some information about current efforts to define "fair use" on behalf of documentary filmmakers is offered at the back of the book in the notes to Chapter 23.

RECREATIONS AND DOCUDRAMA

Many filmmakers use what are known as *recreations* to suggest an historical past, either to augment a sparse visual record or because the recreations better serve their storytelling (and at times, budgetary) needs. There are many ways to film recreations; it's a good idea to watch a range of styles to decide which works best for your film or determine an innovative new approach. You may choose to shoot partial reenactments—a hand here, legs marching, a wagon wheel. Human figures may be kept in the distance, silhouettes against a skyline, or people may be filmed close up and asked to convey emotions. Entire scenes might be played out, whether by individuals who specialize in staging actual battles from the past, or by actors hired to perform for the film. You also need to decide what role recreations play in your film; will they be part of your evocation of the past, as in Ric Burns's *The Donner Party*, or will they play a central role in the storytelling, as in *Murder at Harvard*, discussed below?

A film moves from recreation toward "docudrama" as elements are fictionalized, even when they closely adhere to known facts. This is especially true when actors speak dialogue that is based on something other than factual transcript; for example, when they improvise a murder scene based on evidence alone. In effect, they're choosing and recreating a single version of what happened, when other versions may be possible: Was the murderer really that angry? Did the victim actually see him coming?

Some filmmakers make the process of recreation and its inherent doubt a part of their storytelling. Errol Morris's *The Thin Blue Line* offers several versions, depending on testimony, of the shooting of a police officer. Laurie Kahn-Leavitt's *A Midwife's Tale* focuses on the efforts of historian Laurel Thatcher Ulrich to tease meaning and understanding from a diary kept by a Maine midwife between the years 1775 and 1812. Once the viewer understands how Ulrich knows what she knows from the historical record, the midwife's story comes increasingly to the fore, in detailed recreation. Another example of this is *Murder at Harvard*, produced by Eric Stange and Melissa Banta, which explores the 1849 murder of Dr. George Parkman and the subsequent trial of Harvard chemistry professor John Webster. The film includes actors performing scenes and speaking dialogue that have been imagined for these historical figures. But in this documentary, the imagining is attributed to historian Simon Schama, who wrote about the case in his 1991 book, *Dead Certainties (Unwarranted Speculations)*. In the documentary, he and other historians discuss the line between fact and informed speculation, and those elements of the past that can't be truly known, such as emotions and motivation. In working on the case, Schama had found that there were even variations in the trial testimony. "The testimony in the trial is from the record," notes Boyd Estus, the project's director of photography. "But there was no court stenographer in the sense that we know it today. What would happen was that several different people would compile their notes, and often the lawyers would get together and say, 'We think this is what happened.'" The film plays out several possible scenarios, and Schama explains why he finds a particular one to be the most compelling.

Recreations that pretend to be something other than they are, such as footage that you shoot and then manipulate to appear to be archival (altering it to appear grainy, black and white or sepia-toned, or scratched), are questionable unless you make the artifice of what you're doing transparent to the viewer. In other words, you set the rules of your documentary storytelling. As long as you make those rules apparent, there is plenty of room for creativity.

SCIENCE FILMS

The approach to science filmmaking varies widely, with one standard being set by the long-running PBS series *Nova*, which in turn was inspired by the BBC series *Horizon*. Michael Ambrosino says that when he created *Nova* in 1973, American broadcasters were skeptical. "People thought that a science series would be nice to have in the schedule," Ambrosino says. "It probably wouldn't get a big audience, but it was something that should be done." He was convinced that the show would not only succeed but that it would draw a larger audience than anything else on air at that time, he says, "and in its first season, *Nova* proved just that."

The reason? "We conceived *Nova* as a series that would explore and explain the way the world worked. We would use science as a tool, but we would primarily think of ourselves as journalists looking for the stories of science," Ambrosino says. "It's not possible to make a film about the crab nebula and have you be interested in it or understand it. It *is* possible to tell the story of the dozen or so men and women who are trying to find out what was the core of the crab nebula. And in telling *their* story of discovery, you had a story that was understandable."

Opportunities exist across the broadcast spectrum for science programming—not just programs that teach science, but also programs in which science, like history or politics, is the setting for a compelling story. Things may be changing, but the trend still seems to be toward tabloid science, whether stories are about extreme behavior (animals that kill, insects that swarm), extreme weather, or the paranormal. These films often use documentary techniques, including interviews and narrated questions ("Was it possible that aliens had left these marks?"), that lead viewers to conclusions that may have no factual basis. Fortunes are spent to bring dinosaurs to life through the magic of computer technology, but not enough resources are devoted to stories that advance beyond predator and prey scenarios. Why not present science with as much substance as possible, using storytelling to motivate viewers to want to know more? Rather than posit that these experts with this equipment can figure out the height and age of the victim, for example, why not allow viewers into the process so that they understand *how* the expert knows? Creative documentary filmmaking could make a difference, as those concerned with science literacy, including potential financiers, are aware.

5

Structure

We've all sat through documentaries that seemed pointless and meandering. Maybe they had great beginnings, but then they seemed to start again, and again, and again. The film seemed to be about one thing, but the rousing conclusion was about something altogether different. The story started in the present, and then quickly plunged into background and never resurfaced. Or the situation and characters were so weakly developed that we found ourselves caring little about the outcome. These are often

The aftermath of hurricane Katrina, from *When the Levees Broke: A Requiem in Four Acts*. Photo credit David Lee/40 Acres & A Mule.

problems of structure. *Structure* is the foundation on which story is built, whether that story is being told in person, in a book, or on screen. Already described as the film's "train" (Chapter 2), it's the narrative spine that determines where you start the story, where you end it, and how you parcel out information along the way. Structure works in response to the audience's built-in expectations; it's human nature to try to make sense of patterns and arrangements, to work at filling in the blanks and guessing what happens next. Filmmakers can heighten or confound those expectations, thereby increasing the viewer's involvement in a story and investment in its outcome. There's no such thing as a lack of structure; even in an experimental film, something's stringing those images together. That something, for better or worse, is structure.

ELEMENTS OF STRUCTURE

The building blocks of a film are shots, scenes, sequences, and, in some but not all cases, acts. Because these are commonly used words that at times have conflicting meanings, the following definitions clarify how they're being used here.

Shot

A shot is a single "take" on an image. There may be camera movement during the shot, or it may be static. It may be a close-up, a wide shot, a pan, or a tilt. But it begins and ends with the action of the cinematographer turning on and off the camera; later, the editor will further refine the shot by selecting from within it, giving it a new beginning and end point. Individual shots can convey a great deal of storytelling information: point of view, time of day, mood, emotion, character, rhythm, theme. A single shot may also include a "reversal," which is a twist in the plot, sometimes described as a change in values from one state to another. An example of a shot that contains a reversal can be found in *Yosemite: The Fate of Heaven*: We follow a cascading waterfall down through what appears to be pristine wilderness—until we land in a crowded tram full of noisy tourists. The reversal is from isolation to crowds, nature to humankind, pristine to polluted.

Scene

A scene is a consecutive group of shots within a single location. You might have a "scene at the courthouse" or a "scene on the boat." A scene is usually more than simply a snapshot of a location, however; it's a subset of the overall action.

A scene is made up of a series of beats. In *Born into Brothels*, the scene "The children ride a bus to the beach" might be broken down like this:

- A few shots (interior, then exterior) show the children's excitement that a bus has arrived and is waiting;
- From inside the bus, we see a child ask if she can sit by a window, because she wants to take pictures. Everyone's on board; another quick shot, and then Briski makes sure the children all have their cameras;
- With a honk, we see the driver's point of view (POV) as the trip gets under way. From inside and outside the bus, we see a range of shots: children looking, taking pictures, their point of view as they look out; the bus moving forward;
- Inside the bus, the children eat and begin to sing (various shots);
- One child is sick;
- The music shifts as the bus gets into a more rural area (seen from various points of view);
- Inside the bus, several of the children have fallen asleep (various shots), intercut with more traveling shots, as the landscape becomes more rural;
- The bus has stopped; the children gather their things and look out at the ocean.

In other words, the scene started with the excited shout "Hurry up. The bus is here," and ended with "Look at the water!" Like shots, sequences, and acts, scenes like this contain a beginning, middle, and end, and often, they culminate in a reversal, called a *turning point*, that motivates a shift in action of the overall story. Here, the reversal ties in with some of the film's themes. Boarding a bus in a congested, dirty city, the children arrive at the bright, open seaside. This reversal motivates the next scene—enjoying and photographing the beach.

To be satisfying, a scene should feel complete, which means that those filming the scene need to remain aware that events being witnessed will need to be condensed in the editing room — and shot accordingly. "I've got to get cutaways, I've got to get an end point of the scene, and I've got to get into the scene in some way," says director Susan Froemke (*Lalee's Kin*). Filmmaker Steven Ascher (*So Much So Fast*) adds, "Filming real life is a constant struggle to distill reality into a meaningful subset of itself . . . the telling moments, the telling gestures, the lines of dialogue that will suggest the rest of the scene without actually having to see the rest of the scene."

Sequence

A sequence is a collection of shots and scenes that together tell a more or less continuous story of an event that is a piece of your bigger story. Something like a book's chapter, a sequence also has a beginning, middle, and end. Note that a turning point at the end of a sequence will usually be bigger than one at the end of a scene or a shot. Story expert Robert McKee says that ideally, each scene creates a shift or reversal that is at least minor; each sequence, a change that is *moderate*; and each act, a change that is *major*.

Sequences can generally be summarized by the job they do in the overall storytelling. They're different from scenes in that they may cover a series of locations. *Frankie goes to the prom*, for example, is a sequence that might begin with Frankie rushing home from her job at the mall and continue with her emerging from her bedroom in a long white gown, dancing with her boyfriend, crying in the ladies' room because she's been dumped, and then arriving home, where she collapses into her mother's arms.

It's important that the overall sequence advance the larger story you're telling. If, for example, you're doing a film about Frankie working doggedly to earn a college scholarship, you might not have as much use for a sequence about Frankie going to the prom as you would for one such as *Frankie gets an internship* or *Frankie retakes her SATs*. (The latter might begin with Frankie hiring a private tutor and continue with a montage of her studying late at night and on Saturdays, getting ready to take the test, entering the test room, and end with her nervously taking the envelope, with her results, out of the mailbox.) If *Frankie going to the prom* is just a pleasant distraction from her real task at hand—and your story—it's probably not worth the time and effort to film.

Going back to *Born into Brothels*, we can see how the bus *scene* fits into a bigger *sequence*, which might be called "the day at the beach." The sequence begins with two quick exterior shots before the girl announces the bus's arrival, and continues through the bus ride and into a long scene of the children at the beach, discovering the ocean, playing in the waves, doing cartwheels, and taking pictures. And then it's night, and they're dancing on the bus as it heads back to Calcutta. It arrives, and we see the children make their way up the street, past "the line" of sex workers, and inside the narrow passages to their homes. (The entire sequence runs from a fade in at 36:48 (timed from the film's from first frame of action) to a fade out at 43:53.

This sequence achieves a number of things that serve the overall film. It shows the children interacting as a group and as independent, lively, spirited people. The pictures, especially Avijit's "Bucket," will be featured later in the film. Furthermore, the joy of the scene is immediately contrasted by the next scene, in which we see one of the children being beaten and his mother (and possibly grandmother) screaming obscenities at him and at neighbors. In the scene after that, we see some of the children in a car and hear Briski, voice-over: "I'm not a social worker, I'm not a teacher, even. That's my fear, you know, that I really can't do anything and that even helping them to get an education's not going to do anything. But without help, they're doomed." Having seen them in a brief day's escape, we want more than ever for her to succeed.

Act

An act is a series of sequences that drives to a major turning point—a climactic moment that springs directly from the story and makes necessary the next series of sequences in the act that follows. Each act plays a role in the overall storytelling, and the tension and momentum within each should be increasing. In traditional three-act (also known as dramatic) structure, the first act covers the bulk of the story's exposition and, to paraphrase the late showman and writer George M. Cohan, gets your hero up a tree. In the second act, you throw rocks at him, forcing him higher up in the tree. In the third act, you force him to the edge of a branch that looks as if it might break at any moment . . . and then you turn the corner to your story's resolution, and let your hero climb down.

There are three important things to know about acts. The first is that there is something about dramatic structure that seems built into the way we receive and enjoy stories. The second is that many documentaries do not fit neatly into this structure, but an approximation of it. Third, there are many ways to create a compelling structural throughline—what fiction writer Madison Smartt Bell describes as "narrative design"—in a documentary without going anywhere near dramatic three-act structure. The film still needs to have compelling characters and rising tension, each scene should move the narrative forward, and the film should satisfactorily conclude the story (or mission, essay, journey, etc.) with which it began. But it doesn't have to do it in three acts.

Before we move into some specifics of act structure, here are a few other useful terms.

Inciting Incident

The inciting incident is the event that sets the action of the story (the actions that relate to the *train*, not the subject) into motion. It may be something that's occurred before you start filming. In *Troublesome Creek*, for example (discussed in Chapter 16), it's the decision of the Jordan family, faced with debt, to farm one more year before auctioning off everything but their land. It's this decision that sets the story of the film in motion. In *Spellbound*, the inciting incident for each of the competitors we meet is that they are qualifying, or have qualified, to compete in the National Spelling Bee. In *Super Size Me*, the inciting incident, arguably, occurs when filmmaker Morgan Spurlock first learns of the lawsuit against McDonald's, and comes up with the notion of filming a 30-day McDiet.

Point of Attack

Not to be confused with the inciting incident, the point of attack is where *you*, as the filmmaker, enter the story. It's generally agreed that this is one of the hardest decisions to make over the course of production. In fact, it's often made and unmade many times before the right point of attack is found, and you can't imagine why you ever tried anything else. The point of attack ushers the viewer into the world of your film and its themes and characters. Discussing the opening visuals of his film *The City and the World*, episode seven of *New York* (1945–present), Ric Burns (Chapter 18) says, "It wasn't until fairly late in the editing process that we realized the beginning of the film was a moment in 1944 when Helen Leavitt borrows a 16mm movie camera and takes it up to the streets of East Harlem, and with a couple of friends, including James Agee, begins to shoot the footage that becomes her extraordinary film, *In the Streets*. That scene is absolutely, in my view, the best way to start that film, and it seems so completely inevitable— but it wasn't inevitable in the sense that we knew it from the beginning."

Where you begin your film is a critical decision, because it sets your train in motion and draws the audience into your story and its themes. As they discuss in Chapter 17, filmmakers Victoria Bruce and Karin Hayes attracted attention at the Slamdance Film Festival with their documentary, *Missing Peace*, about a Colombian presidential candidate who'd been kidnapped before the election and was still in captivity. But the film as shown had a soft start. "We had a slow build of getting to know this woman," Bruce says. When HBO Cinemax bought the film after the festival, HBO editor Geof Bartz moved the kidnapping up. The film now begins with images of a woman campaigning; a title card reads, *In January 2002, Ingrid Betancourt campaigned to become president of war-torn Columbia.* After a bit more campaign footage, the filmmakers cut to a view of mountains, as the credits and title appear onscreen: *The Kidnapping of Ingrid Betancourt.* The film then goes to previously-filmed footage of Betancourt with her children, as the story (beginning well before the kidnapping) gets under way. "It's brilliant," Bruce says, crediting the move to HBO executive producer Sheila Nevins, who argued that audiences would care more about Betancourt's time with her kids if they knew she'd be gone soon. In other words, the point of attack is the kidnapping. The film then goes back in time, and as in the cut at Slamdance, the first act continues with exposition about who Betancourt is and how she came to be running for president.

Your point of attack is very likely to change as you grow closer to your material and see which themes best serve the story you want to tell. You simply start with the best opening you have at that time and let it evolve from there.

Backstory

Backstory is a form of exposition, but the two terms are not always synonymous. The backstory includes the events that happened before (sometimes long before) the main story being told; it often includes material a filmmaker thinks is critical for the audiences to understand in order to "get" the story.

Backstory can be conveyed in a number of ways, including title cards (text on screen), interviews, narration, and conversation. To some extent, backstory involves the details of exposition that are revealed over the course of the film and add complexity to the story and its characters. Far along in *Grizzly Man*, for example, we learn that Timothy Treadwell very nearly won the role in the television series *Cheers* that went to actor Woody Harrelson. It is backstory—part of the complex journey that led Treadwell to live dangerously close to bears in the Alaskan wilderness. Placed where it is in the film, the detail adds a further layer of complexity to our understanding—and the filmmaker's—of the forces that led to Treadwell's death.

Often, and sometimes painfully, backstory gets dropped in the cutting room because the story itself has become so compelling and the themes so evident that the backstory is more of an interruption than a necessity. Backstory is most likely to stay in if it directly enhances and enriches the story unfolding on screen, adding depth to a character's motivation, illuminating themes and issues, or underscoring irony or historical continuity. A little goes a long way, however. If the backstory starts taking over your film, you might need to rethink which story, past or present, you really want to tell.

You may also need to look at where it's placed. In *The Kidnapping of Ingrid Betancourt*, the backstory (details about who the kidnapped candidate is, and how she came to be running for president) worked best after the train was under way: a candidate is kidnapped, and her family continues the campaign in her absence. In *When the Levees Broke*, a segment that presents the backstory of New Orleans's history doesn't appear until the third hour of the film. That hour "deals with the whole notion of coming back or staying—are people going to go back to New Orleans or stay where they are, are their lives better now in other places?" explains coproducer Sam Pollard. The notion of connection to the history and culture of the city motivates a look back at New Orleans in the years before the hurricane.

THREE-ACT STRUCTURE

For those who want to tread into the world of three-act structure, the following is a basic introduction. Three-act, or dramatic, structure is a staple of the Hollywood system, so one of the best ways to study it is to rent some mainstream films (it may be easiest to do this with popular dramatic films such as *My Cousin Vinny* or *Legally Blonde*, which are more likely to be built around a traditional three-act formula) and map them out, scene by scene, using a stopwatch or the video counter on your screen. You may not be able to really "see" the act structure until you're all the way through the film, but what you'll tend to find is that it *roughly* divides as follows:

Act One

The first act generally runs about one-quarter the length of the story. In this act, you introduce your characters and the problem or conflict (in other words, this act will contain most of your important exposition). Act One often contains the "inciting incident"—the event that gets everything rolling—although this event sometimes has already occurred when the story begins. There tends to be a "first turning point," which is somewhat smaller than the turning point that ends the act. By the end of Act One, the audience knows who and what your story is about and, at least initially, what's at stake. The first act drives to an emotional peak, the highest in the film so far, necessitating the action that launches the second act.

Act Two

The second act is the longest in the film, about one-half the length of the story. The stage has been set in Act One and the conflict introduced. In the second act, the story's pace increases as complications emerge, unexpected twists and reversals take place, and the stakes continue to rise. The second act can be difficult, because there is a risk that the story will bog down or become a succession of "and then this happened, and then this." You need your second act to continue to build as new information and new stakes are woven into your story. The second act drives to an emotional peak even greater than at the end of Act One, necessitating the action that launches the third act.

Act Three

The third act is usually slightly less than one-quarter the length of the story. As this act unfolds, the character is approaching defeat; he or she will reach the darkest moment just as the third act comes to a close. It's a common misperception that your third act resolves the story, but it doesn't. It intensifies it; the tension at the end of the third act should be even greater than the tension at the end of Act Two. That tension then pushes you into the *resolution*, those last moments where you resolve the story, tie up loose ends as necessary, and let your hero out of the tree.

Structuring Multiple Story Lines

Although you can only tell one primary story, it's possible to follow two or even three story lines within that story. In Hollywood terms, these are "A" stories, "B" stories, and possibly even "C" stories. The "A" story carries the primary weight and is the story around which the piece is structured, but the other stories should also have emotional peaks and valleys.

Most importantly, the stories should inform each other, meaning that at some point they should connect to form a coherent whole and advance a single overall story line. With *Lalee's Kin* (Chapter 21), matriarch Lalee Wallace and school superintendent Reggie Barnes are the protagonists of separate but related stories. Both want what's best for the children in their care and both see education as the route to getting it. Lalee's grandchildren and great-grandchildren attend the schools that Barnes oversees; they embody the difficulty and hope of Barnes's work.

When she was filming *Lalee's Kin*, Susan Froemke also began pursuing a third story line, about a man who taught literacy to young fathers in prison. It fit the program's themes, but there was no direct overlap and eventually the story was dropped. "In terms of storytelling and in terms of a budget, it became almost overwhelming," Froemke says. "We found that the more questions we had and the more questions we answered we still had to keep simplifying." (About a year after the filming was complete, she adds, the stories did unexpectedly intersect, through the imprisonment of Lalee's son, Eddie Reed.)

Yosemite: The Fate of Heaven contrasts the primeval Yosemite that survived until the 19th century with the national park that today accommodates several million visitors a year. The filmmakers interweave two stories, one more clearly narrative than the other. The first is built around an 1854 diary kept by Lafayette Bunnell, who was part of a battalion that entered Yosemite on an Indian raid. "It was a search and destroy story, eerily reminiscent of Vietnam," says filmmaker Jon Else, "an old-fashioned war story of a bunch of soldiers looking for a bunch of Indians, and going out and driving the Indians from their home." The second is a more impressionistic look at the ongoing, day-to-day struggle to balance use of the park by those who love it with the needs of those who maintain it and are working to preserve it for the future.

The use of multiple story lines often enables filmmakers to create films that are more complex than would be possible with a strictly linear approach. Rather than tell everything in the order in which it occurred, they select an event *within* a life and use that to focus the primary film narrative, which frees them to look back into the past or even ahead into the future as needed. This format can be seen in the upcoming case studies (Chapter 7) of *Daughter from Danang* and *Murderball*.

What Three-Act Structure Is Not

Three-act structure does not mean taking a film and dividing it into three parts and calling each part an act. An act can only be considered as such if it advances the one overall story (or essay) that you set out to tell. For example, a film that looks at early settlements in the United States can't be structured, "Act One, Plymouth, Massachusetts; Act Two, Jamestown, Virginia; Act Three, New York, New York." There is no common story there; there may be common themes and this may work as an organizational construct for a film, but these aren't acts. On the other hand, you could tell three individual dramatic stories within that structure, one within each location that you then combine into a film.

Three Acts in Five or One or Two

Whether your film is described as having five acts or one, it can still follow dramatic (three-act) structure. There are many practical reasons to divide a story, including breaks for commercials (television) or audience intermission (theater). But "one-act" plays and "five-act" television specials can often still be divided into three acts. For example, while David Auburn wrote *Proof* as a fictional, two-act stage play, the action can easily be broken into three-act dramatic structure. Auburn's "first act" actually contains all of Act One and the first half of Act Two; his "second act" contains the balance of Act Two and all of Act Three. Where you break a story for reasons like commercials or intermissions is part of the structural discussion, but does not necessarily interfere with your use of dramatic storytelling. With stakes rising throughout, there are natural places in most stories (e.g., the first turning point in the first act, the midpoint of the second act) that lend themselves to breaks.

Conversely, simply because a story is divided up for commercial breaks doesn't mean it's divided into acts. Many biographical films, for example, are shaped more by chronology than by a story being told, so that breaks come at dramatic moments but do not generally represent an underlying three-act structure.

APPLYING FILM STRUCTURE

Some documentary filmmakers think about structure over the course of production but don't focus on it until they're editing. Others play with structure from the start, creating outlines that they return to during production and postproduction, revising them and reshaping them as needed. No matter how you anticipate structuring your film or what your process is, structure is a type of grid that allows you to anticipate and critique the rhythms of your storytelling—structure is not a formula for production. In fact, in terms of actually weighing the relative length of scenes, sequences, and acts, it's safe to say that most filmmakers don't do it; storytelling is usually more intuitive. However, if a film feels like it takes forever to get going, or your test audiences love the opening but lose interest from there, or your audience is thoroughly confused by a terrific ending that seems to have nothing to do with the film you introduced at the beginning, mapping structure can be a good idea. I do it all the time in my consulting; I go through the film with a stop watch (or watch it with a counter on my computer screen) and sketch out the story, when and where it reaches its various peaks and how (or if) they relate to the film's train. Seeing the film on a single piece of paper like that, it's often very easy to see that it began twice, or that the first act is twice as long as it should be, or that the third act drives to a climactic moment that may be emotional but is unsatisfying because it has nothing to do with the train that got under way in Act One.

What's interesting is how many successful documentaries, even those that seem vastly different in style and approach, can be analyzed in terms of acts. This is true even with many films that in whole or in part defy some of the more formulaic rules of Hollywood storytelling. **But act structure or not, the important thing to keep in mind is that if your film is working—even if the charts and stopwatches say it shouldn't be—leave it alone.** Storytelling is an art, not a science. Go with your gut. If the film's great, who cares what "rules" you broke?

6

Manipulating Time

Film is a linear medium. People watch it from beginning to end, with one shot following another, one sequence following another, until the film is over. "I've never seen an even vaguely success-ful documentary film that does not move forward through time," says filmmaker Jon Else, citing a number of disparate examples. "*Night and Fog* has an absolutely traditional, very simple forward chronological motion through the late 1930s to the end of World War II. *Tongues Untied*, Marlon Riggs's film, appears to be a non-linear rumination about what it means to be young and gay and black in America in the 1980s, but in fact it moves through his life. Even Chris Marker's *Sans Soleil*, which is often described as being nonlinear, moves forward through time. This whole business of a plot moving forward, I think, is just so inextricably embedded in our cultural DNA."

Moving a story forward through time, as evidenced by the preceding examples, does not mean resorting to a plodding narrative that is strictly a chronological recitation of events in the order that they occurred. Often, it involves the interweaving of chronological and nonchronological elements to form a cohe-sive and satisfying whole; a film that drives forward while being enriched and made complex by elements outside or apart from the chronology. *Daughter from Danang* selects an event within the chronology of Heidi Bub's life—her trip to Vietnam in 1997 to meet her birthmother—as the framework, or train, through which to explore issues and events that cover the entire span of her life, including her birth in 1968 and, especially, her mother's decision to give her up for adoption in 1975.

There are many ways to present a chronological story in an order that satisfies the requirements of good dramatic storytelling. This doesn't mean fictionalizing actual events, but *presenting* those events in a different order, provided you are true to the underlying facts. While this kind of structuring may change over the course of production and especially during editing, your approach to a story's underlying chronology is also a big part of how you think about a film's train. Think back to the example of Jim Jones and Guyana, from Chapter 2. The hypothetical film started with a congressman's fact-finding mission in 1978, and the events that immediately followed formed the film's train. But the bigger story that was told, about Jim Jones and the People's Temple, actually began decades earlier.

TELLING A CHRONOLOGICAL STORY, BUT NOT CHRONOLOGICALLY

As a documentary storyteller, you decide where to begin and end the story. You can begin in the middle, go back to the beginning, catch up with your story, and then move ahead to the end. You can start at the end before moving to the beginning to ask, "How did we get here?" You can flash forward or back. The only thing you can't do, in a documentary that's driven by a narrative sequence of events, is change the important facts of the main underlying chronology.

Suppose you've unearthed a story in the archives of your local historical society. The following are the events in chronological order:

- A young man becomes engaged;
- His older brother enlists to fight in World War II;
- The young man also enlists;
- Their father dies;
- The young man is shipped overseas;
- He learns that his brother has been killed;
- His fiancée sends a letter, breaking off their engagement.

These events haven't happened in an order that's particularly dramatic, and there's no way to tell, on the surface, which events are linked by cause and effect. It may be that because his brother enlisted, the young man also felt obligated, but there could be other reasons. If you can verify your characters' motivations, whether through records or eyewitnesses, you can state them; otherwise, present the facts and let the audience draw its own conclusions. By the same token, you may not rearrange the underlying chronology to imply a more interesting cause and effect. For example, based on the above chronology, you might be tempted to:

- Show the two sons enlisting *after* their father's death, to create the impression that they enlisted in his honor;
- Film a recreation in which the young man, already in uniform, proposes marriage;
- Present the fiancée's letter in voice-over as the young man enlists, implying that he's enlisting in reaction to the breakup.

Each of these might be dramatic, but they all lead the audience to a false understanding of cause and effect. But respecting cause and effect, there are still some more dramatic choices. Start with the young man's rejection by his fiancée, for example, and then reveal that this is another in a string of losses. Leave the father and fiancée out of the story and focus on the two brothers at war. Tell the story of the young man going to war, and then go back to follow the story of his engagement. There's plenty of room for creativity.

An example of a documentary that creates a false impression of chronology, to the detriment of an otherwise powerful argument and film, is Michael Moore's *Roger & Me*. Critic Harlan Jacobson published a detailed review of this film in *Film Comment*, outlining some of the problems. The film's present-day narrative begins in late 1986, when, according to Moore, General Motors chairman Roger Smith closed 11 plants in Flint, Michigan, leaving 30,000 people jobless and sending the city on a downward spiral.

Moore then presents a series of events, including these, in this order:

- Eleven GM plants are opened in Mexico, where, Moore says, workers can be paid 70 cents an hour;
- The last vehicle rolls off the assembly line in Flint;

- Ronald Reagan visits Flint; over archival news footage, Moore narrates, *Just when things were beginning to look bleak, Ronald Reagan arrived in Flint. . . .* At the end of the scene, Moore says someone *borrowed the cash register on his way out the door;*
- A parade is held in Flint, and Moore interviews Miss Michigan shortly before she'll compete to be Miss America;
- Evangelist Robert Schuller comes to Flint to cheer people up;
- As Moore presents an abandoned and decaying Flint, he says, *The city had become the unemployment capitol of the country. Just when it looked like all was lost, the city fathers came up with one last great idea.* This plan includes the building of a Hyatt Regency hotel downtown; the Water Street Pavilion, a new shopping center; and the opening of Auto World.

Remember that the film began with the closing of 11 plants in Flint, late in 1986. From Harlan Jacobson's article, here is the actual chronology of the events:

- In 1980, Ronald Reagan arrives in town as a presidential candidate and buys folks pizza. Two days before his visit, the cash register was stolen;
- In 1982, Reverend Schuller comes to Flint and the Hyatt Regency is opened;
- Auto World opens in mid-1984 and closes in early 1985;
- In 1986, the Water Street Pavilion opens, the result of a plan that may have been under way since the early 1970s. Also in 1986, the number of layoffs at GM do not total 30,000 but about 10,000, according to Jacobson. The real "watershed" of layoffs had occurred much earlier, in 1974. The net loss of jobs since 1974 was about 32,000.
- In the fall of 1988, shortly after the parade, Miss Michigan is crowned Miss America.

In other words, many of the events presented as the efforts of the powers-that-be to staunch the bleeding from the 1986 layoffs actually occurred, or were under way, long before those lay-offs took place. Jacobson's article includes an interview with Moore, in which he asks the filmmaker about these issues. "The movie is about essentially what happened to this town during the

1980s," Moore responded. "As far as I'm concerned, a period of seven or eight years . . . is pretty immediate and pretty devastating" [*ellipses in the original*]. Moore argued that he was trying to "tell a documentary in a way they don't usually get told. The reason why people don't watch documentaries is they are so bogged down with 'Now in 1980 . . . then in '82 five thousand were called back . . . in '84 ten thousand were laid off . . . but then in '86 three thousand were called back . . . but later in '86 ten thousand more were laid off.' "

In fact, telling an accurate story doesn't have to mean getting bogged down in detail or needing to tell the story sequentially. Arguably, you could leave the edit of *Roger & Me* exactly as it is and simply rewrite Moore's narration. For example, there's nothing to stop your use of footage of candidate Reagan stumping through Flint years before the plant closings; you simply write into it in a way that acknowledges the time shift. Here's Moore's narration, building on the aftermath of the 1986 layoff: *Just when things were beginning to look bleak, Ronald Reagan arrived in Flint and took a dozen unemployed workers out for a pizza. He told them he had come up with a great idea, and if they tried it they'd all be working again.* (In archival footage, a woman then explains that Reagan suggested they move to another state to find work.)

Alternative narration: *People had been trying to help the unemployed in Flint for years. As a candidate in 1980, future president Ronald Reagan took a dozen workers out for some pizza and inspiration.*

The narration needs to keep track of where you are in the film's present—in this case, somewhere between 1986 and 1988—while letting us know that what we're seeing is from the past, and how it informs the present. What to do about the cash register theft? This sounds like one of those facts that is "too good to check," but it must be done. If you know that the theft occurred two days before Reagan's visit, and you really want to use it, you have to be a bit creative.

Moore's words: *None of Reagan's luncheon guests got back into the factories in the ensuing years, and the only bright spot to come out of the whole affair was the individual who borrowed the cash register on his way out the door.*

It's unclear whether these luncheon guests were already laid off before Reagan arrived (and stayed that way) or if they were employed between Reagan's visit and the layoffs later in the 1980s.

In any case (or if you can't find out the specifics about the individuals in this footage), you could say something more general, such as: *In the years to come, Reagan's luncheon guests may have wished that instead of listening to the candidate, they'd taken a cue from the guy who'd robbed the pizza parlor two days earlier and made off with the cash register.*

While mine is not brilliant voice-over, it's a quick example of how you can tell a story out of order, with as much irreverence as you want, without building a case that has a weak or inaccurate foundation. To imply that the visits of Reverend Schuller and Ronald Reagan and the opening of the Hyatt Regency and Auto World occurred both after and because of a plant closing in 1986 is simply inaccurate. In his defense, Moore told Jacobson that *Roger & Me* isn't a documentary but "an entertaining movie that hopefully will get people to think a little bit about what is going on." However, audiences and critics received the film as a documentary, and it's highly regarded as such. The power of documentaries comes from their veracity, and it's undermined if people discover that in the interest of a compelling argument, they've been misled.

Not all documentaries, or sequences within them, need to adhere to a strict chronology; filmmakers may rearrange filmed sequences if they are typical but not necessarily specific to a time line, such as routine events (skateboard practice, Sunday church, an annual holiday). Where you place this material in the film, regardless of when it was shot, is generally up to you. If you're following a group of people—residents in an assisted living center, for example—your choice of which scenes and stories to present and when may be driven by the emotional argument you're building, rather than any specific chronology or the order in which stories were filmed. (Within each story, however, rules of cause and effect still apply. If a woman suffers a heart attack, recovers, and then dances with her husband at a formal dinner, it would be dishonest to edit the sequence to imply that the dancing led to the heart attack.)

Material filmed for thematic reasons may also stand apart from the chronological sequence. An example of this can be found in *Troublesome Creek: A Midwestern.* The chronology is built on the Jordans's efforts to pay off a bank debt by auctioning off their belongings. For thematic reasons, the filmmakers asked the Jordans to return to a farm they'd rented for many years before moving to the farm they're now at risk of losing. The scene's exact placement in the film, other than sometime before the auction, isn't specific. Jordan's voice-over simply says, "Early one morning we took a trip to Rolfe to visit . . . the farm I grew up on." Jordan's parents are upset to discover that the old place is abandoned, but their visit doesn't motivate any action. Instead, it serves a filmmaking purpose—shedding light on the historical context of the overall film and on themes of change and loss.

COLLAPSING AND EXPANDING TIME

Filmmaking, from shooting through editing, is a process of expanding and/or collapsing real time. "Filming real life is a constant struggle to distill reality into a meaningful subset of itself, into the telling moments, the telling gestures, the lines of dialogue that will suggest the rest of the scene without actually having to see the rest of the scene," says Steven Ascher. The event needs to be covered with the editor in mind, so that there is enough variety of shots, cutaways, and transitional material to make a creative edit possible.

For the most part, simple editing can imply a passage of time. Your characters are at home, seated around the breakfast table, and then they're on the school basketball court; or your character is trying on a tux for the prom, and then he's at the prom. If the story has been taking place in the summertime, and you cut to children playing in the snow, the season has changed. Sometimes, filmmakers emphasize passage of time with dissolves, time-lapse photography, an interlude with music, or a montage. If the passage of time is part of the story, the filmmaker might comment on that visually. Errol Morris used a clock to mark the hours that passed while Randall Adams was being pressured to confess in *The Thin Blue Line*.

Some scenes may be granted more or less emotional weight than others through the length of time you devote to them. For example, you might spend two minutes of screen time bringing the audience up to date on 10 years of history prior to a candidate's decision to run for office, and then spend the next 45 minutes on an eight-month campaign; you've collapsed the first part of the chronological story in order to focus more time on the campaign itself. And sometimes you expand time because you've built to an emotional moment and you need to let it play, as was true in at the end of *Bridge to Freedom*, or the last hour of the first season of the series *Eyes on the Prize*.

FILMING OVER TIME

In some cases, a documentary's complexity comes not only from its immediate story but from an opportunity to check in on characters months or even years later. A recent example of this is the Spanish film *Braceros*. The film begins in 1994 and follows a handful of determined emigrants who risk their lives in order to reach the shores of the United States, traveling on dangerous, makeshift rafts. Some don't make it far offshore; others are picked up by the U.S. Coast Guard and held in detention at Guntánamo for many months. Eventually, though, each makes his or her way to the United States, and we see them settling down in small towns and big cities throughout the country. The filmmakers check in on them nine months later, to see how they're doing, and then they check in on them again five *years* later. The result is a look at immigration and the American dream, at opportunities seized and squandered, and at choices and mistakes that can have a lasting impact.

Another noted example is British filmmaker Michael Apted's *Up* series. In the 1960s, Apted worked on *Seven Up!*, a documentary in which 14 seven-year-olds of various economic backgrounds were interviewed about their lives and hopes for the future. Apted, who is also known as a feature film director (*Coal Miner's Daughter, The World Is Not Enough*), assumed direction of the project, returning in seven-year intervals to see how the children and their dreams were holding up at ages 14, 21, 28, 35, 42, and most recently, 49. A few of the original subjects dropped out of the project over the years, but most continue to participate, and in their achievements and frustrations audiences get a profound look at what it means to live ordinary, extraordinary lives.

COLLAPSING INTERVIEWS

There are two primary reasons to edit an interview: to focus information and to shorten the time it takes to convey that information.

A person will talk to you for 10 minutes, an hour, maybe two or three hours, and you'll usually end up using only a few bites, unless the entire film is "a conversation with." You must condense the interview material in a way that does not alter its initial meaning and remains true to the intent of the speaker. For example, here's the raw transcript of a witness describing your character, Sanders:

> *CHARLIE: Sanders wasn't a bad man, in fact I'd have to say he was a pretty good guy, overall, which is why nobody could figure out—at least I couldn't figure out—uh, what the, what he was doing even thinking about embezzlement. I don't know, but I think, I mean, who knows, but in my opinion, he was just panicked about money. I mean for crying out loud, this guy's got three, uh, three, uh, you know, he's got three kids and another one on the uh, on the way—maybe it got to him, I don't know, maybe he just couldn't figure out how he was going to support all these little ones or whatever, you know? He was selling auto parts, used auto parts. Besides, embezzlement's a white collar crime, he's a blue collar guy—well, not really, he's not working with the auto parts, he's more the manager of the store, driving to work in his, oh, what was it, Tercel, his blue Tercel, shirt and tie and all the while I guess he's thinking nobody above him would miss that thirty thou. Arrogance, I guess. Yeah. Arrogance.*

What can't you use? No matter how catchy it sounds, I wouldn't use, "embezzlement's a white collar crime, he's a blue collar guy" for two reasons. Sanders is not, in fact, blue collar, and furthermore, the witness *himself* corrects this statement.

In terms of editing for time, however, condensing the essence of this paragraph, you could do any number of cuts depending on the point you want Charlie to make and where it will be used in the film. What material is the interview bite following? What will it precede? One of the ways to see this before trying it in the editing room is to make the cut on paper, which you can then give to the editor. Two things to remember. First, don't make the editor crazy by cutting out every third word and expecting her to construct a sentence or a paragraph out of the bits and pieces. This is very difficult and very time-consuming, and furthermore, any interview material that's hacked to bits will have to be used as a voice-over. In any case, if you're hacking an interview to bits, chances are good that either you've interviewed the wrong person or you're asking this interview to do a job in the film that it wasn't meant to do, and you should probably look for other solutions.

The second thing to remember is that a cut on paper may not work on film. The way people speak often reads differently than it sounds. People end sentences with a question, or they run two sentences together, or they burp or sigh or a plane flies overhead or their energy level shifts so much that you can't cut between two bites. You do the best you can to note the big issues when you're watching rushes (the raw footage) with the transcripts in hand, but there will still be times when something that should work just doesn't.

With that said, there are a few tricks to increasing the odds that your paper cut will work. It's generally easier to cut into a hard consonant, such as *b*, *t*, or *v*. Words that begin with soft consonants, such as *s* or *h*, can be more difficult. Note that just because you cut the "Well" from "Well, I think it started" doesn't mean that the editor can make the excision. Usually, though, if one bite or cut doesn't work, there will be something else available that's close enough. Finally, there is a rhythm to how long a person needs to be on camera before you can cut away from him, depending in part on whether you've seen the person on camera before. While this is something you can anticipate in a paper cut, it can't really be decided until the editor is working with the material. (And, as will be discussed in Chapter 13, another common problem is that as the schedule wears on, the production team gets tired of interview bites they once found exciting and cuts them too close.)

Whether or not you "cover" the edits with cutaways is a stylistic choice. When you cut from two different parts of an interview, especially when the focal length (e.g., close-up, medium shot) hasn't changed, the cut—known as a jump cut—can be jarring. Some filmmakers find an elegance or at least an honesty in a jump cut; there is no disguising that the material has been edited. Others "cover" the edit with a cutaway, so that the soundtrack continues, apparently seamlessly. (For example, you're on someone's face as they talk; while they're still talking, the film cuts to the person's hands, fidgeting; then to a neighbor, listening from a nearby chair; then to a clock on the wall, and then back to the speaker's face.) How long you cut away from someone before you need to see them speaking again is a matter of taste, as is the decision about how long you can hear someone's voice "over" before you show who is speaking. Sometimes, you let an interview play simply because you don't want to interrupt the answer. And sometimes, the entire interview will be voice-over (v/o), especially if the footage is all of one person and/or it's very obvious who is speaking. Effective portraits of people at work—a zookeeper, an underwater explorer—have been done this way.

Of course, editing *within* an interview is only one solution. You can also synthesize a story by using multiple storytellers and cutting between them, or using narration to reduce the amount of interview needed or to state concisely something with which the interviewee struggled. For this discussion, the focus is on reducing the length of the interview in a way that is consistent with generally accepted principles of documentary ethics. For example, here are some ways to shorten the interview in which Charlie discusses his friend, Sanders:

> CHARLIE: *Sanders wasn't a bad man, in fact I'd have to say he was a pretty good guy, overall, which is why nobody could figure out — at least I couldn't figure out, uh, what the, what he was doing even thinking about embezzlement. . . . . Arrogance, I guess. Yeah. Arrogance.*

> CHARLIE: *(beginning v/o) . . . he was just panicked about money. I mean for crying out loud, this guy's got three, uh, you know, (now, possibly on camera) he's got three kids and another one on the uh, on the way—maybe it got to him, I don't know, maybe he just couldn't figure out how he was going to support all these little ones or whatever, you know?*

> CHARLIE: *(beginning v/o) He was selling auto parts, used auto parts. Besides, embezzlement's a white collar crime, he's a blue collar guy — well, not really, he's not working with the auto parts, he's more the manager of the store, driving to work in his, oh, what was it, Tercel, his blue Tercel, shirt and tie and all the while I guess he's thinking nobody above him would miss that thirty thou.*

Depending on what your story is and where you're going with it, each of these edits might work. The first gets to the root of why Sanders did it, at least in Charlie's opinion—arrogance. The second explores a more sympathetic reason behind the crime. And the third paints a picture and gives some specific information about Sanders and his job. If you already have Sanders's wife describing him staying up late at night panicked by bills, you might not want to use version 2. If in fact he was not at all arrogant, just blindly panicked, you might not use 1. And if you find out that he drove a used BMW, you can't use #3 because it's not accurate. Your talking heads must be fact checked, and errors can't be left in simply because you, the filmmaker, didn't say it. By leaving it in, you are saying it. Note that a significant exception is when the falsehood is part of the story, as was the case with the "eyewitnesses" rounded up by law enforcement personnel in *The Thin Blue Line*.

Another problem to watch out for when condensing interview material (or any sync material, which includes footage of people talking to others on camera) is that out of context, something may honestly seem to mean one thing, but those who were on the shoot know that it meant something else. This is why it's important that someone connected with the original shooting be involved in the edit, or at least given a chance to sign off on it. Usually, the director and/or producer maintain this oversight, but cost cutting has led some venues to farm out bits of production and effectively separate the editing and packaging of a documentary from the shooting of it. When that happens, all editorial decisions are made by people with no direct connection to those filmed, which can be risky. (For the same reason, a writer or consultant who begins work on a film late in the process of editing should refer back to original transcripts and unedited footage.)

Throughout the editing process, and perhaps especially when collapsing interviews, filmmakers need to be careful to maintain accuracy. Something as simple as taking a sentence from late in the interview and putting it at the beginning might make sense for the overall film argument, but if it distorts the meaning of the specific interview, you can't do it. "You've always got to try to know when to back away from that stuff," says filmmaker Sam Pollard (Chapter 22), "not to manipulate it to such a degree that it's like a lie."

Case Studies

7

One of the best ways to understand documentary films is to analyze them. Rent or buy a DVD (or VHS) copy and plan to spend a few hours with each film. Have a pad of paper and a pen handy, or split your computer screen so that you can see the film and type notes at the same time. You'll need to be able to see a time counter in the frame.

First, pay attention to the title. What does it set you up to anticipate? Next, make note of how long the film is. As a *very* rough guide, divide the total number of minutes by four. In films that employ three-act dramatic structure (or simply follow its rhythms), it's likely that in many cases—but by no means all—the end of the first quarter will *roughly* correspond to the end of the first act. The end of the third quarter will roughly correspond to the end of the second act. The end of the fourth quarter, or shortly before it, is the end of your third act, with the remaining film time spent (briefly) on resolution. (It's rarely this simple, but I find that it offers a good benchmark for beginning to map the structure.) As you watch, pay attention to casting: Who comes on screen, what role do they play in the film? Pay attention to when you're confused, and see if or when the filmmaker answers your confusion. Also note where and how you feel tension or concern for the characters or situation, and whether (or how) that tension is resolved.

CASE STUDY: *DAUGHTER FROM DANANG*

Daughter from Danang, nominated for an Academy Award in 2003, is roughly 78 minutes in length. As discussed elsewhere, the film tells the story of Heidi Bub, an Amerasian woman raised in

Tennessee who travels to Vietnam to meet the birth mother who gave her up for adoption. Elements of the film include live-action shooting, archival footage and stills (including personal artifacts), and interviews.

Filmmakers Gail Dolgin and Vicente Franco shot in Vietnam for about a week with Bub and did additional shooting in Vietnam after she went home. After they returned to the United States, they conducted a follow-up interview with her. "Everything happened quickly, and we were really just gathering material," Dolgin says. "We came back with the story we had and then started doing research for the backstory of Bub's experience in the U.S., the babylift, and what the mother's experience might be, and it wasn't until after we accumulated all of that and started looking at it that we said, 'Wow, we've got a lot of material here, what do we do with it?'"

At that point, the filmmakers began approaching financiers, who wanted to know how the film would be structured. "They weren't asking for a script," she says, "but they wanted a clear sense of how we were going to tell the story." The filmmakers didn't want to tell a strictly chronological story, one that would begin with Bub's Vietnamese mother giving her up (in 1975) and move forward to the reunion (in 1997). "We were playing with the concept of memory; it's so capricious," Dolgin says. "Heidi's memories of her past with her mother—she says at different times in the film, 'I had such great memories' and 'The memories are so painful, they're all going to heal when I go to Vietnam.'" Because of this, they decided to structure the film around Bub's trip to Vietnam, using moments within the trip to motivate her memories of the past. "Working with that structure allowed us to figure out what story to craft out of this very complicated journey that we had all been on," she says.

The film took about a year to edit (Kim Roberts edited), and the final version offers an excellent example of three-act dramatic structure as applied to a documentary film. Note, however, that the timings and outline that follow are an analysis done by me, not the filmmakers. Dolgin says that the process of structuring their film was more organic, and that although they tried outlining material on the computer, "ultimately, having an Avid or any of the nonlinear (digital editing) systems, you can do so much of that trial-and-error with the actual material that it just made more sense to work that way."

Act One/Title Sequence

Zeroing the counter (00:00) at the first frame of action, the film begins with text on screen (with music in the background) that sets up basic information: In 1975, the U.S. government launched "Operation Babylift," through which over 2,000 Amerasian children were brought to the United States for adoption. Archival images of the war follow, as a voice-over begins in Vietnamese, with English subtitles: "There were so many rumors. I was so frightened. If I didn't send my child away"—we now see the speaker, an older woman—"both she and I would die." Over more archival footage, we hear another speaker, revealed to be a young woman, as she remembers being torn from her family. "How could she do this to me? How could you just give up a child like that?" After some archival shots of airplanes, the title comes up: *Daughter from Danang*. Briefly, in this opening sequence, we've seen the *inciting incident* (the separation), the *protagonist and antagonist* (daughter and mother), and a foreshadowing of the conflict that will emerge between them.

After the title and opening credits, the film opens on a beach in Danang, and we learn more about Heidi's mother, who has missed her daughter for 20 years: "Finding her would be like giving birth a second time," she says. We learn that Heidi, too, has always hoped for a reunion, and is now getting ready to go and see her birth mother "face-to-face, for the first time in 22 years." This reunion is the film's train; it is the present-day narrative spine that drives the story forward. Once the train is under way, the filmmakers are free to take motivated detours into the past. Sitting on the airplane, for example—"going home," as she puts it—Heidi Bub tells us that the trip is bringing back memories, adding, "I was born in Danang, in 1968." The filmmakers use this opening to return to the past. We learn more about Bub's birth (her mother says Bub "had no father"), the war, and why her mother decided to send her away. (Note that the filmmakers are only telling us what we need to know at this point. Later, for example, will we learn important details about Bub's father.)

Bub's mother brought her to the orphanage, telling her she "must never forget" (6:02). This is the first big turning point; it also provides motivation for the filmmakers to explore the historic issues of Operation Babylift and what it meant in terms of U.S. policy. Among the storytellers in this section is Tran Tuog (T. T.) Nhu, identified as a journalist. She and her husband talk about their awareness, even then, that some of these "orphans" had families in Vietnam; through archival footage we see American social workers pressuring Vietnamese mothers to give up their children, a detail that adds complexity to the specific story of Bub and her mother. (Note that Nhu is not simply an expert in this story, but someone who plays a role in the reunion of Heidi and her mother.)

A little more than 10 minutes into the film, Bub describes meeting her adoptive mother, with whom she moved to Tennessee, assuming an American identity. The sequence culminates with Bub being told, "If anybody asks where you were born, you tell 'em Columbia, South Carolina" (16:27).

But Bub's birth mother has begun searching for her daughter, and, by coincidence, gives a letter to an American who knows T. T. Nhu. Through Nhu, the mother's letter reaches the Holt Adoption Agency. In the meantime, Bub, at the age of 20 or 21, starts looking for her birth mother, and she, too, ends up at Holt. She contacts Nhu, and together they make plans to go to Vietnam for the reunion. This is the end of Act One, roughly a quarter of the way into the film. Note that once the filmmakers get the train under way, they are free to spend the first act on backstory, establishing who the characters are, how they became separated, and what it took to get to the verge of reunion.

Act Two

Act Two begins on the plane, as T. T. Nhu and Heidi Bub head to Vietnam. Bub begins to worry; she's been "101 percent Americanized" and has "no earthly idea" of her family's expectations. In this act, the filmmakers show how out of place Bub is in her native Vietnam; they set up her nervousness about meeting her mother, and her high hopes for what this meeting will mean. "It's going to be so healing for both of us to see each other," Bub says. "It's going to make all of those bad memories go away, and all of those last years not matter anymore."

At around 24:00, Bub and the filmmakers meet Bub's mother and other members of her family in Vietnam. Had this moment come earlier, the audience would not have been as prepared as they are, by this point in the film, to experience it. We are emotionally invested in the reunion because we've gotten to know something about Bub and her mother, and we're curious about the growing number of questions that remain unanswered: Where is Bub's adoptive mother? Who was her father? Are Bub's expectations realistic?

The reunion plays on screen for a while before the filmmakers use another interview statement to again motivate a return to the past. "I always wanted the feeling that someone would love me no matter what," Bub says. "And I never had that with Ann [her adoptive mother]." This time, the filmmakers' exploration of the past drives to a painful revelation: Escalating tension between Bub and her adoptive mother led to a severing of their relationship when Bub was still in college. By presenting this information here, the filmmakers have raised the stakes on the reunion currently under way in Vietnam: Bub has felt rejected by two mothers, so this reunion with the first has added significance. We carry this new information with us as we return to Vietnam, and the visit continues.

Act Two continues in this fashion, balancing the story on screen with events that have led to these moments. We learn more about Bub's husband and two children, and about her birth father,

Mai Thi Kim and her daughter, Heidi Bub, in *Daughter from Danang*. Photo courtesy of the filmmakers.

an American soldier. We also see a new complexity in the visit. Bub is getting homesick; she is overwhelmed by the poverty and lack of opportunity she encounters in Vietnam, and is newly appreciative of what her life in the United States has afforded her.

At this point, events themselves raise the stakes on Bub's story, as her Vietnamese family begins asking her for money. T. T. Nhu, serving as cultural interpreter for the viewers as well as for Bub, explains that having a relative overseas can be an important lifeline to those in Vietnam. But Bub says she doesn't want to be anybody's salvation; she came here to be reunited (50:00). Tension continues to build as we realize that Bub and her family each have a very different understanding of what this visit might lead to. Increasingly critical of her mother and feeling smothered by her family's attention, Bub finally says, "I can't wait to get out of here."

Act Three

The worst is yet to come, which is part of what makes the third act so strong. (Contrary to a common misperception, the stakes should continue to rise in Act Three, until the issue or conflict reaches its most extreme point. Only then, in the last minutes, should there be resolution.) T. T. Nhu has to leave, so a new translator is brought in to help Bub through a lengthy and painful family meeting in which all of the misunderstandings come to a head. Bub's brothers ask her to bring their mother to the United States; then they suggest that she assume her "filial responsibility" by sending a monthly stipend. Bub is hurt, then outraged, even refusing to allow her mother to comfort her (63:36). Speaking to the filmmakers, Bub takes a position almost opposite to the one with which she began the journey: "I wish I could have just kept the memories I had— they were so happy. I wish this trip never happened now." She leaves Vietnam, and when the filmmakers visit her at her home in Rhode Island shortly afterward, she's not even sure she wants to write to her mother; "I wouldn't know what to say." Arguably, Act Three ends either when Bub leaves Vietnam (off screen), or here, at around 75:00. Although she's achieved her initial goal, to reunite with her birth mother, Bub has not succeeded in forming a bond with her or "erasing" bad memories. In some ways, the two women seem farther apart than they were before the story began, because their hopes for the reunion are gone.

Resolution

The resolution in this film comes in the form of a brief epilogue, which begins with a caption that reads: *Two Years Later*. Bub and her children are seen visiting her adoptive grandmother. In an interview, Bub summarizes her current feelings about her Vietnamese family. "I guess I have closed the door on them," she says, adding, "but I didn't lock the door. It's closed, but it's not locked." The ending, in part because of this ambiguity, is a satisfying resolution to the story that began the film.

CASE STUDY: *MURDERBALL*

Winner of the Documentary Audience Award and a Special Jury Prize for Editing at the 2005 Sundance Film Festival, *Murderball* is a terrific example of a modern documentary. Underneath an energetic soundtrack and some athletic competition is scientific information about spinal cord injury and an unsentimental look at disability. Like *Daughter from Danang*, *Murderball* generally follows a three-act dramatic structure. "During the shooting, we discussed fiction films, not docs," said co-director and cinematographer Henry-Alex Rubin, in the film's online publicity material. Citing dramas including *The Great Santini* and *Rocky*, he said, "We tried hard to follow an old screenwriting rule: show, not tell." The film has multiple protagonists and two story lines. The first and most prominent one is the rivalry between U.S. and Canadian teams, embodied by American player Mark Zupan and Canadian coach Joe Soares, who is also American. The second follows newly-injured Keith Cavill as he adapts to life as a paraplegic. The film is about 82 minutes long, and features vérité footage, interviews, and animation.

Act One/Title Sequence

The film fades up on a man in a wheelchair (later identified as Zupan) changing from jeans into workout clothes. There is no music or voice-over, just natural sound. A credit interrupts the scene, and then the man removes his t-shirt and begins to wheel himself out of frame. In a series of vignettes intercut with credits, we meet three other men. Two tell stories that mock people's reactions to their wheelchairs: "They say 'It's good to see you out,' " one says, adding, "Where am I supposed to be, in a closet?" A third, with only partial limbs, is seen getting into a van. "What I can do that probably people don't think I can do," he says, "is I can cook, and I can drive." Finally, a garage door opens, and we see the first man (Zupan), sitting in a specialized chair, looking fierce. Beginning voice-over, he says (an in interview that continues at a gym), "I've gone up to people, start talking shit and they're like, 'Oh, oh, oh,' I go 'What, you're not gonna hit a kid in a chair? Fucking hit me. I'll hit you back.' " The musical soundtrack kicks in and soon we see wheelchair rugby players on an indoor court, smashing into each other until a chair tips over and players cheer. The title comes up: *Murderball* (2:55). This opening sequence has effectively introduced some but not all of the film's main characters (by attitude, not by name), and set an irreverent, tough-guy tone for the story to come.

Immediately after the title, two referees introduce quadriplegic rugby, developed in Canada and originally called "murderball." We see players' chairs being fixed up as a man (identified on screen as *Marty/USA pit crew*) talks about the gear involved. Zupan (still not identified) introduces the fact that the majority of players have had neck injuries, which motivates a drawn animation illustrating the location of the injury and the "rods, plates, screws" that are now inside. A match dissolve from the animation back to the scar on a player's neck transitions to the next important piece of exposition, one that anticipates confusion in at least some of the audience: "The biggest misconception," Zupan says, "is, 'You're quadriplegic? I thought they couldn't move their arms.' I'm like, 'No. I have impairment in all four limbs.' " Footage of a player on the court again dissolves to animation, as we learn that the higher up the neck is broken, the less mobility a person has. Quad rugby players are given a point value ranging from 0.5 to 3.5 points, "based on what you can move." (The four men we've met so far pose, and over their heads we see their numbers: 3.0, 2.0, 2.0, 1.0.) With four men on court at one time, the total ability can't exceed eight points.

Having set up some basics of the game (exposition), the filmmakers then begin to introduce the players (more exposition), both through conversations with them and through brief onscreen words: *ANDY/Car crash/10 years ago, HOGSETT/Fist fight/13 years ago, ZUPAN/Car accident/11 years ago.* We get to know a bit more about Zupan through an interview with his parents (4:12), rugby colleagues, and some friends in a bar. Zupan is also shown clowning around with some guys in what seems to be a hotel lobby. When one falls backward, chair and all, an older, able-bodied couple standing nearby asks the cinematographer, "Do you want us to call security?" It doesn't matter when or where the scene was actually filmed. Its placement here is interesting because not only does it show Zupan acting playfully aggressive, it also shows that, as Andy remarked early on, "people say the dumbest things."

Six minutes into the film, the filmmakers get the first story, the U.S./Canada competition, under way. Through text on screen, shots of banners ("Wheelchair Rugby World Championship 2002 Gothenburg"), and shots of players, we learn that 12 countries are competing and that the United States has been on top for the last 10 years. Those are *stakes* they need to defend.

Seven and a half minutes in, we finally meet Zupan's nemesis, *JOE/Polio/43 years ago*. Through visits to his home, where we see his trophy wall and hear from his nephew and wife, and through news reports, we learn that Joe Soares was arguably the best quad rugby player in the world. But he got older and was cut from the U.S. team, so he began to coach Canada (9:08) and took American plays with him. "U.S.A., learn a new way," he says without sympathy. Zupan responds in an interview, "If Joe was on the side of the road, on fire, I wouldn't piss on him to put it out."

At 9:55, Canada and the United States have both made the finals at Gothenburg. The filmmakers raise the stakes with text on screen: *For the first time, Joe will face his former U.S.A. teammates*. In other words, this isn't just any game. But, having increased the tension in the main story, the filmmakers now take another detour, to let Bob Lujano (now identified, but by name only—we still don't know how he lost his limbs) give more details about the rules of the game, with animation to help. The placement of this information is excellent; these details would have been lost earlier, when there were too many other pieces of information vying for the audience's attention. Now, we know that it's team against team, man against man, and we're willing to take a moment to learn more about how this battle will be played. In addition, because these rules are fresh, the audience is prepared to just *watch* as the U.S./Canada match gets under way. It's fast and furious, with cameras mounted on and under chairs, and the editing (by Geoffrey Richman, with co-editor Conor O'Neill) is first rate. Through a combination of text on screen, wall clocks, and cutaways to coaches and crowd, the filmmakers condense this close-scoring game. At 13:21 in the film, Canada wins. The Americans taunt Soares: "How's it feel to betray your country, man?" He appears to be hurt, revealing a new layer of complexity.

The film is far from over—we're only halfway through the first act—so the filmmakers need to quickly move the story and the stakes forward. Note that they did not set up a single goal early on and instead have been *revealing* a rivalry between the United States and Canada, and to a lesser extent between Zupan and Soares. Immediately after the win at Gothenburg, the filmmakers tell us (through text on screen) that the United States and Canada will face each other again at the 2004 Paralympics in Athens, Greece— so the rivalry has a new focus, a new goal. This motivates a cut to Birmingham, Alabama, to the Team USA training camp.

We learn that out of 500 players, coaches will select 12 to compete in Greece, although this is not a big source of tension in the storytelling. The camp seems to be more of an opportunity to get to know the guys better and, more importantly, explore the issue of disability. At 17:41, Andy introduces this shift: "Everybody who gets hurt thinks they're gonna walk again," he says, explaining that this hindered his ability to move forward. Hogsett talks about how hard the first two years are, after a spinal cord injury. In quick shots, the filmmakers begin introducing a new location, a rehab hospital, and at 18:30, we're behind a young man with a large scar on the back of his neck; we then meet him, staring impassively at the strangeness of the hospital around him: he's *KEITH/Motocross accident/4 months ago.*

The casting of Keith is critical to this film. Without him, you see extraordinary athletes who are past the most difficult part of their journeys from injury to altered ability. "He anchors the film— narratively and emotionally—because without him, you don't see what [the other] guys lost," says Dana Adam Shapiro, the film's co-director and producer, in publicity material. At the Kessler Institute for Rehabilitation (an exterior shot of the building establishes this), the effort Keith makes to perform basic tasks—get himself into a sitting position, for example, or undo the Velcro straps on his shoes—shows, better than any words could tell, how far the rugby players have come. And interestingly, it's Keith's story, and not the rivalry, that structures the acts in this film. At the end of Act One, we see Keith at the start of his rehab journey.

Act Two

The second act (and this is my analysis, not necessarily one the filmmakers would agree with) begins as the film shifts back to its primary story line, the rivalry. Just under 21 minutes into the film, we see coach Joe Soares at his home in Florida. He's having a Super Bowl party, and for the first time, we meet his son, Robert. The relationship between this hard-driving, athletic man and his studious, musical son adds complexity to Soares's story, both personal and professional. Grilling steak, for example, he seems distant and demanding of his son; soon after, he tells his Canadian team that "in a year and a half, we've become the strongest family I've ever had, strongest second family. You guys are my boys." This sequence with Soares, his family, and friends lasts almost five minutes.

At about 26:30, the filmmakers turn their attention to Soares's rival, Mark Zupan. We see Mark in personal moments as well, swimming and hanging out with his girlfriend, which opens the door to the issue of sexuality after injury. The filmmakers cut to the hospital, where Keith asks a doctor if he'll be able to be sexually active again. His doctor, who's able-bodied, introduces an instructional video (hosted by the doctor); the filmmakers cut to their own footage of a disabled man talking about sex, followed by Andy Cohn and then Scott Hogsett, who articulates the question: "Can you do it?" For these guys, the answer is yes, and they (and Keith's doctor, in his video) offer details. This sequence also lasts a bit more than five minutes, and then the film returns to its train: the U.S./Canada rivalry (31:40), with text on screen: *Team Canada Training/8 months before Paralympics*. (Note the effective use of *signposts* in this film, occasional reminders about *who, what*, and especially *when* as the film returns to its train, to reground the audience in the story line.)

We don't stay at the training camp for long. A brief scene with Soares and his team as he tells them his theories on discipline motivates a cut to an interview with Soares, in which he reveals that his father was a police officer who used to hit Joe "really hard." His own treatment of his son, he argues, is "not even close." In the following scenes, we see Soares at an anniversary dinner with his wife, meet his sisters, and learn that a doctor is concerned about his stress. After a quick montage of his volatile coaching, text on screen announces that Soares has suffered a heart attack

(35:00). He looks small and vulnerable in the hospital bed, but the filmmakers don't milk this moment unnecessarily; by 36:25, we know that he's out of the woods, and the scene shifts to Mark Zupan's 10-year high school reunion.

Note how long it's been since we've seen athletic competition—it's the train, but not the *point*, of this film. As structured by the filmmakers, the sequence about the reunion is really about Mark's accident (11 years ago) and the estrangement between him and the friend (Christopher Igoe) who was driving the night he was hurt. We hear from Zupan's classmates, parents, and Igoe. The sequence motivates an interview with Zupan, in which he remembers how hard it was for him when he first came out of rehab—which in turn allows for a smooth transition, at 42:15, to Keith, who is at the same point in his own recovery. After 10 months in rehab, he's going home. This is the film's *midpoint* (and note again that it's pegged to Keith's journey). The scene begins on a note of achievement but ends in frustration, as Keith realizes, he says, "what was once normal will never be the same" (46:12).

Cut to a banner (with the Olympic logo), setting a new scene: "USA Lakeshore Foundation Official U.S. Training Site." With six months to go, Team USA is making its final cuts. The selection is edited for some tension, but all of our characters make the 2004 team. A visit from some Camp Fire Girls gives the filmmakers an opportunity to tell us more about Bob Lujano. (Note that you don't have to introduce everybody right away, nor do you have to introduce everyone in the same way. Several recent documentaries, including *Spellbound* and *Born into Brothels*, also feature multiple protagonists. It's worth watching them to see how they handle introductions and the balance of story lines to avoid repetition.)

At 51:40, coach Joe Soares is out of the hospital. On a visit to his childhood home in Rhode Island, he tells us a bit more about himself. Born in Portugal, he describes himself as living the American dream—in other words, this adds even more texture to the fact that he's coaching Canada. But as we see him play with children at the house, we have a sense, confirmed by his sisters, that Joe is different; we see him bragging to childhood neighbors about his son. (A transformation like this, while important to good drama, can *never* be manufactured or overstated. If it happened, great; if it didn't, you aren't free to even suggest that it did.) Here, the change in Soares begs the question, does he still have the edge he needs to lead Canada to victory?

At 54:39, the scene shifts to Vancouver, Canada. Text on screen continues the countdown: *3 months before the Paralympics/The US is facing Canada to determine the #1 seed*. This is the first we've heard about this interim match (we were aiming for the Paralympics), and it's a bit of a risk. You never want to have three versions of the same basic event played out in three locations: The stakes, style, and purpose of each should be different, and they need to build in importance. (For example, you wouldn't want to start with an Olympic match and then follow with two exhibition games merely to see the rivalry in action.) Here, the filmmakers skillfully use the match to remind us of the stakes and players and get us back into the game (we haven't seen actual competition for more than 40 minutes). First, they intercut a tense-looking Joe Soares and an equally tense-looking Mark Zupan, the core rivals. Then, they use a somewhat different editing style from the previous game, and this time, the U.S. team wins, so the power position as they go to the Paralympics has changed. In sync footage right after the game, Zupan reminds us that the Paralympics are still two and a half months away—this was just a warm-up. Finally, and a key reason to keep this sequence, about 58:00 into the film, the coach of the losing team, Soares, gets a call from his son, asking him to hurry home to attend a viola concert. The scene that follows visualizes, more than the conversations in Providence, that Soares has changed.

In the next sequence, about an hour into the film, the "A" and "B" stories come together elegantly, as Keith attends a demonstration about quad rugby led by Mark Zupan. Act Two ends as Keith tries out a specialized rugby chair (63:44).

Act Three

The filmmakers take advantage of a "US Olympic media summit" (a press conference) to add a bit more exposition about the Athens Paralympics, and Mark Zupan describes his visit to the rehab hospital and how "fulfilling" it was to see the response of one patient (Keith). The inclusion of this moment is nice, in part because it tells us that the sequencing of these events is real. From there, the film moves on to *1 Month to Paralympics* (65:14). The filmmakers add some breathing room here, as the team plays a practical joke; they also erase what may be a confusion in the minds of some audience members about the distinction between Paralympics and

Special Olympics. Then, with a week to go, we learn that Zupan has invited Christopher Igoe to see him play, pulling together strands of an earlier sequence. There's a bit of an interlude as Igoe makes his way to Athens (in part, perhaps, to give the audience a chance to remember who Igoe is and why this meeting matters).

At 71:00, it's "game on" at the Paralympics, the culmination of the film. The editing of this game is unusual: We see people scoring, cheering, the score changing, but the natural sound has been replaced by a fairly quiet musical score. The effect is powerful; the music swells and natural sound returns gradually at the end, as tension mounts and Canada pulls ahead. At 75:00, it's over. Now, the filmmakers focus on the Americans as they are comforted by family and friends, followed by a bittersweet conclusion: Team USA didn't win the gold (they came in third) but neither did Team Canada. They came in second, after New Zealand.

Epilogue

We see the team traveling together, and hear quick voice-overs of the guys' stories about how they became injured. Only gradually do we understand that they're addressing wounded Iraq war veterans at Walter Reed Army Hospital in Virginia. After a cheer, "USA Rugby!" (79:00), the film goes to black. Interrupting the end credits, the filmmakers then show a series of "where are they now" vignettes all of the major characters, including Keith and young Robert.

CASE STUDY: *SUPER SIZE ME*

Nominated for an Academy Award in 2004, and one of the top-grossing documentaries of all time, *Super Size Me* is a science documentary that's funny, thought-provoking, and fast-moving. The film is probably best described as an essay, but there is a protagonist (filmmaker Morgan Spurlock, who won the Best Director award for the film at the 2004 Sundance Film Festival) and goal (to see what happens if he eats only at McDonald's for 30 days). He faces opposition not from an individual, but from the effect this diet may have on his health and well-being, which may force him to end the experiment early. From first frame of action to closing credits, the film is about 95 minutes long.

Act One/Title Sequence

The first frame of action shows children singing, invoking the names of fast-food restaurants. Following a text-on-screen quote from McDonald's founder Ray Kroc, a professional-sounding narrator (who turns out to be Morgan Spurlock) tells us that "everything's bigger in America." In a fast-paced, fact-filled setup, he defines the problem: "Nearly 100 million Americans are today either overweight or obese. That's more than 60 percent of all U.S. adults." He suggests a cause: When he was growing up, his mother cooked dinner every single day. Now, he says, families eat out all the time, and pay for it with their wallets *and* waistlines. He notes a cost: "Obesity is now second only to smoking as a major cause of preventable death in America."

Spurlock then introduces the lawsuit that inspired the film: "In 2002, a few Americans got fed up with being overweight, and did what we do best: They sued the bastards." Using a magazine cover and animation, he lays out the basics of the case, which was filed on behalf of two teenaged girls: a 14-year-old, who was 4'10" and weighed 170 pounds, and a 19-year-old, 5'6", who weighed 270 pounds. Sounding astounded, Spurlock says the "unthinkable" was happening: People were suing McDonald's "for selling them food that most of us know isn't good for you to begin with." But he offers evidence to show that we eat it anyway, millions of us worldwide. Returning to the lawsuit, he highlights a statement by the judge, which he paraphrases: "If lawyers for the teens could show that McDonald's intends for people to eat its food for every meal of every day, and that doing so would be unreasonably dangerous, they may be able to state a claim." Spurlock seizes on this challenge but also notes a question, a theme that will inform the entire film: "Where does personal responsibility stop, and corporate responsibility begin?"

At 3:48, we see him for the first time on camera as he sets out the design of his experiment: "What would happen if I ate nothing but McDonald's for 30 days straight? Would I suddenly be on the fast track to becoming an obese American? Would it be unreasonably dangerous? Let's find out. I'm ready. Super Size Me" (4:04). This 30-day regimen is the film's *train*, the narrative framework that, once under way, allows the filmmaker to take detours into issues that, on their own, would probably not have packed audiences into theaters worldwide. (It's also likely that a similar 30-day experiment in the hands of someone bent on "proving" the evils of fast food and McDonald's wouldn't have been as effective. Spurlock is credible as he takes us on this journey because he seems genuinely open to gray areas, as described later.)

After the opening titles, Spurlock spends time establishing a baseline for his own physical condition. Three doctors, a nutritionist, and a physiologist confirm that his health is excellent. They aren't thrilled by the experiment, but don't expect anything too terrible to happen in just 30 days. Roughly 10.5 minutes into the show, Spurlock adds a further wrinkle: Because more than 60 percent of Americans get no form of exercise, neither will he, other than routine walking. (This prompts a sidetrack about walking in general, walking in Manhattan, and how many McDonald's there are to walk by in Manhattan.)

At 12:03, we're back to the train as we meet Spurlock's girlfriend Alex, a vegan chef. She prepares *The Last Supper*, one of a handful of chapters named on screen over original artwork. A little over a minute later, the experiment gets under way, as *Day 1* is identified with text on screen. Spurlock orders an Egg McMuffin and eats. (Here, as in several places throughout the film, he breaks up blocks of narration with musical interludes. These breaks are important; they add humor and breathing room, giving the audience a chance to process information.) In a quick scene, we see Spurlock writing down what he's eaten. We need to see this record keeping at least once, because it's part of the experiment: The log provides the data the nutritionist uses to calculate his food intake. We then see Spurlock on the street, asking people about fast food. Interspersed at various points throughout the film, these interviews also add humor and alter the rhythm of the film, while providing a range of what are presumably "typical" responses.

Around 15 minutes into the film, standing in line at McDonald's, Spurlock expands on the experiment's rules (he talks on camera to his film crew, and also in scripted voice-over). After getting this additional exposition out of the way, he bites happily into a Big Mac (gray area—he enjoys some fast food). At 15:47: another artwork, another title: *Sue the Bastards*. We see Spurlock again on the street conducting interviews, this time about the lawsuit. All three of the people consulted think the lawsuit is ridiculous—which at this point in the film may also be the attitude of the audience. Spurlock interviews John F. Banzhaf, a law professor "spearheading the attacks against the food industry" and advising the suit's lawyers. Spurlock gives Banzhaf's work a bit of credibility (to counter the man-on-the-street responses) by noting that people thought Banzhaf was crazy when he was going after tobacco companies, too—"until he won." Banzhaf adds an important detail about why McDonald's is a particular target: The company markets to children.

Another man worried about the children, Spurlock says, is Samuel Hirsch, lawyer for the two girls in the lawsuit. But look at the gray area in this interview. Over a shot of Hirsch, we hear Spurlock ask, "Why are you suing the fast-food establishment?" The shot continues, unedited, as Hirsch considers, smiling. "You mean motives besides monetary re—, compensation? You mean you want to hear a noble cause? Is that it?" The lawyer seems to consider a bit longer, and then Spurlock cuts away from him, and that's the end of Hirsch's time on screen. It's funny, but perhaps more importantly, this willingness to paint various sides of the argument in less-than-flattering light is part of what makes this film engaging. Audiences have to stay on their toes and be willing to not only see complexity, but figure out for themselves what they think.

David Satcher, former U.S. Surgeon General, introduces the problem of "super sizing," which allows Spurlock (and other experts) to explore the issue of portion size. In other words, Spurlock is building an argument and letting one idea flow to the next. Finally, it's just under 21 minutes into the film and we've been away from the "train" for about five minutes, so Spurlock drives up to a McDonald's, and text on screen announces *Day 2.*

Act Two

In the second act, the experiment really gets under way. Fortunately for Spurlock, he was asked on Day 2 if he wanted to super size, and by the rules he's established, he must say yes. (There might be a temptation, in a film like this, to let Day 4 stand in for Day 2, if it provided an opportunity like this. You can't. You don't need to give each day equal weight—some days are barely mentioned—and you don't need to show all meals each day. But the time line of these meals needs to be factual, as does the time line of Spurlock's health.) Watch how Spurlock condenses time in this scene: He starts out laughing, kissing his double quarter-pounder, calling it "a little bit of heaven." The image fades to black, and white lettering comes up: *5 minutes later*. Fade up: He's still eating. (The visual point, underscored by the card and by the screen time given to the scene, is that this is a *lot* of food, and for Spurlock, it's an effort to eat it.) Fade to black again: *10 minutes later*. Spurlock says that a "Mcstomach ache" is kicking in. To black, *15 minutes later*. He's leaning back in his seat. To black, *22 minutes later*. He's *still* forcing the food down. A cut, and we see him leaning out the window and vomiting. A meal that lasted at least 45 minutes has been effectively compressed into a sequence that's 2.5 minutes long.

At about 23:18, we see a new illustrated chapter title, *The Toxic Environment*. Experts and Spurlock introduce the problem of "constant access to cheap, fat-laden foods" and soda vending machines, compounded by a reliance on cars. After a brief health concern on Day 3, he cuts to Day 4 and takes a detour to further compare obesity and tobacco use, including marketing to children. This sequence is followed by another "meadow" (or musical interlude), in which we see Spurlock enjoying a McDonald's play area.

At 28:21, a new chapter, *The Impact*, explores the lifelong health implications, including liver failure, of obesity in children. At 30:38, Spurlock cuts to a 16-year-old, Caitlin, cooking in a fast-food restaurant. Here again, his ambivalence seems to leave some of the work to the audience. In an interview, Caitlin talks about how hard it is for overweight teenagers like herself because they see the pictures of the "thin, pretty, popular girls" and think "aren't I supposed to look like that?" As she's talking, Spurlock fills the screen with images of thin young women, until he's covered Caitlin's face. Just before she disappears, she concludes: "It's not realistic, it's not a realistic way to live."

Is Spurlock implying that Caitlin is letting herself off the hook too easily? This may be the case, because the scene is immediately followed (32:07) by a sequence in which motivational speaker Jared Fogle, who lost 245 pounds on a Subway diet, gives a talk at what appears to be a school. An overweight eighth grader argues, like Caitlin, that weight loss isn't realistic: "I can't afford to like, go there [to Subway] every single day and buy a sandwich like two times a day, and that's what he's talking about."

As if to offer a contrast, the film then cuts to a sequence about a man who did take personal responsibility for his health: Baskin-Robbins heir John Robbins. According to headlines on screen, he walked away from a fortune because ice cream is so unhealthy.

Robbins, a health advocate, runs through a litany of health-related problems involving not only his own family but also one of the founders of Ben & Jerry's ice cream. (This sequence, like the many shots in the film of fast-food companies other than McDonald's, helps expand the argument beyond one company to look at larger issues of food choice and health.)

At 35:09, it's Day 5 of the experiment. We see Spurlock ordering food but don't see the meal; instead, we follow Spurlock into his nutritionist's office, where we learn that he's eating about 5000 calories a day, twice what his body requires, and has already gained nine pounds. Hitting the streets again (about 37:00), he asks a range of people about fast food (they like it) and exercise (only some do it).

About a minute later, Day 6 finds him in Los Angeles, ordering chicken McNuggets. This meal motivates another look at the lawsuit and McDonald's statements about processed foods; Spurlock augments this with a cartoon about the creation of McNuggets, which he says the judge in the case called "a McFrankenstein creation."

Back to the experiment, Day 7, and Spurlock isn't feeling well. Within 30 seconds, it's Day 8, and he's disgusted by the fish sandwich he's unwrapping. Less than 30 seconds later, it's Day 9, and he's eating a double quarter-pounder with cheese and feeling "really depressed." He's begun to notice not only physical but also emotional changes. The following sequence, with an extreme "Big Mac" enthusiast, doesn't add to the argument but is quirky and entertaining.

With that, we return (at 43:00) to an idea raised earlier, the notion of advertising to children. An expert offers data on the amount of advertising aimed at kids, and how ineffective parental messages are when countered with this. Another expert points out that most children know the word "McDonald's," so Spurlock—in a scene set up for the purposes of the film—tests this out, asking a group of first graders to identify pictures of George Washington, Jesus Christ, Wendy (from the restaurant), and Ronald McDonald. He also uses a cartoon to demonstrate how much money the biggest companies spend on direct media advertising worldwide.

At 46:34, we're back to the experiment: *Day 10*. But once again, we leave the experiment quickly. By 47:02, a new illustrated chapter title appears, *Nutrition*. This sequence doesn't actually look at nutrition, but at how difficult it is to get nutrition information in stores. As John Banzhaf argues, how can people exercise personal responsibility if they don't have the information on which to base it? At 49:20 (roughly midway through the film), we're back to the experiment, as Spurlock gets his first blood test. He now weighs 203 pounds, 17 more than when he started.

Around 50:30, a new chapter: *It's for kids.* Spurlock takes the essay even wider, with narration: "The one place where the impact of our fast-food world has become more and more evident is in our nation's schools." This is a long sequence in which he visits three schools in three different states. In Illinois, the lunch staff and a representative for Sodexo School Services (a private company that services school districts nationwide) seem willing to believe that students make smart food choices, even though Spurlock shows evidence that they don't. In West Virginia, Spurlock visits a school served by the U.S. federal school lunch program. Here, students eat reheated, reconstituted packaged foods, with a single meal some-times exceeding 1,000 calories. Finally, Spurlock goes to a school in Wisconsin, where a company called Natural Ovens provides food for students with "truancy and behavioral problems." The food here is not fried or canned, and the school has no candy or soda machines. (It's almost a shock at this point to see fresh veg-etables and fruit and realize how brightly-colored they are.) The behavioral improvements in the students here, administrators tell us, are significant. And, Spurlock notes, the program "costs about the same as any other school lunch program. So my question is, why isn't everyone doing this?" (56:02).

Over footage of the Wisconsin lunch line, we hear a phone interview in which the founder of the Natural Ovens Bakery is allowed to answer Spurlock's question: "There's an awful lot of resistance from the junk food companies that make huge profits off of schools at the present time," he says. To me, this is a misstep in an otherwise powerful sequence. Unlike several of the experts who've been interviewed, this man's ability to speak for or about "the junk food companies" hasn't been established. (I'm not say-ing it doesn't exist, just that it's not set here.) The *information* he conveys may be fact-checked and 100 percent accurate, but to me, a better way to convey it might be through facts, such as how much money per year the fast-food companies actually make in the nation's public schools. (That companies resist being removed from schools is a point made, effectively, in the following scene, when the Honorable Marlene Canter talks about the Los Angeles Unified School District's ban on soda machines.)

At about 57:08—roughly 60 percent of the way through the film—Spurlock returns to the experiment. It's Day 13, and he's in Texas, home to five of the top 15 "fattest" cities in America. Day 14 finds him in the #1 city, Houston, but he quickly goes into a new sidetrack: a visit with the Grocery Manufacturers of America, a lobbying firm based in Washington, D.C. The group's vice president says the issue is education, teaching good nutrition, and teaching physical education. It's a bit of a thin transition, but this leads Spurlock to explore the fact that only one state, Illinois, requires physical education for grades K–12. Returning to the Illinois school, he films an exceptional program, and then for contrast, shows an elementary school in Massachusetts where physical education involves running around a gym once a week for 45 minutes. At 61:00, Spurlock suggests a reason for the issue, the "No Child Left Behind" education reforms of President George W. Bush, which an expert says explains cuts to "phys ed, nutrition, health." This, in turn, motivates Spurlock to ask students in a ninth-grade health class what a calorie is. They struggle to answer—but so do six out of six adults interviewed on the street.

At 63:02, it's Day 16, "still in Texas," but in about 20 seconds, it's Day 17 and he's back in New York. We learn that the experiment is getting to Spurlock; his girlfriend says he's exhausted and their sex life is suffering. The following day, the doctor says his blood pressure and cholesterol are up and his liver "is sick." He's advised to stop. We see him talking on the phone to his mother; they're both concerned. She's afraid the damage he's doing will be irreversible, but Spurlock reassures her that "they" think things should get back on track once it's done. Act Two ends here.

Act Three

At 69:26, Act Three (and again, as with the other films, this is my analysis, not the filmmaker's) begins with a look at the "drug effect" of food, with input from a new expert, a cartoon about McDonald's use of the terms "heavy user" and "super heavy user," and an informal phone survey. Spurlock learns that his nutritionist's company is closing, and uses this as an opportunity to explore the amount spent on diet products and weight loss programs compared to the amount spent on health and fitness. This motivates a transition to an extreme weight loss option, gastric bypass surgery, filmed in Houston (74:03). Note that this sequence may have been filmed anywhere during this production; its placement here in the film makes sense, because things are reaching their extremes.

The stakes for Spurlock have also continued to rise, which helps to make this third act strong. At 97:33, in New York, Spurlock wakes at 2:00 a.m.; he's having heart palpitations and difficulty breathing. "I want to finish," he says, "but don't want anything real bad to happen, either." More visits to doctors result not only in specific warnings about what symptoms should send him immediately to an emergency room, but also the realization that these results are well beyond anything the doctors anticipated. But at 81:20, Spurlock is back at it: *Day 22*. In short order, he sets out to answer a new question that he's posed: "How much influence on government legislators does the food industry have?" He visits again with the Grocery Manufacturers of America, before finally (at 83:26) attempting to contact McDonald's directly.

These efforts, ultimately unsuccessful, will punctuate the rest of the film. Spurlock gets through Days 25, 26, and 27 quickly. At Day 29, he's having a hard time getting up stairs. By Day 30, his girlfriend has a detox diet all planned out. First, there's *The Last McSupper*—a party at McDonald's with many of the people we've seen throughout the film. Then it's off to a final medical weigh-in. Fifteen calls later, still no response from McDonald's.

Resolution

At 89:34, Spurlock is nearing the end of his film, and essay. He returns again to the court case. "After six months of deliberation, Judge Robert Sweet dismissed the lawsuit against McDonald's," he says. "The big reason—the two girls failed to show that eating McDonald's food was what caused their injuries." Spurlock counters by tallying up the injuries he's suffered in just 30 days. He challenges the fast-food companies: "Why not do away with your super size options?" But he also challenges the audience to change, warning: "Over time you may find yourself getting as sick as I did. And you may wind up here (we see an emergency room) or here (a cemetery). I guess the big question is, who do you want to see go first—you or them?"

Epilogue

Prior to the credits, the filmmakers do a quick wrap-up, including information about how long it took Spurlock to get back to his original weight and regain his health and the fact that six weeks after the film screened at Sundance, McDonald's eliminated its super size option. At 96:23, the credits roll.

Part II

IDEAS TO TREATMENTS

8

Research

Good documentary storytelling, with few exceptions, depends on good research. You need to find a subject, understand your story, and be sure you're presenting a balanced and accurate point of view—at least, you do if you want to get the program to a general audience. Remember that balance and accuracy do not mean that you can't, as the filmmaker, take a particular position, or that your subjects can't take one. But if you expect the audience to take you seriously, you must allow them to weigh the evidence for themselves, which means that you need to research and present that evidence. This is true for what may seem like a surprising range of filmmaking styles. In an interview by Jason Silverman, filmmaker Alan Berliner describes working on his personal documentary, *The Sweetest Sound.* "I began where I always begin, with a tremendous amount of research, with a passion to understand the total landscape of whatever subject I'm entering."

Susan Froemke and assistants at Maysles Films, the noted vérité company, spent about six months researching poverty and looking for potential stories in several states, including Wisconsin, Maine, Iowa, and Missouri, before they settled on the stories and characters of *Lalee's Kin*, filmed in the Mississippi Delta (see Chapter 21). Filmmaker Jay Rosenblatt creates unusual documentary stories from bits of old films and "found footage." In press material submitted to the San Francisco Jewish Film Festival, Rosenblatt says that it took about eight months to do the research for *Human Remains*, a half-hour film about the banality of evil. In it, he presents black-and-white footage of five of the 20th century's most notorious leaders—Hitler, Mussolini, Stalin, Franco, and Mao—over reminiscences voiced by actors but scripted from actual quotes and/or factual biographical information. "One of the challenges," Rosenblatt notes, "was to find images of the dictators that didn't include hats or uniforms, since they had to look . . . like the guy next door."

Do all documentaries require research? No. Liane Brandon's memorable and deceptively simple film, *Betty Tells Her Story*, while evoking powerful themes, began when the filmmaker heard something of interest in a colleague's story and asked her to tell it on camera (see Chapter 13). Not everything has to involve experts and advisors and location scouting. But many films, if not most, do involve research to some degree. With that in mind, here are a few suggestions.

Ask Questions, Dig Deeper

Whether you're looking for a story or finding the best way to tell it, a good film is one that surprises, challenges, and, often, informs. This means that the information going into that film needs to be surprising. All too often, documentaries just repeat information that everybody knows. The easiest way out of that trap is to stop and challenge yourself. "Energy equals mass"—what does that mean? The Apollo 13 space mission—why was it named Apollo? "Everybody knows" that Rosa Parks was the tired seamstress who didn't feel like giving up her seat on that bus in Montgomery in 1955, right? It's a nice story, this downtrodden woman who has reached her breaking point. What if you found out that she was an active member of the Montgomery chapter of the NAACP, a group fighting for civil rights? Suddenly she's not so much a victim of oppression as an activist who sees an opportunity to fight it. You're telling better history and bringing fresh details to an old story that everybody thought they knew.

Good research is a sequence of questions, answers, and more questions. As mentioned previously, why start a project if you just want to prove a point? We've all seen films like this, where the filmmakers are out to prove that strip mining is bad or that a certain election was rigged. Have you ever seen a group of people telling each other what they already know and agreeing with each other since no one disagrees? That's how stimulating your film is going to be. If you want to change someone's mind, or at least raise doubts, hopes, and ideas, you have to trust in that person's ability to make an informed decision. Give him or her information that will lead to that decision. That kind of information comes from a research process that is open-minded.

Do Your Own Research

One of the problems of faster and cheaper filmmaking is that original and up-to-date research is often beyond the scope of a project's resources and budget. It's much easier for producers to rely on a few articles or books rather than explore what's new in a field, who's doing innovative work, or what a more diverse group of storytellers might add to the audience's understanding of a familiar topic. The same tired experts are approached time and again to speak about the same subjects, in part because the producers have already seen them on TV and know both what they look like and how well they speak on camera. But why tell the same story again, particularly if you could explore a newer or more complex angle? It may take more effort to gather and master up-to-date information and balance it with previous understanding of an issue, but as a documentary filmmaker, especially if your work has a life beyond broadcast (many documentaries end up being used by classroom teachers and community organizers, for example), this is exactly what you want to be doing.

Don't Be Afraid to Ask Basic Questions

Although you should gain a thorough grounding in your subject, you can't possibly, in a few days or weeks or even months, become an expert. Don't, in the interest of appearing "professional" to your advisors or experts, fake an understanding that you don't have; if you're confused, speak up. Your expertise is in knowing how to communicate a complex subject to a general audience; it's important that you understand the subject well, and that's why the experts are there. Most people who have spent their lifetimes mastering a subject are also passionate about it, whether it's professional football or nuclear physics, and enjoy sharing their knowledge with others, particularly when the person asking the questions is prepared and professional.

Bayard Rustin, late 1940s, from *Brother Outsider: The Life of Bayard Rustin*. Photo courtesy of the estate of Bayard Rustin.

WHEN DO YOU RESEARCH?

The amount of research you do, and when you do it, varies from project to project and depends, to some degree, on your chosen topic, your approach, and your strategies for fund-raising. Some public funding sources, as well as some private foundations, require that your grant application include evidence that your film project is built on a solid and current academic foundation. Projects that are funded "in house"—by public or commercial broadcasters directly—may be less rigorous in their up-front requirements, but producers will still need to do at least some research in order to effectively pitch their ideas and make their programs.

With many films, therefore, research begins with the development of the initial proposal(s), but begins again—and at greater depth—once financial support is available. (As discussed in Chapter 10, support may come in stages: development, scripting, production, postproduction, etc.) Research generally is ongoing through the development of outlines and shooting treatments, and continues as needed until the film is complete. A flurry of fact checking often occurs in the last weeks of editing.

ADVISORS

The input of academic and nonacademic advisors can be crucial to a project. These people offer their insight and experience behind the scenes; some of them may also be asked to appear on camera as experts, if that fits the program's style. On any film that's intended to be the least bit authoritative about a subject, advisors can help tremendously by getting you up to date quickly on current research in the field and directing you to people, places, and content to be explored. They can help you to see how your film might contribute to the public's understanding of a subject and who, beyond a general audience, might be able to use the film (in classrooms, for example). It's useful to seek out advisors and experts who represent a variety of viewpoints. If you're doing a film about the role of first ladies over the years, for example, you might find biographers of specific first ladies, as well as scholars whose specialties cover presidential history, American history, women's studies, and political history. You might also look for nonacademic experts, such as a former or current first lady or someone who has worked closely with her.

Advisors tend to be paid an honorarium for their services; the work might include a couple of meetings, as well as reviews of outlines and/or treatments and consultation on at least one, if not two, cuts of the film as editing is under way.

Good advisors—and they are often extraordinary—understand that they are advisors and you are a filmmaker, and that their job is to push for content and inclusion and yours is to try to tell the strongest and most accurate story you can. What a film can do best is excite viewers about new and complex material; it's up to library and web resources to satisfy the hunger you may create for extensive detail. You won't and can't do everything the advisors want, but if you have truly considered their expertise and understood their concerns, chances are you've found a way to address them that also serves your purposes as a filmmaker.

When do you approach advisors? As filmmaker Jon Else summarizes, "You read the ten most important and widely respected books about the subject, and then you read the two fringe books at either end of the subject. Then you do the basic primary research; you figure out who are the ten important living people and what are the ten important available documents or pieces of stock footage. And then you call the experts." As mentioned, some of the people you'll be contacting as advisors may turn out to be people you want to interview. It's good to avoid confusing these roles initially, because what you need at first is background help. If someone asks whether or not he or she will also be asked to appear on camera, you can honestly say that it's too soon to tell.

Advisors' Meetings

On some larger-budget documentaries and documentary series, funds are raised to enable at least one in-person gathering of filmmakers, advisors, and invited experts. These meetings might take place as the funding proposal is taking shape, and maybe again as production gets under way. With *Eyes on the Prize* and other major series produced by Blackside, Inc., production began with what was called "school." Production teams, researchers, and others joined invited scholars and other experts in panel discussions that continued over a period of several days and were invaluable in setting out the work ahead. If you can afford them, in-person meetings spark an exchange of information and ideas that isn't possible when the filmmaker speaks individually to this advisor, then that one. Valuable information can result from their interaction not only with you but with each other.

Professional Conferences

Another way to conduct a lot of research quickly, as well as find potential advisors or candidates for on-screen appearances, is through attending professional conferences in the subject you're researching. For a film she was developing to help teachers and other education professionals understand and protect the civil rights of gay and lesbian students, filmmaker Liane Brandon and some colleagues attended an all-day conference that allowed them, as a group, to immerse themselves in nearly 40 sessions on the subject. Brandon took a similar approach when researching her documentary, *How to Prevent a Nuclear War*. "I spent a year just meeting with different grassroots groups to see what they were doing, what they thought was effective, who was doing it, how they did it," she says. The diversity of the groups she met also allowed her to select individuals who could represent a variety of perspectives on screen, in terms of age, occupation, and location.

TELEPHONE RESEARCH

Some of your research, whether searching for people, fact checking, or just trying to get a handle on a subject, will inevitably be done by phone. Be as prepared as possible for these calls. Knowing as much as you can (within time limitations) about the person you're calling and his or her area of expertise will sharpen your questions and make the call more productive.

FACT CHECKING

Fact checking means being able to footnote your treatment and eventually, your script. Any fact stated, whether by you as the filmmaker or by someone on camera, needs to be verified through not one but at least two credible sources. Even authors of highly reputable sources make mistakes, and bias and inaccuracy can be found in both primary and secondary sources. Have you ever been at a rally that seemed packed, only to hear it described on the news as a "small number" of protesters? Or sat through an afternoon in which the majority of speeches were credible and coherent, and the radio coverage featured a couple of speakers who clearly had no grasp of the issues? The reports may be factual, but do they accurately represent the events?

Another example: A writer profiling an anti-poverty activist might point out that the activist grew up in a town that, she notes, is "a wealthy suburb of New York." The fact may be true, but 50 years earlier, the town was still quite rural and had not yet become a bedroom community for the city. And even then, the activist was from a family living well below the means of other townspeople. Yet the reporter has used factual material to create a false impression, whether intentionally or not, that the activist grew up wealthy—an impression that has a direct bearing on any portrayal of the activist's current work.

Suppose you're making a film about this activist's life. Because you're using multiple sources, you should realize that the picture being painted by this reporter doesn't match others that you're seeing. You should also be doing your own reality checks: Is it really possible that the description of a town in 2006 also applies to the same town in 1956? Furthermore, even if the majority of townspeople were mega-wealthy back in 1956, do you know that the activist's family was also wealthy?

Suppose you've plowed ahead without considering this, however, and have become attached to the idea of using the man's childhood in a wealthy town as a motivating factor behind his work on behalf of the poor. Maybe you've even talked to experts (unfamiliar with the activist in question) who explain that growing up wealthy can have this type of impact on children. So the information and motivation end up in your narration, whether they are accurate or not. This is a situation in which having advisors on your side can be invaluable. A biographer of the activist, if given a chance to read a treatment of your film or screen a rough cut, will respond to narration such as "He grew up in the wealthy community of X," and cry foul. This doesn't mean that you have to remove the fact; it does mean that you will need to put it into a more accurate context.

THE TELLING DETAIL

Facts are not just something to ensure accuracy; they can also be the lifeblood of the "telling detail" that will enrich and inform your storytelling (depending, of course, on the kind of film you're making). Facts can be a source of humor and irony; they can illuminate character, heighten tension, and underscore themes. So throw the line in the water, pull up what you can, organize it and file it, and then throw the line back in. Bess Myerson is known as the first Jewish Miss America. She was also the first to have a college degree. Which detail will you choose to use? Hold on to them both, for now. Famed Norwegian playwright Henrik Ibsen liked to read the comics. Russian author Fyodor Dostoevsky loved ice cream. Are these useful details? Maybe. They certainly add a human face to authors who've attained a certain stone-like presence in literary catalogs. As you do your research, begin to keep track of the details and tidbits that strike your fancy, as well as the ones that answer questions essential to your storytelling.

Find a way to keep track not only of the information but also its source. Make sure to note the source material as completely as possible, so that (1) you don't have to track it down again and (2) you could track it down again if necessary.

STATISTICS AND OTHER FORMS OF DATA

Statistics must be scrutinized and put into context. It's always a good idea, when you come across a statistic you want to use, to trace it back to its source. Suppose you find an article in a magazine that says that a certain percentage of teenagers smoked in the 1950s. Somewhere in the article you may be able to find the source of that information, such as "according to the National Institutes of Health." You should always question someone else's interpretation of raw data, meaning that if you really want to use this statistic, you need to go back to the NIH data yourself. Maybe it was X percent of all 17-year-olds who smoked, or maybe it was X percent of 17- and 18-year-olds in Philadelphia. People often misinterpret statistical information, whether intentionally or not. The interpretation may satisfy your story, but don't trust it until you can get it corroborated by someone with sufficient expertise.

CHRONOLOGIES

Chronologies are one of my favorite tools for storytelling, especially in the early stages of a film. I begin by going through the material that directly relates to my story and charting in sequence what happens and when. This helps me to see the story more clearly, without the overlay of someone else's narrative. Second, I add other columns to my notes that indicate what's happening in the world beyond my immediate story. (Various "Timetables of

History" are available in bookstores.) By putting these chronologies together, I can see new areas of research to be explored. For example, the first Miss America pageant was held in 1921. Prior to that, according to scholars, beauty contests were held in the pages of America's newspapers. But this wasn't possible until the photographic halftone was invented—in 1880, I find out when I look that up. What else was happening between then and 1921? A flood of immigration and migration was increasing the ethnic and racial diversity in America's growing cities, sparking differences of opinion about what constituted an American feminine "ideal." Add to all of this the emergence of mass media and a consumer culture, and the stage is set for the first official Miss America pageant in 1921. But note the date. A year earlier, in 1920, American women had finally won the right to vote. Is this relevant? The truthful answer is "Not necessarily." So while you can note the interesting dateline, you can't draw any conclusions about it. Cause and effect is a slippery slope; the fact that two things happen in succession does not mean there is a link. This is an excellent example of the kind of question you explore with your advisors, which is just what the production team of *Miss America: A Documentary Film* did.

The extent of the chronology depends entirely on the project. We did several chronologies for the series *I'll Make Me A World: A Century of African-American Arts*. The initial chronology was a grid, containing 10 columns, left to right (one for each decade of the century), and then six rows down (one each for literature, theater and dance, music, the visual arts, African-American political history, and American social and cultural events). As the series developed, separate chronologies were made for each story. The lives and vaudeville career of Bert Williams and George Walker, for example, were charted by month and year alongside events in American history. This may not work for everyone, but I find that a chronology helps me to keep track of a story, look for a structure within it, and find some telling details that might enrich it and prevent mistakes. A song commonly believed to have been popular among soldiers during the First World War may, in fact, have been written in 1919—which a good chronology will show you is after the war's end. In addition, by listing the major events in your story in chronological sequence, you can sometimes see possible points of attack—places to begin the story—and from there you can think about what moments you might drive toward and why, and which events can serve as backstory.

In my experience working with people doing films that involve any kind of time line, one of the biggest mistakes made early on is not to do a careful, detailed chronology right from the beginning. Even for a student assignment (for example, to write a treatment for a historical documentary), a chronology is your first best tool. Why not take good notes from the beginning? Instead, most people, students included, jot down a few details that are so vague they're essentially useless: *19th century, Ellis Island opens, thousands of immigrants arrive; 1950s, Ellis Island closes its doors*. If your film is about immigrant arrivals at Ellis Island, even if you're trying to figure out a story from *within* that history, you'll need a time line that includes dates, numbers, countries of origin, and references to legislation governing immigration. If a few particular immigrants pop out at you, note the date (and ship) they arrive on. If you don't do it in the beginning, it's almost a certainty that you'll be going back to those same sources, over and over, and adding to the chronology in bits and pieces over the next several weeks (for a student project) and months, if not years, for projects where there's no semester deadline.

PRINT AND INTERNET RESEARCH

I love the Internet. It's a tool that puts unbelievable amounts of information into your hands almost too easily. But the Internet augments libraries; it doesn't replace them. Keyword and subject searches on the Internet are limited by your ability to come up with the right combination of magic words, spelled correctly (or the way they were misspelled by someone else) to find what you want, and if you don't come up with those words, you'll wind up empty-handed. Perhaps even more frustrating, web searches can land you at sites that are not sufficiently credible.

Libraries and bookstores are also great places to go when you're looking for ideas or you have a topic in mind but aren't sure how to approach it. By wandering among the shelves, you can cast a fairly wide net, finding books and connections you might not have considered and information that you wouldn't have known to search for on the web. Even better, you can find material, such as magazines and newspapers, that significantly predates the limits of most web databases. Furthermore, you can see this material in the context of everything else on the page and in the issue; you can see the price of shoes and mattresses at the time, read reviews of whatever entertainment form was being offered, and look at the way stories in general were covered. Not only do you get a better sense of the period (whether the 1970s or the 1870s), you also get ideas for visual storytelling and narrative context.

Be Organized

You'll need to keep track of the material you're citing. If you are taking notes on published text, make it clear that you are copying. Note the source, put it in quotes—do whatever it takes to make sure that six months from now, you don't go back to this material, think that you've written it yourself, and incorporate it into narration, only to find out that you've lifted entire sentences from Stephen Hawking or Alice Walker.

A few other tips:

- *Note the source.* An article that's not referenced is a waste of everyone's time. On the copy of the document itself, note the bibliographic data. It's also useful to note which library you found it in and even write down the call numbers. Otherwise, you may very well find yourself having to look it up again.
- *Be sure you've got the whole article.* If you're photocopying an article or printing one off a microfilm reader, check to be sure that the entire piece is actually readable. If it's not, try again or take out a pen and fill in the gaps. If an article is footnoted, photocopy the footnotes. It's very frustrating to the producer to find great material in the body of an article and not be able to use it without sending the researcher back to the library.
- *Don't editorialize.* Do not, as the researcher, take it upon yourself to annotate the photocopy (unless you're asked to do so). Pages and pages of underlined and highlighted material can be annoying. Steer the production team to relevant passages, but let them form their own impressions.
- *Be organized.* For example, do your best to keep bibliographies in alphabetical order. It will save you from looking

up the same source more than once, by mistake, as you go down the list.

- *Make use of file folders,* so that you don't end up with a massive stack of paper that you will find yourself sorting through over and over.
- *Neatness counts.* Research is a lot of work, and everybody gets tired. But you must take the time to write legibly, or at least to copy any scribbled notes within a short period of time, before you can no longer decipher them. And if you're keeping a research notebook, keep it current.
- A plea on behalf of libraries: *Never mark up in a library-owned book or magazine.* Never bend the pages down, and if you must spread the book face down to photocopy or scan, do it gently.
- *Go a step further.* If you're doing research for someone else, get the material you've been asked to retrieve and then look through it. As mentioned, photocopy footnotes if they accompany an article. But then scan those footnotes to see if there's additional material you could pick up while you're at the library. Does a more current book by the same author come to your attention? If there's a reference to a primary source within a secondary source, can you dig up the original material? Come back with these unexpected treasures and you will make the producers very happy. Primary sources, especially, tend to be wonderful finds that take more than Internet digging.
- Again, *be cautious about what you find on the Internet.* It's an amazing tool. In a matter of minutes, it's possible to learn the population in Sioux City, Iowa, in 1910, or learn how many American presidents were married to a woman named Eleanor. But the web also contains a lot of beautifully produced, but less-than-useful, information. An impressive-looking history of the civil rights movement might turn out to have been produced by Mr. Crabtree's eighth-grade social studies class; a scientific-looking report on the "myths" of global warming might have been produced both by and for the oil industry. As you search the web, pay careful attention to the source of the material and read everything with a skeptical eye.

VISUAL ARCHIVES

Depending on the story you're telling, you may or may not need to explore what's available in terms of stills or motion picture footage in the archives, whether public (such as the National Archives in Washington, D.C.) or private (such as Corbis). Extensive visual research is most commonly done once a film is at least partially funded; the visual research becomes part of the overall research and development leading to a shooting treatment, and often continues as needed (or begins again) as the story takes further shape in the editing room. Knowledge of at least some of what's available can add a note of veracity to your fundraising material, whether you're submitting a treatment or script. For example, "Grainy black-and-white photos, a recent find in the collection of the McGooey Foundation, show the inventor as a child hammering together a contraption that he clearly meant as a flying machine."

As with the print material, organization of your visual research is everything. Many productions have a separate person (or people) responsible for keeping track of archival material, in part because the effort of acquiring rights to use footage (after it's been definitely selected for use in the film), as well as the logistics of ordering broadcast-quality reproductions, can be significant. In any event, you will have to find some way to keep track of visual images, such as a "stills" notebook that the production team can refer to when searching for images. However you choose to keep this visual record, it is critical that source information be recorded; it's very frustrating to realize that a particular image is perfect, only to find that the researcher doesn't remember the source or whether it was photocopied from a book or printed from the web.

Archival stills and motion picture footage, no less than print materials, should be subject to scrutiny in terms of its veracity and completeness. Sure, that footage undeniably shows teenagers looting a store, but you can't tell from the few kids crowding the frame how representative their behavior was of the event as a whole. Archival material, whether motion picture or stills, was created for a purpose. To the extent possible, you need to understand what the source of the material is and what else might be available to balance out that one particular viewpoint.

Archival research is a specialty, although plenty of first-timers have made their way to the various film, video, and photographic archives to search through material. (Some searching can now be done online.) As with print materials, it's important to do your own research as much as possible. Archivist Kenn Rabin, interviewed in Chapter 23, says that all too frequently these days, filmmakers research archival material mostly, or even solely, by screening other films that have used archival material on the topic. This creates problems for a number of reasons. In the first place, it will be very difficult to find out exactly where the shots came from; an edited sequence may have shots and stills from a variety of sources. You have to go to the original source, not the previous filmmaker, for rights. Secondly, you're trusting the journalism of the previous filmmaker, who may be trusting the journalism of a previous filmmaker. Suppose Producer A uses a shot labeled by the archive as "civil rights protester, Chicago, 1934" to stand in for a shot that doesn't exist (or he wasn't able to find) of Jonathan Miller, leader of a fledgling union of black workers in Detroit in 1937. Suppose Producer B then uses that shot, labels it "Jonathan Miller, labor leader," and uses it for a story that explores the extent to which charges of communism among labor organizers were or were not true. Producer C might take that same footage, drop the "Jonathan Miller," and label the guy "communist sympathizer, 1930s." It gets messy.

MOVING FORWARD

Research of every sort will be ongoing for most of the film's production, but there comes a point when the filmmaker has to decide that it's time to move to the next stage—production. But first, at least some of this information must be put down on paper, whether for your own use (a production treatment), for funding, or for the go-ahead (the "green light") from a supervising or commissioning executive. Knowing when to stop researching, at least for now, can be tough. There's always more to learn, and the more you learn, the more you want everybody to know what you've found out. Just because something is fascinating or important doesn't mean it can or should make it into your final, edited film. As Alan Berliner said about working on *The Sweetest Sound* (in the same interview that started this chapter), "one of the hardest things I had to do was let go of everything I knew—to accept that the film could not possibly contain everything I had learned about names."

9

Casting

Not all documentary filmmakers would call it "casting," yet all would agree that the people you see on screen—whether they're interacting with each other, talking to an off-screen interviewer, or acting as narrator or host—need to be researched, contacted, and brought onto the project with care. Decisions about who will be filmed, how they will be chosen, and what they're expected to contribute to the storytelling are important. Even the people who appear through archival means, whether in archival footage or through a reading of their letters, diaries, and other artifacts of the past, are important to the overall casting of a story. In fact, how you cast your documentary is so important that some executives want to see footage of your main characters before they'll approve or commission a project.

WHEN TO CAST

In general, you begin thinking about casting even as you're considering a topic and story to film; it's part of the conception of a film's style and approach. If there are specific people whose involvement is critical, you'll need to cast them (or at least know that they would be available and amenable) prior to your inclusion of them in any pitch. After that, casting takes shape as the outline and treatment do, and you begin to know who or what type of people you're looking for and why.

WHOM TO CAST

For a film that requires experts, it's wise to cast a range of viewpoints. This means that instead of just shooting "five experts" on a subject, you know how each of the five differs from the others in expertise and outlook, offering a means of adding complexity and balance to the overall film. There are only so many people an audience can follow in a half-hour or an hour, and you don't want all of those people talking about the same issues from the same perspective.

One way to think about casting is to regard each individual who appears on screen, whether as a character you're following or as someone you interview (or both), as having a *job* to do in the overall film. Sometimes they stand in for a particular aspect of an argument; sometimes they represent an element that you could not otherwise film. For example, you could get three people to talk in general about Title IX legislation in the United States, but it might be stronger to find a lawyer who'd fought for its enforcement, a female athlete who got a college scholarship because of it, and an athletic director who opposed it out of fear that it would limit resources for his school's football program. They may each know a little bit or even a lot about each other's areas of expertise, but it muddies the storytelling if they don't stick to the part of the story that they best serve.

Along the same lines, if you're creating a historical film, you might want a biographer to stand in for Martha Washington, for example. He or she would be asked to comment specifically and only on your story as it relates to Martha. Without attention being called to it, the audience will learn this cue. When they see that expert, they'll know that—in a way—Martha, or at least her proxy, is now on screen.

Do Your Homework

A significant part of casting effectively is doing some research before you start indiscriminately calling around looking for experts or "types." The less generic the casting is, the stronger the film will be.

Casting Nonexperts

Sometimes, you're not looking for experts but for real people willing to give you access to lives and situations that embody themes and ideas you've set out to explore. Some examples:

- For their film *Troublesome Creek*, Jeanne Jordan and Steven Ascher decided against casting or interviewing any experts, and instead focused on Jordan's family members, especially her parents. "We absolutely did not want any expert testimony about anything having to do with farming or economics that would make it seem like this was a subject being studied as opposed to a subject that was being lived," Ascher says.
- The producers of *Hoop Dreams* were fortunate in their discovery of the two young basketball players featured in their film, Arthur Agee and William Gates. According to their press material, filmmakers Steve James, Frederick Marx, and Peter Gilbert initially planned to make a half-hour documentary on street basketball in Chicago. In 1986, they approached producer Gordon Quinn of Kartemquin Films, and Quinn, in turn, approached KTCA, the PBS station in St. Paul. By this time, the filmmakers had found Agee and Williams, both freshmen in high school. The plan now shifted, and they followed the players over a period of years to see where their basketball dreams would take them. Each player, on his own, would have been interesting, but their two stories interwoven provide a far more insightful look at the various ways in which opportunity, family, skill, and luck can affect an athletic career.

On-the-Fly Casting

A popular device in television advertising these days is to put a group of young people into a car with a camera and portray them as making a documentary, apparently winging it. They pull up in unfamiliar places, shout questions to strangers, and then move on. There are circumstances in which you might want to do this, but in general, this isn't an effective use of time, unless of course it's part of a thought-out film design. In *Super Size Me*, Morgan Spurlock effectively conducts a number of these "man-on-the-street" interviews. While not a random sampling, these people seem to represent the average person and his or her knowledge of fast food, nutrition, and in one case, the lyrics to an old McDonald's jingle. This can be fun and effective.

Casting Opposing Voices

How do you get people to participate in a film when it's likely that the viewpoint they hold is contrary to yours or the audience's? A primary way is by making it clear that you are open to what they have to say, intend to treat them fairly on screen, and believe that their point of view, while you might disagree with it, is important to the subject at hand and the public's understanding of it.

Don't misrepresent yourself or your project just to gain someone's cooperation. If you want to explore the notion that the 1969 moonwalk was faked, don't imply that your film is a look at manned space flight. Does this mean that you can't approach credible experts on subjects that strain credibility? No. It means that you need to bring them with you, not trick them into cooperating. Give them the option of adding their credibility to the project, and then use their credibility responsibly. (If you are an expert and are approached for a documentary, do some homework before saying yes. A quick web search should tell you a bit about the producer and/or the series that will be airing the interview.)

Main and Redman, from *Lalee's Kin: The Legacy of Cotton*. Photo courtesy of the filmmakers.

Casting for Balance

Balancing the point of view of a film does not mean simply presenting opposing sides. In fact, it almost never means that. Two opposing sides talking past each other do not advance anyone's understanding of an issue. When the opposing sides are actually very uneven, such as when a majority of credible experts takes one position and a small (and often fringe or invested) minority disagrees, then giving these two views equal time and weight creates a false impression that the issues are more uncertain than they actually are. This is not balanced; it's inaccurate. Instead, you should look for people who can offer shades of gray, complexity, within an issue.

Note that casting for balance also means letting the appropriate people present their own points of view. This doesn't mean that individuals can't speak to experiences outside their own; a French historian whose expertise is Native-American education at the turn of the century, for example, might be well qualified to discuss life on a particular Oklahoma reservation in 1910. It's more of a stretch to ask a biology major who happens to be protesting foreign sweatshops to tell you what goes on in an overseas sneaker factory, unless you limit your questioning to a frame of reference relevant to that person: "Why am I here? I'm here because I read an article that said . . ." If your film storytelling requires that you convey conditions in the factory, you'd be better off trying to find someone who has witnessed those conditions firsthand (as a worker or owner, for example, or as someone who toured the facilities on a fact-finding tour) and/or a labor expert who has studied those specific conditions.

When you hear someone on camera talking about "them"— for example, "The people living in government housing thought we were being unfair to them"—it's likely you need to find individuals from within that community who can speak for themselves, or experts uniquely qualified to speak on their behalf.

Expanding the Perspective

It's very easy, when casting (and especially when casting quickly), to go after the people at the top, the leaders and figureheads. Often, they are known to be charismatic and articulate. But they rarely represent the whole story or, often, the most interesting part of it.

Dig deeper, and ask yourself who else might add perspective to a story. If you're talking to policy experts for a film on education, you might want to explore what a second-grade teacher would add. If you're doing a film about corporate scandals, an interesting perspective might come from a realtor trying to sell the homes of some former executives who are now in prison.

Be careful, also, to avoid perpetuating misconceptions about gender, ethnicity, or nationality. From the leaders to the line workers, seek out a range of individuals and experiences, rather than rely on what may be a less expansive cast from a previous documentary or news report. If you can't find female and minority astrophysicists, structural engineers, construction workers, or social historians, for example, chances are you're not looking very hard. It would be incomplete and inaccurate in today's world (or yesterday's, for that matter) to portray it as less diverse and complex than it truly is (or was). You should reflect that complexity in your casting.

HOSTS AND NARRATORS

There is a wide range in how and why people use on-camera hosts for documentary films. Sometimes a broadcaster will want the producer to use a celebrity, such as an actor, sports figure, or politician. With celebrities known to be involved in particular political, social, or health issues, for example, this can give the project added credibility. A celebrity's reputation—as a humorist, for example—can set the tone for a project. Finally, the involvement of a celebrity can help boost a project's promotion and raise audience interest. (Using a celebrity who is not a trained actor can be frustrating, however, because it's harder than it looks to walk and talk naturally on camera, and it takes skill to maintain tone and energy during a voice-over recording session.)

Some programs involve the host in the filmed story line, as when *Wild Nature* took celebrities on journeys around the world. These hosts help to bring a narrative structure to the filmmaking, as discussed in Chapter 3. It's also possible to have one person introduce a show and another narrate it. And it's possible—in fact, quite common—for a celebrity or noncelebrity to narrate the show without ever being seen on camera. Actor Peter Coyote, for example, narrated *Enron: The Smartest Guys in the Room*; actor

Morgan Freeman narrated *March of the Penguins*. In any case, you want the narration to be recorded by someone who can enunciate and whose voice will carry even when placed against music or sync sound.

The narrator's voice sets a tone for the film. Will it be male or female, or have an identifiable accent? How old do you want your narrator to sound? How do you want this person to come across to the audience? As an expert or a friend? Sounding humorous, somber, remote, or warm? Even an unseen narrator has a distinct presence in the film and is part of the overall balance of voices that are heard. Alternatively, some films are "narrated" in voice-over by the filmmaker, who may appear on screen. *Grizzly Man* (Werner Herzog), *My Architect* (Nathaniel Kahn), and *Super Size Me* (Morgan Spurlock) are examples of films in which the narrator/filmmaker plays a role in the story.

There are many creative ways to narrate films. In *The Kidnapping of Ingrid Betancourt*, discussed in Chapter 17, the filmmakers were about to start shooting when the subject of their intended film, Colombian presidential candidate Ingrid Betancourt, was kidnapped. Just prior to that, however, she had been on a book tour in the United States, where she conducted several radio interviews in English. The filmmakers used this material to construct a voice-over that allows Betancourt to introduce herself and her ambitions during the film's first act, which leads up to the kidnapping.

PAYING YOUR SUBJECTS

The general rule in journalism is that if you start paying for stories, people will come up with stories for which they want to be paid. There is a big difference between paying an actor to portray Thomas Jefferson and paying a scholar or expert to discuss him. One is a craftsman in an art frequently supported through freelance employment such as this. The other is usually a career scholar and/or author who benefits by advancing his or her expertise and, in many cases, published work, for whom you are providing a significant audience. Some filmmakers may decide to pay subjects indirectly, whether through buying them groceries or making a contribution to a charity. Scholars and experts who appear on screen (and are not also advisors) are not paid, although this is usually under debate and some new precedents are being set.

Don't be confused by the difference between experts who appear on camera and those who work off camera as advisors, and don't assume that they are the same people. As discussed previously, advisors work behind the scenes, often for the duration of the project. They are usually paid an honorarium for their time and given a credit that flies by all too quickly at the end of the film. What about those people who agree to appear on camera but have nothing to gain, no book to build an audience for or business that benefits from publicity? People participate in films for a number of reasons. They believe in their work or struggle and hope that their stories may raise awareness or help others; they've suffered an injustice or a personal loss and hope that publicity may gain them support or bring perpetrators to the attention of law enforcement agents; or they are asked to cooperate by their employers or sponsors. There are a number of good reasons to participate in a documentary. Being paid shouldn't be the most significant one.

10

Pitching and Proposal Writing

Chances are, you'll be pitching your story until the day it's broadcast or screened, if not after. Your pitch is the way to excite people about your project, which you need to do in order to get them to fund you, work with you, work for you, give you a broadcast slot, or distribute your film. Your pitch is your first and best ticket in; it's also, it turns out, a very good way to see if you really have a good film story. There are exceptions, but in general, if you can't pitch your story clearly and succinctly, it's likely that you don't yet have a handle on it.

PITCHING

A pitch very quickly lets the listener or reader "see" your film and understand why it needs to be made. An ineffective pitch introduces the topic but not the story, as in "This is a film about the ethics of genetic testing and about how some people face hard choices." An effective pitch does both. "This is a film about genetic testing in which we follow an actress making the tough decision about whether to be tested for the disease that claimed her mother's life." The pitch works because it compels the listener to ask follow-up questions: What will she do if the test is positive? Will she let you follow her through the process? What if she doesn't take the test?

Here's another example of a weak pitch. "Four years ago, Vietnam veteran Martin Robinson decided he would scale the

heights of Mount Whatsit at the age of 53—with one leg. He succeeded, and in the years since has inspired veterans' groups across
America." There's just one hitch. Where's the story here? There *was*
a story (his efforts four years ago), but unless you have some plan
for telling it now, what's holding the film together? A 57-year-old
man standing before various groups of veterans.

A better version of this pitch, assuming you can find a more
dynamic angle, would go something like this: "Four years ago,
Vietnam veteran Martin Robinson became the first amputee to
scale the heights of Mount Whatsit. Now, he's going back—and
bringing two Gulf War veterans, amputees who thought their best
athletic days were behind them—along with him." Not a bad pitch,
especially if you can follow it up with good access to these people
and some information about your own skills as both a filmmaker
and a mountaineer (to show you'll be capable of following them
up the mountain). In many cases, the pitch will be even stronger
if you show a tape that introduces your main characters, allowing
people to see that they're appealing and will work on camera.

Tailoring the Pitch

If you're pitching to a specific program or foundation, you'll want
to emphasize those aspects of the story and your treatment of
it that meet the needs of that group. If you were pitching the
film about genetic testing to a foundation concerned with issues
of medicine and the public's ability to make informed choices,
that would be your emphasis. The exact same film, pitched to a
television executive, might play up the emotional aspect of a young
woman facing tough life choices. Tailoring the pitch doesn't mean
changing the film to suit the financier; it means highlighting those
elements of your project that are likely to be of greatest interest and
helping the reader or reviewer see the relevance of your material
to his or her goals or mandate.

This means, of course, that you need to know as much as
you can about the individuals or groups to whom you're pitching.
Don't throw ideas at just anybody. If you're pitching to a network
or the producers of an existing series, watch their programs, go to
their websites, and find out everything you can about the programming they've done and if they're moving in any new directions.
Are they interested in character-driven stories? Would they want

an historical survey film? Do they tend to use on-screen presenters? Can you submit a magazine-length story, or do they only want broadcast hours? If they commission work, do they tend to work with the same handful of known producers? In panel after panel, commissioning editors complain that people approach them without knowing enough about who they are, how they work, or what kind of programming they do. So do your homework, and be prepared before you pitch.

This is no less true if you are approaching government or private agencies. Not all foundations support media projects, and those that do have a mandate for the work they support. Go to their websites, which generally offer detailed information about the kinds of programming they support. Often, foundations also have program officers who are willing to answer questions. It can take time to find your way around the various funding agencies, but the good news is that, while some potential financiers require detailed and lengthy proposals, others only require an initial query letter.

With the caveat that fundraising is an area of expertise beyond the scope of this book, what follows are some tips for presenting your story as effectively as possible, as part of your overall fundraising strategy. No matter how serious the mission of the

Ken "Spike" Kirkland, in *Sing Faster: The Stagehands' Ring Cycle*. Photo courtesy of Jon Else.

foundation, the bottom line of your approach is as writer to reader, filmmaker to audience.

When to Pitch

There is no single way to raise money or support for a project. Some filmmakers pitch an idea verbally or in an introductory letter. Others walk into a meeting with a handful of ideas, none of which has, as yet, been significantly researched and developed. It can be very difficult for independents to get financial support for development, but the odds of doing so increase as you establish a solid track record in production. In addition, you may find yourself pitching as a staff person, or you may be pitching to an independent company that regularly provides programming to a network and therefore has some funds for development. Every scenario is different. But for many documentarians, it all gets a bit jumbled together—pitching, development, and proposal writing—in a cycle that's generally underfunded. The process is bearable for the following two reasons: the passion you feel for the story, and the conviction that the film will eventually get the support it needs.

Pitching on Screen

At times, you'll run across programmers who would rather see footage than paperwork, and many times people want to see both. What this means varies, depending on the scale of the project. Sometimes, you only have to provide footage of other films or tapes you've made, as evidence of your skill as a filmmaker. But it's not uncommon for people to want to see even raw footage of your story as a way of seeing your characters in action. In any case, a good, short promo reel can be an effective way to excite people about your project and make it clear that you know what you're doing. As Nick Fraser explains in Chapter 20, you want your trailer to reflect your final film in pacing and tone, rather than be a slick sort of "ad" for the film.

Pitching to Hone Storytelling

Outsiders aren't the only ones to whom you might be pitching. On some projects, producers pitch their stories at in-house development meetings, not once but several times as the films or series take shape. The following is adapted from an in-house pitch that I helped to construct for the opening hour of *I'll Make Me a World*. The six-hour series told two to three stories in each hour, and the hours themselves were arranged sequentially, in an order that was both chronological and thematic.

The pitch: Hour One: Lift Every Voice *(1900–1924)*

This film begins at the turn of the 20th century, a time when the United States is emerging as a modern, industrialized nation and the culture that will come to be known as "American" is still being formed. The first generation of African Americans to be born in freedom is also coming of age. This hour is about their efforts to add their voices, ideas, and visions during this time of possibility and hope. This hour includes three stories:

"Nobody" follows Bert Williams as he teams up with George Walker and they head for the Broadway stage, where they face an audience whose expectations of black entertainment have been shaped by 60 years of minstrel traditions. Can they reject these stereotypes and still attract a mainstream audience? This story continues through the death of George Walker; we end with Bert Williams performing with the Ziegfeld Follies alongside stars including W. C. Fields, Will Rogers, and Fannie Brice—and yet, as actor Ben Vereen portrays him, still facing racial discrimination.

Our second story, "The Good Mad Music," follows a talented young trombone player, Edward "Kid" Ory, as he arrives in New Orleans in 1908 and sets about creating his "Creole Jazz Band," drawing together such future notables as Sidney Bechet and King Oliver. Together, they help to create the controversial new sounds that many call America's first original music: jazz.

Our last story, "Within These Gates," explores the promise of the brand-new motion picture industry and the efforts of filmmaker Oscar Michaux to create films that present the complexity of African-American life at a time of growing racial division, embodied in 1915 by D. W. Griffith's acclaimed epic, The Birth of a Nation, *a dramatic portrayal of the rise of the Ku Klux Klan. We follow Michaux to his artistic triumph of 1924,* Body and Soul, *starring activist and actor Paul Robeson.*

By the end of the first hour, white resistance to African-American advancement has closed doors to opportunity in jobs, education, housing, and voting rights. African-American leaders seize upon one of the few avenues open to opportunity: the arts. They launch a movement that— as we see in the series' next hour—comes to be known as the Harlem Renaissance.

The story titles listed above were never used on screen; they were simply a way to summarize the stories within each hour and differentiate them from the other stories. (In the editing room, these stories were woven together, meaning that one story would start, continue part way, and then be put on hold while a second story got under way.)

Pitching helps you to streamline how you think about a story, its themes, and its important action. Eventually, if the story is to be told using a three-act structure, you'll want to be able to pitch it as such. In other words, "Our first act begins here . . . . We drive to the moment when . . . . As the second act begins, such-and-such is happening. The second act drives to the point where . . . ," etc."

If you're pitching out loud, it's a good idea to practice beforehand so that you don't get bogged down in unnecessary details and sidebar information that will lose your listener. ("Oh, and you'll find out along the way that he's gotten married to so-and-so and I should have mentioned that they toured in Europe . . . .") You want to tell a clean and exciting story, which means that as your pitch changes over time—as your familiarity with the story and how you want to tell it evolves—you'll need to continue to revise and practice your pitch.

PROPOSAL WRITING

Many filmmakers in the United States complain that they spend more time writing proposals than they do making films. Proposals are the documents you submit in order to request funding from grant-making agencies, whether public or private. In general, the following are stages at which financial support might be available prior to the completion of your film: planning, scripting, production, postproduction, and finishing. The first two fall under the category of "development" and can be very difficult funds to raise. The easiest, arguably, are finishing funds, which are awarded at or after the rough cut stage. At that point, the financier can see your film, there are few surprises, and there is a higher likelihood that you'll be able to complete the project.

While each proposal must be tailored to the guidelines and mandates of the particular agency, there are a few basic things that they'll usually want to know, whether in a letter of introduction, a 3-page summary, or a 25-page narrative. They include the following:

Nature of the Request

Who you are, what your project is ("a 90-minute program to be shot on digital video on the history of the can opener and its impact on American cuisine"), how much you're requesting at this time from this grant maker ("$X,000 for scripting" or "$XXX,000 for production of one hour of this four-part series"), what activities are to be supported for the amount requested, and what the end result of the grant will be. (For example, if you ask for a scripting grant, you should end up with a script or, in some cases, a production-ready treatment.)

Introduction to the Subject

This section offers the proposal reviewer a general grounding in the *subject matter* to be treated on film. In other words, this is not your film treatment and does not have to include detail about how you will treat the subject on screen. It's an overview of the subject, presented clearly and concisely, and written in a way that will hopefully bring the reader to share your conviction that the subject is interesting, relevant, and worth a commitment of resources.

Rationale

A more focused opportunity to convey the significance of the project and, in particular, its relevance to the financier. Another way to look at it is, "Why this project now? How will it advance public understanding and awareness of the topic? Why is it useful for this topic to be presented on film? In what way will audiences be served by this project?" A few carefully chosen facts often speak volumes when making the case for a film.

Goals and Objectives

What your project is designed to accomplish. There will be a handful of these; for example, *Goal: To explore the historical context in which Title IX legislation was originally passed and the inequalities it sought to address, and to evaluate the law's impact, intended and unintended, in the context of current efforts to repeal it. Objective: Viewers will better understand the complexity of Title IX legislation beyond the issue of school sports, and appreciate the social and political processes by which legal change is brought about.*

Related Projects

What other films have been done on the same or related subjects, how does their success (or lack of success) inform your approach to your story, and how does your story build on or differ from these projects? As mentioned previously, the fact that a topic has been covered is not necessarily a deterrent, given all the different ways a topic can be treated and the different venues available. But you should demonstrate that you know what's out there.

Ancillary Projects

These are sometimes also called "related projects," which makes for confusion. An ancillary project is something that you're developing to bolster your film's shelf life and reach. These might include web-based materials, radio broadcasts, material for educational outreach, and/or material for community engagement, which uses media as the catalyst for action and discussion within and between community groups. At a time when the television landscape is cluttered with choices, including documentary choices, it's becoming increasingly important to financiers, especially those who support public television programming, that you demonstrate ways in which you will extend the impact of a broadcast.

History of the Project

Some information on how the project got under way and on the financial or institutional support you've received to date. Your passion for the project and your connection to the story are likely to come through here, as well as in other places, because this is where you tell people how you got involved in the project, why the story appealed to you and/or seemed vitally important to tell, and what you've done, so far, to tell it.

Audience and Broadcast Prospects

Information on your target audience(s) and how you intend to reach them.

Organization History

Information about the organizations involved in submitting the proposal, including the production company and possibly the fiscal sponsor. As elsewhere, you may want to highlight those areas of your expertise that mesh with the interests of the potential financiers.

Project Staff

Information on the media team and academic advisors (where appropriate). If you or your media team aren't experienced in the kind of production you're proposing, consider taking on other team members who will add to your credibility. If it's your idea but your first film, figure out what you need to get out of it, personally and professionally, and then determine what you might be able to give up in the interest of getting it made. It's very difficult to get anything funded these days, so you need to do what you can to be competitive. (Alternatively, if you can afford to do so, you might work to get farther into the production before requesting funds, so that you have a film-in-progress that demonstrates your ability.)

Plan of Work

A detailed description of the work that will be done, and by whom, with the funding requested. Be sure that this plan of work doesn't exceed the scope or length of the grant period; if you're asking for scripting money, your plan of work shouldn't continue through production and editing.

Appendices

Résumés, letters of commitment, research bibliography, lists of films on this or related subjects, description of materials to be used, if appropriate. For example, for a film that will rely on archival footage, a list—even a preliminary one—of archival materials pertinent to the subject should be included.

Treatment

Many financiers want to see some form of written treatment in order to consider a request for scripting or production funds. A treatment is a prose description of the film as you envision it; in other words, it is not a research document, but a "good read" that conveys, in print, the film as it will unfold on screen (more on this in the next chapter). Depending on where you are in your research and development, this treatment may be fairly preliminary. Even so, it should be well written and make the strongest case possible for your film.

Budget

Financiers often want to see a breakdown of how you'll spend the money you're asking them to provide. They're also likely to want to see your entire production budget, to get a sense of how funds will be allocated overall.

A Few Extra Pointers

Much of the advice for proposal writing can be applied to the entire production, including the editing. From my own experience as a consultant and proposal writer and my experience as a proposal reviewer, here are a few tips:

- *Accuracy is important.* It's standard practice for potential sponsors to send proposals out for review by people who know the subject well. If you spell names incorrectly, get titles and dates wrong, or misrepresent factual information, it will (and should) be held against you. The proposal and the quality of work that goes into it are indicative of the film to come. Besides, the fact checking you do now, if filed carefully, will be useful later.
- *The storytelling matters.* The people reviewing your proposal, whether they're scientists, historians, mathematicians, or teachers, are as aware as you are that audiences don't watch a film because the topic is important; they watch because they're interested in a story. So while reviewers will be on guard to see that you don't cut academic corners, they'll

also be checking to see that you know how to attract and hold an audience's interest.

- *Good writing goes a long way.* Beyond the basics of spelling and facts, the proposal should present a coherent argument that flows from paragraph to paragraph. Be concise. Your readers are likely to be plowing through several proposals, and you don't want to trip them up with writing that's unedited, unclear, or ungrammatical.

- *Be your own first audience.* Ask yourself if you'd be interested in the film you're pitching, and if the answer is no, work on it some more.

- *Anticipate resistance.* If you are going to propose a history of the American soap opera as a way to look at important themes in American cultural and social history and women's history, be prepared for the reviewer whose first instinct is to laugh. Get some experts on your side and, with them, make your case. Answer the naysayers with solid research. Producers have gotten funding for films on all sorts of subjects that might not, at first glance, have seemed "suitable."

- *Arm people with what they need to know to understand the proposal.* A producer can sometimes get so close to a topic that he or she forgets that other people aren't immersed in the subject and may need either to be reminded or introduced to key characters and events. Assume that your audience is smart, but seed information throughout your proposal in a way that brings readers along with you.

- *Passion is important.* It comes across in the presentation of a proposal in subtle ways, but mostly it shows in the quality of the work—how thorough the groundwork was, how creatively the ideas have been transformed into a story, and how well that story is presented on paper.

- *Avoid overproduction.* Teachers are known to be wary when they receive papers with fancy, multicolored covers that clearly took hours to design and execute because they doubt the same effort went into the actual paper. The same is true of proposals. Put the effort into the contents (and where appropriate, a sample reel); include a few pictures as well as charts and chronologies where they're helpful, but otherwise, don't worry about fancy graphics.

- *Avoid unfounded hyperbole.* "This is the most amazing story that the XYZ foundation will ever help to produce, and nothing that XYZ has done to date will have the kind of impact this film will have." This kind of language is always a turn-off for readers.
- *Avoid paranoia.* "While we are pleased to share this proposal with you, we ask that you keep it in strictest confidence as we are certain that others would grab this idea the minute they got wind of it." Foundations keep proposals in confidence unless or until they are funded and produced.

PROTECTING YOUR IDEAS

When you become passionate about an idea, you're convinced that it's great—great enough to steal. The truth is, ideas are cheap, and it's the whole package—your experience, your treatment of the idea, your ability to make the film happen—that will sell the project, not the idea alone. With that said, there are ways to protect your work. In the United States, the first is through copyright, which is a form of intellectual property law. You cannot copyright an idea, but you can copyright your treatment of an idea, whether as an outline, treatment, script, finished film, or published article. Completed films are also subject to copyright. For more information, go to the Library of Congress website (www.loc.gov).

Another way to protect your work is through a guild. In the United States, the Writer's Guild of America (WGA; www.wga.org) represents writers in the motion picture, broadcast, cable, and new technologies industries. The WGA offers a registration service to nonmembers as well as members. For a fee ($22 for nonmembers as of 2006), you can register anything from an idea to a scenario, synopsis, outline, treatment, or script. By writing down your pitch—the basic story and your unique approach to telling it—and then registering it, you'll have a record of the idea's origination, should it become necessary to prove that you came up with it first. It's best to register at least an outline or treatment (e.g., enough detail to indicate how you'll be approaching the story and what story you'll tell). For example, "a look at skydiving" is far too vague. "A film about skydiving that follows the stars of *Grey's Anatomy* as they learn together how to do it and then take their first skydive together" is better; a 2-page, 10-page, even 25-page treatment is even better.

Know, however, that ideas are in the air. A story that caught your attention on the local news probably caught someone else's attention as well, and it was probably picked up and carried in newspapers all across the country. Books, other films, and current events all trigger film ideas. Anyone who's reviewed proposals, whether for a station or a financier, will tell you that ideas often come in waves—surprisingly comparable proposals from disparate sources.

At the same time, it's not a perfect world. Keep track of where your material's been, who's seen it, and when. In other words, don't be paranoid, but do be organized.

11

Outlines, Treatments, and Scripts

The role of outlines, treatments, and even scripts in documentary storytelling varies from project to project, but their basic purpose is the same. They're to help you and others see, on paper, the film as you imagine it at various points in production—while you're raising funds, before you shoot, before or during your edit. Taking the time to express yourself coherently in print, thinking through what you're doing, how you're doing it, and why, can save you a lot of time, effort, and money.

There is no single way to work. The level of detail in these documents depends, to a large degree, on your schedule, budget, and reasons for writing them. For some filmmakers, it's necessary to write out the story (usually in treatment or preliminary script form) because a potential financier requires it. For others, such as those shooting a film designated for a specific series or broadcaster, a treatment or script may be necessary in order to get the go-ahead to film. But even for filmmakers working more independently, creating written material at various stages can focus the storytelling and ensure that a team shares the basic vision for the project. Better to see gaping holes in logic, casting, or tension on paper than to find out about them in the editing room; if you're 60 pages into your treatment for an hour-long film on China's Cultural Revolution—and you're still not through Act One—chances are your history is a little *too* sweeping.

OUTLINES

An outline is a sketch of your film, written to expose its proposed structure and necessary elements. In most cases, the outline is a working document for you and your team; the prose doesn't need to be polished, and you can use shorthand if your meaning is sufficiently clear. For an hour-long film, a detailed prose outline might be four to five double-spaced pages. It would include a synopsis (one or two paragraphs) of the overall film story, and then a program outline broken down by acts (if applicable) and sequences, with detailed information on elements such as archival footage or specialized photography and interviews.

The outline is a chance to begin imagining your film as it will play on screen. Be careful to focus it as you intend (for now) to focus the final film; in other words, identify the train and point of view. Is the story about the expedition leader or about the group of retirees on the expedition? The parents waging a legal battle against commercialism in the public schools or the budget-starved principal actively courting soft-drink contracts?

If the film is about events in the past or events over which you have control (a series of demonstrations set up for the purpose of an essay, for example), it's easier to begin outlining the film and finding an appropriate structure. For films of events that will unfold as you shoot, it's still possible to draft an outline (and treatment) based on what you anticipate happening. If you intend to follow an eighth grader through a summer at basketball camp, you can do research to find out what the experience is typically like, and what scenes or sequences offer possibilities for meaningful interaction. Do the students board at the camp or go home at night? Do they tend to form close friendships? Are there one-on-one sessions with coaches? Is there much pressure from parents? Knowing these things can help you begin to think about what a sequence will *do*, as opposed to the specifics of what it *is*. If you know, for example, that you want a sequence that you're tentatively calling "The end of innocence"—a sequence that looks at the commercial pressure on young phenoms—then you arrive on location with that focus in mind.

The same is true when considering the people you want to film. As you're doing the outline, you'll begin sketching in the names of people you need to tell your story, from those you "have to have" to those you'd ideally like. Sometimes you won't know who you want specifically, but will have a sense of who they're likely to be, for example, "We need someone who was at the dance with her," or "We want to talk to janitors and others who keep the physical plant operating." An outline can help you see if your story or argument is building and if you have enough variety in casting and sequences, or if too much of your film is doing (and saying) the same thing. Over the course of filming, decisions about story and structure are bound to change, but for now you're taking the first steps in organizing your story into a workable film.

TREATMENTS

Unlike an outline, a treatment has to *show*, not tell. In other words, your outline is a working sketch of your film, and you can discuss what's in it and why. In contrast, the treatment *is* your film, or at least the paper equivalent of it as it exists—most likely in your imagination—at the time you write it.

There are many reasons to write a treatment, and they differ in length and style because of this. As discussed in the previous chapter, if the treatment is your detailed "pitch" to a financier or executive, it should reflect the interests of that audience. Treatments submitted to the National Science Foundation are extremely rigorous; a pitch to a cable science show is likely to be shorter and catchier. A treatment written for use in-house may be less polished in terms of prose, but might include more details about specific shots needed, especially those requiring special gear, as a means of beginning the process of planning for the shoot.

The bottom line, though, is this: The treatment is your way of working out a film story—not necessarily the final film story, but a good working model—on paper, so that even if nothing wonderful and unexpected happens on location to make your film a thousand times better, you'll at least end up with a film that works. Funders aren't the only ones who want to see treatments; many series and/or executive producers will expect to approve at least a brief, workable treatment before allowing producers to shoot. Otherwise, producers may return with a lot of shots and scenes that add up to nothing, and resources will have been wasted.

Even if they're only a few pages long, treatments should demonstrate that the producer has a sense of the film's train, where the story begins and where it's going. This is easier for historical films, but even for films where events are unfolding as you film, you should have some expectation of what the potential middle and end points might be—even a range of possible outcomes. Heidi Bub's reunion with her birth mother might go smoothly, but even then, the filmmakers have an opportunity to explore cultural differences, the historical past, and the meaning of family bonds. Heidi Bub's reunion might *not* go smoothly (as it didn't; see Chapter 7), which makes for an even more complex film but doesn't change the basic train, or the opportunities for exploration.

What Should Come Across in a Treatment?

A basic treatment should draw the reader into a story that begs to be put on screen. From the treatment, your reader should understand:

- Who or what is the film about, what the goals and obstacles are (story);
- Where you're starting the film and how it's organized, at least as you begin to shoot (structure);
- Why you're telling the story (themes and your personal connection);
- Who the major characters are and what role they play in the story (casting).

Treatments for an hour-long film may be 5 pages or 25, depending on what you need. (For some examples, see the end of this chapter.) They should be double spaced, for ease of reading, and written in the present tense—a film story moves forward in time, even if the story is set in the past. The structure of the treatment should mirror the structure of the film. If you plan to start at the grave of a soldier killed in Iraq, for example, your treatment will also start there. If the film is driving toward a meeting between siblings who only recently learned of each other's existence, your treatment should also drive to that point, and not "give away" the drama of that moment by referring to it earlier. If, in your thinking about the film, you envision a three-act dramatic structure and the reunion as being a culmination of Act Two, the reunion should probably not appear until *roughly* three-fourths of the way through your pages.

People, places, and events should be introduced in screen order (meaning the order in which you think they will appear on screen), including a description of how information will be presented. For example, if you plan a sequence about the New York City marathon, it should be clear in the treatment when and how it occurs in your film. Does it start the film, or do you drive to it? If you're going to explore the history of the marathon, will you do so with archival material, interviews, or something else? There's a bit of a balancing act involved—a treatment is *not* a script, nor is it the finished film. You are merely trying to convey not only your story but your approach: "We take this journey with Nils, sitting with him in libraries as he searches through old microfilm, traveling with him to interview elderly relatives and neighbors. Finally, we accompany him to the Venice airport, where the meeting with his long-lost brother will finally take place."

For in-house use, a treatment can refer quickly to references the team already shares. But if your proposal will be read by outsiders (such as reviewers at a grant-making agency), you want to be a bit more explicit. A shorthand line intended for the in-house team might read: "Washington crosses the Delaware; military historians explain; Smith reviews the mythology." More careful and detailed prose might read, "Over Emanuel Gottlieb Leutze's famous painting, *George Washington Crossing the Delaware*, we learn through narration of Washington's triumphant crossing of the Delaware River on the stormy night of December 25, 1776. As our historians make clear, all had seemed lost for the Americans. Now, Washington and his army of 3,000 surprise Britain's mercenary forces at Trenton and capture one-third of the men. They also gain a foothold in New Jersey that puts a halt to the British offensive. It's a decisive moment in the war for independence. We return to the painting, as art historian Jane Smith compares the history to the mythology. The painting was completed in 1851, 75 years after the event...."

Note that this example, which happens to be for a historical film, hasn't said what images you'll be weaving into and out of between historians; hopefully by this point in the treatment, it's clear how you're handling the war history. Nor does it list all of the specific historians talking about this particular event, because by now the reader probably has a sense of which historians you've involved. You can't describe every image and every voice-over and every anticipated sync bite, or you might as well write the script.

What you're doing is making the story and progression of events clear, and including the most important details, in this case, the use of the painting and the art historian. The same would be true if you were imagining a modern-day story for which you were seeking support.

Story, Not Images

Your focus is on story, not photography. In fact, one sure sign that a treatment has been prepared by a less-experienced filmmaker is that it begins by mentioning spectacular sunsets or mists across the valley. If you're focusing on shots or describing the dolleys and cranes and helicopter mounts you'll be using to get them, you're not conveying story. With that said, you can write a treatment that is (occasionally) cinematic. For example, "Work-worn fingers moving rapidly under the sewing machine seem to belong to someone other than the lively 14-year-old operating the machine." That sentence clearly is a close-up that widens out to reveal the person sewing. Or this, from *The Milltail Pack* (see sample pages at the end of this chapter): "The pack [of red wolves] is heading to a corn field just at the end of the road. In the brown, dry stalks of last month's corn live mice, rabbits and voles—tasty appetizers for the Milltail Pack." This is enough of an image to carry the reader through the exposition that follows. Using a different style, here is the first sentence of the treatment for *You Could Grow Aluminum Out There* (for the series *Cadillac Desert*): "In California we name things for what they destroyed. *Real estate signs whiz by the windshield . . . 'Quail Meadows,' 'The Grasslands,' 'Indian Creek,' 'Riverbank Estates,' 'Elk Grove Townhouses,' 'Miwok Village.'* Before the Spaniards came, 300 tribes shared the Central Valley of California."

Note that there's a difference between writing to describe what you *know* you can see, and inventing it as if you were writing the treatment for a dramatic feature. A treatment for a dramatic feature might set a scene like this: "It's late at night. President Truman and his cabinet sit in a smoke-filled room, deliberating their next move." If this is how you're writing a treatment for a factual, historical documentary, either you're aware of stock/archival footage of this scene, or you're planning to recreate it, based on historical evidence that supports your visual interpretation—who was in the room, how late at night it was, what was being discussed. In either case, it should be clear in your treatment how we'll be seeing what we're seeing. For example, "We recreate an impression of this meeting as we hear an actor reading from the president's own diary: It's late at night. He and his cabinet sit in a smoke-filled room. They are deliberating their next move . . . ." Or, "In black-and-white-footage shot by the president's niece, a young art student who happened to be with her uncle that fateful day, we see the late-night meeting, the smoke-filled room. A weary president and his staff, deliberating . . . ."

If this is a scene that you're *anticipating* for a present-day story—for example, you've gotten permission to film a corporation as it unveils a new product—then imagining a scene is permissible, if it is based on research and reasonable expectations. For example, "Our cameras accompany Heather Bourne as she strides into Gotham Towers and rides an elevator to the penthouse, where we'll see her present the new, and somewhat radical, ad campaign to the company's famously traditional board of directors."

Introduce People

You need to let readers know who people are. "Webster describes the carnage at the battlefield" is not enough for outside readers not already steeped in your subject. "Historian Victoria Webster, an expert on World War II military . . . ." Then, if you don't mention Professor Webster for another 10 pages, remind us briefly who she is, for example, "Historian Victoria Webster disagrees."

Explanatory Materials

If you're submitting a treatment for outside review, one way to add information other than what's in the film—because at best, the treatment can't possibly capture everything the film will deliver—is to include a preface, often called "an approach." For example, the filmmaker can state his or her objectives for the program and raise questions to be explored. "Was Father Divine an inspired religious leader who helped to reinvent the rules of social ministry? Or was he a potentially dangerous man deluded by power? This story will examine . . . ." The approach can offer explicit information about the themes and ideas that will be explored in the storytelling; it can also make the filmmaker's position on an issue clear. "We are committed to exploring the overwhelming evidence that manufacturers of XYZ knowingly withheld information about its dangers . . . ." Note, however, that questions must still remain to be explored; in this case, they might be "Were regulatory agencies aware of these dangers, and if so, why didn't they take action sooner?"

Quoting People

Suppose you know whom you want to interview, but you haven't spoken with them yet, either in a pre-interview or a filmed interview. You should never make up quotes based on what you hope someone will say, even if you have a good idea of what it might be, if only because the world is small and if Professor X finds out that you attributed a statement to him that he hasn't or wouldn't make, the chances the he will cooperate with you in the future are slim.

Instead, there are a few options for sprinkling in quotes from sources you haven't spoken with directly. First, you can simply describe what someone will be asked about, for example, "Dr. Hunter offers an introduction to photosynthesis . . . ." Second, you can quote from the individual's published writing. Third, you can quote from interviews that others have conducted with the person. However, if you do any of these, you need to be clear that you have not yet contacted the person directly, and that he or she has not yet agreed to participate in the film. You might say, "Except as noted, quotes are taken from print material published elsewhere." *Suggestion: If you decide to do this, write a version of your treatment with footnotes, so that you can go back to this source if necessary. Remove those footnotes in copies for outside review; they're distracting and unnecessary for readers who are "seeing" your film on paper, not reading a research report.* Another possibility would be, "We have gained the cooperation of Dr. X and Reverend Y, but have not yet spoken with Mr. Z and Dr. P, who are also quoted here." In any case, quotes should be used sparingly. This is your treatment, not your script.

Unknown Information

Even the most polished treatments are written before all of the pieces are in place; you don't know what you'll discover on the film shoot or what terrific visuals you'll find in somebody's attic. Most importantly, it's often the case that you're writing the treatment to raise money to do necessary research; you're doing the best you can with the resources you have, but you know that there's a lot more you need to learn before you can go out to shoot. One solution is to acknowledge these gaps by describing, in general terms, types or scenes that you believe you'll need. For example, "A trainer describes what it's like to work with thoroughbred horses and takes us through the paces of an early-morning work-out." Or, "We are searching for an expert in queuing theory who can apply his or her theoretical work to the design of amusement parks, and we will find parents who know from experience that there is a limit to how long their children, and they themselves, are willing to wait in line."

Writing Treatments for a Series

Writing treatments for a multipart series is not much different than for individual films, except that the approach (and the films themselves) may need to serve a series story, as well as individual film stories. What is the overall series story? Where does each film begin and end? How does one film set the stage for the next film in the series? The build doesn't always need to be chronological; the evolution of a mathematical concept, for example, could form the spine of a series. Sometimes a series has no overall story. Each film simply explores a different aspect of a subject.

Reflect the Work You've Done

Surprisingly, one of the most common problems I encounter when reviewing treatments is that they seem to be based on an afternoon's worth of research, when in fact, the filmmakers have spent weeks or even months on the project and, in some cases, have shot a significant portion of the footage. Your treatment should sell your project and play to its strengths. Add the details that will make your efforts show. For example, "In an interview filmed last May on the steps of her home in Leeds, author Celia Jones offers her perspective on the housing crisis." Or "Our crew follows Mr. Smith down spiral stairs leading to a dusty basement filled with old newspapers, magazines, and a rare collection of photographs that he offers to show us." Provide enough detail to make it clear that you know your subject inside and out, even if you also know that there is a lot more you need to learn.

Tell a Good Story

An important trick of writing treatments is to convey your passion early on. You think you've found an excellent subject for a film—convince the reader. A good story, well researched and well told, goes a long way. As someone who's reviewed proposals, I can say from experience that many submitted treatments are little more than research documents, or, even worse, ideas that haven't progressed much beyond a basic topic. Treatments that attract attention are those that set up and deliver a compelling story, one that's informed by research and enlivened by something different—an unusual perspective, a new angle, unique access to people or places.

Tell a good story as best you can. Then run your treatment past someone who knows nothing about your movie, and preferably is not related to you, so that you get impartial feedback before you send your material to the people you're likely to need most at this stage—financiers.

THE SHOOTING TREATMENT

A *shooting treatment*, if you create one, is the culmination of your work prior to shooting. If you did a treatment to raise development and scripting funds, a shooting treatment reflects the research and creative thinking that those funds enabled. Usually, a shooting treatment is for use by the filmmaking team; if a preliminary treatment got you some development funds from a commissioning editor or executive producer, a shooting treatment may be required to get the go-ahead to head out into the field with a crew. It's the baseline guide to the elements you need to tell the story that you anticipate telling, a document that can be shared (as discussed by Boyd Estus in Chapter 12) with cinematographers, sound recordists, and others to help ensure that opportunities aren't missed.

SCRIPTS

Documentary scripts tend to evolve over the course of production. In the case of programs that are significantly driven by narration (whether spoken anonymously, such as actor Peter Coyote's narration of *Enron*, or as voice-over by the filmmaker, such as Werner Herzog's narration of *Grizzly Man*), the script might begin to take shape during preproduction, only to be significantly revised and rewritten during editing.

For most programs, narration augments visual storytelling, so scripts are not written until editing is about to start or under way. Once transcripts are available, filmmakers will often assemble a paper script. This script builds on the original treatment but takes into account changes to the story as filmed, and it incorporates interview, sync, and archival material in proposed screen order as a blueprint for the editor to follow (for more details, see Chapter 13). As editing progresses, this script is revised and rewritten, until no more changes are to be made (script lock and picture lock). Note that not all films are edited in this way, and some editors rely solely on an outline that is revised over the course of editing.

Scripts for Fundraising

Some funding agencies require a script as a condition of granting production money. If you are already editing, you will be able to submit a draft of your script in progress. If you are still seeking funding for production, however, what you submit is more akin to a very developed treatment or a document that is part treatment, part script. You do the best you can, adhering to the guidelines for a treatment but generally presenting the material in a more script-like format.

Script Format

Don't go out and buy a commercial screenwriting software program; these are designed specifically for dramatic feature films and serve that function well, but they're of little use for documentaries. Most documentary filmmakers seem to use Word or WordPerfect (files cross these platforms without much difficulty), using them to create scripts that are formatted in either one or two columns.

If two columns are used, one is for visuals, the other for audio. With a single-column format, visuals, if mentioned, are put in parentheses. In either case, narration and interview bites should stand out from each other; for example, the narration might be in bold, or the interview bites indented. On films with significant interview material, whether or not there will also be narration, it can be helpful to create a separate block (whether you're working with one column or two) for each interview bite that's pulled, so they can be quickly moved around. Some filmmakers also use the outlining function to keep sequences intact, again, so they can be quickly rearranged.

Narration Script

When it comes time to record narration, your narration pieces are generally numbered and then isolated into a script of their own—a *narration script*—which is often a single-column, double-spaced document, with very wide margins to the left and right for ease of reading. Don't put the narration in all capitals, because this makes it more difficult to read.

TREATMENTS AS A CLASSROOM EXERCISE

I recently led a seminar that looked at the presentation of history on screen. It was a nonproduction course, and only a few of the students had film experience. I wanted them to evaluate the storytelling in others' films and learn how to apply it to their own (hypothetical) documentaries. For the first half of the semester, we screened and critiqued several historical documentaries as well as three fictionalized histories, *Mississippi Burning, JFK*, and *Glory*.

During the second half of the semester, each student developed ideas and wrote a detailed treatment (20 to 25 pages) for a film on a subject of his or her choosing. To give them all a common set of ground rules, the topics and treatments had to suit guidelines for the PBS historical series, *American Experience*. The series seeks "dramatic and compelling stories about the American past—stories about people both ordinary and extraordinary," according to its website, www.pbs.org/wgbh/amex/guidelines/. "We are particularly interested in stories that offer a unique or rarely seen perspective on our history and that have a clear narrative arc and strong characters. We are least interested in films that take a survey-type approach to history." Series guidelines allow for programs that raise issues which resonate to the present, but not for programs where the historical information is merely a bridge into "contemporary issues and conflict."

In the professional world, treatments for historical films can take many weeks, if not months, to research and write. My expectations for the students' treatments were scaled back to accommodate the realities of their academic schedules. I strongly recommended that they start with subjects for which at least one, if not two, secondary sources existed (preferably books that had been well reviewed), because that meant that professionals had done the time-consuming and highly-skilled work of digesting raw historical data. I also wanted them to explore at least two primary sources, to have the experience of working with period documents and/or artifacts. Otherwise, my emphasis for the assignment was on turning a subject into a story, one exciting enough to draw and hold general viewers even as it offered historical evidence and complexity. I stressed that someone reading the treatment should enjoy the experience the way one enjoys reading a well-written magazine article, and that this "article" should give a good sense of the film as it would unfold on screen.

A few lessons learned:

- It helps to do a quick academic web search to see where scholars stand on your story. Is there cutting-edge research or controversy? Don't find just any secondary source and go with it—find the *best* source or two, and then a couple of backups. (An excellent article in a reputable journal, for the purpose of this exercise, was also acceptable.)
- It makes as little sense to be completely skeptical of all filmmakers as it does to be completely gullible. At the same time understand that creative arrangement in nonfiction is not the same thing as "artistic license" in fiction. In fictionalized history, "artistic license" is the freedom (with some constraints) to create composite characters, to put real people into imagined situations and vice versa, or to mix fiction and nonfiction elements. This is not permissable with documentaries. (The use of dramatized footage and

stills to illustrate the past can arguably be seen as mixing fiction—the imagined past as visualized by the filmmaker—with nonfiction, the factual history. This is a complex subject, but for this discussion, we're following the generally accepted notion that limited recreations, if it's clear that that's what they are and they're done responsibly, fit within the purview of documentary.)

- It's also important to note that not only does "creative arrangement" (in other words, narrative design) not automatically mean sleight of hand, it also does not mean that the history being conveyed will necessarily be dumbed down. While film can never convey the detail of print, what it *can* do is make the experience of history more immediate and experiential than can most books or articles. In fact, while it might at first seem counterintuitive, by structuring a story on film in a way that's compelling to the nonexpert as well as the expert, a filmmaker can create a framework that allows for the conveyance of history that's *more*, not less, detailed.

- Treatments are not theses. With some exceptions, historical documentary filmmakers don't come up with an original take on the *history*; they come up with original, compelling, and thought-provoking ways to present current scholarship (sometimes from a single point of view, more often from a range of perspectives) to audiences.

- Chronologies matter. Take the time to do them well.

- In considering your film's approach, think not only about the subject but also the kinds of films you like to watch, including dramatic features. Even historical documentaries come in a range of styles, from mysteries to biographies to epics.

- Pay attention to what excites you about the subject and what stands out as you go through books and articles. Look at how the historians have structured their narratives—what's their point of attack, who have they chosen to follow through the history? Finally, pay attention to what you tell your friends or family as you discuss the subject and story you're exploring. These details are what's exciting you, and chances are they will be what excites your audience, too.

- Think easier, work backwards. Find the nugget of a *story* within historical headlines ("Tokyo Rose pardoned by President Ford") and then dig deeper to enrich it. Doing it the other way—going after a general topic like "advertising" or "poverty" or "World War I" and then searching for stories within these broad topics may take more time.

On the way to their treatments, students pitched ideas, identified their film's trains (one of the toughest parts of this assignment), and wrote outlines that broke the films into sequences. (As described elsewhere, a sequence is akin to a chapter. Breaking their stories into sequences—*roughly* 8–12 per hour-long film, but there's no hard-and-fast rule—seemed to help make the stories and history more manageable.) They then wrote at least one preliminary draft of the treatment for my review before moving on to the final version.

SAMPLE PAGES FROM BROADCAST FILMS AND SERIES

In the pages that follow, I've included some sample pages of outlines, treatments, and scripts for a range of programs that have already been broadcast. The samples reflect diversity in the program styles and the varied uses of the print material. The editing outline for *Lalee's Kin*, for example, was created for in-house use only. In contrast, the treatment for *Getting Over* (an hour of the six-part series *This Far By Faith*) was submitted to numerous public and private funding agencies, including the National Endowment for the Humanities.

Sample page, outline, *Ain't Gonna Shuffle No More*[i]

PROGRAM TITLE: *Ain't Gonna Shuffle No More* (1964–1972)

Synopsis: This hour looks at rising Black consciousness through the transformations of Cassius Clay, who becomes Muhammad Ali and takes a stand against the war in Vietnam; students at Howard University, who fight for a curriculum that recognizes their Black heritage; and elected officials who join Black nationalists at a National Black Political Convention in Gary, Indiana.

Program outline:

Sequence 1:   Tease: Black is Beautiful

 A montage of archival images and sync material that introduce the Black Arts and Black consciousness movements of the 1960s.

 PEOPLE: Interview with Sonia Sanchez, poet

 FOOTAGE: Archival of Amiri Baraka (at the Congress of African Peoples, 1970) and the Last Poets

Sequence 2: "I Shook Up The World"

 We begin the first act of our first story: Olympic champion Cassius Clay challenges World Heavyweight Champion Sonny Liston. Rumors are spread that Clay is spending time with Malcolm X, spokesperson for the Nation of Islam. Fight promoters want Clay to deny the rumors; he refuses, and after he defeats Liston, he publicly announces his new Muslim identity: Muhammad Ali.

 PEOPLE: Edwin Pope, sportswriter; Kareem-Abdul Jabbar, student; Angelo Dundee, trainer; Herbert Muhammad, son of Elijah Muhammad

 FOOTAGE: Archival of Muhammad Ali, Ali with Malcolm X, the Liston fight

Sequence 3: A Heavy Price

 As associates and the press react to Muhammad Ali's new identity, he embarks on a tour of Ghana, Nigeria, and Africa, where he is welcomed as a hero. Returning to the U.S., he

---

[i] Episode five of the second season of *Eyes on the Prize*. This page was written as demonstration only. The initial outline for *Ain't Gonna Shuffle No More* was for a program called *New Definitions.*

Sample page, preliminary treatment, *You Could Grow Aluminum Out There*[1]

Not fact checked/interview subjects not confirmed   4

ACT I, THE CENTRAL VALLEY PROJECT

FIRST CAUSES

In California we name things for what they destroyed.

Real estate signs whiz by the windshield....."Quail Meadows," "The Grasslands," "Indian Creek," "Riverbank Estates," "Elk Grove Townhouses," "Miwok Village."

Before the Spaniards came, 300 tribes shared the Central Valley of California...Maidu, Miwok, Patwin. A few weeks of flooding each winter fed the great marshes and seasonal lakes, but for most of the year—the seven month dry season when Indians moved to the cooler surrounding foothills—the Great Central Valley got, and still gets, less rain than North Africa. It was the American Serengeti.

Spanish maps.

Richard Rodriguez, or perhaps Maxine Hong Kingston or Jesse De La Cruz pick up the story.

The wet winters and dry summers unique to California had gone on for a hundred thousand years before Europeans came. A rich, complex ecosystem had evolved with such intelligence that the great condors, elk, delta smelt, cougars and bunch grass could survive in the natural cycles of drought and flood. Each carried genetic information for the next generation to thrive in arid land, and the next and the next. Bidwell saw 40 grizzlies in a single day, and Central Valley salmon ran in the millions. Muir, standing on a hill south of San Francisco looked 100 miles east toward the Sierra and saw "...a carpet of wildflowers, a continuous sheet of bloom bounded only by mountains."

---

[1] Program produced, directed and written by Jon Else; page 4 of 40, episode three of *Cadillac Desert*, broadcast as *The Mercy of Nature.* © 1995 Jon Else, reprinted with permission.

Sample pages, NEH treatment, *Getting Over*[j]

HOUR THREE: *Getting Over* (1910−1939)

Tell me how we got over, Lord;
Had a mighty hard time, comin' on over.
You know, my soul looks back in wonder,
How did we make it over?

Tell me how we got over, Lord;
I've been falling and rising all these years.
But you know, my soul looks back in wonder,
How did I make it over?

"How I Got Over" (gospel song)

THE PRESENT:

"Where is hope? Hope is closer than we know!" declares the Reverend Cecil Williams, pastor of the Glide Memorial United Methodist Church in San Francisco.

> I want you to know this morning that this is Bethlehem! The rejected are here. The wretched of the earth are here. Poor folks, rich folks, middle-class folks. You can be yourself here. You don't have to run from yourself here. You don't have to put yourself down here. You can embrace love here. Where is hope? Hope is here! Amen!

Glide Memorial Church in the Tenderloin district of San Francisco, an area of tenements, crack houses, and shooting galleries, lies at what Rev. Williams calls "the intersection of despair and hope." Williams took over the church in 1966, when the congregation included about 35 people, nearly all of them middle-class whites. Today, it has 6,400 members and a reputation, as *Psychology Today* reported in 1995, as "an urban refuge for the spiritually disenfranchised…a faith steeped more in heart and soul than in scripture."

Powerful and influential visitors like Oprah Winfrey and President Bill Clinton speak of Glide as a model religious institution. Poet Maya Angelou, a parishioner for nearly 30 years, calls it "a church for the 21st century." Glide is San Francisco's largest provider of social services, offering recovery centers for substance abusers, domestic-violence workshops for batterers and victims, anger management classes for youth, job skills and computer training for the unemployed or those wishing to further their education. Its tradition of outreach is a hallmark of African-American religion, especially as it developed in the decades following the Great Migration.

3 –3

On a Sunday morning, we watch as Rev. Williams evokes the past in his demands for the future:

> Faith and resistance are the fuels that power the train of freedom and transformation....
> The train of freedom and recovery chugs on daily. Claim your place on this train. The
> freedom train is passing you by. Catch it. Then listen. Listen carefully. Those on the
> train are singing. Can you hear the voices of a New Generation? They are singing and
> shouting with unchained abandon. Lift your voice, raise your fist. You sing, too.

We will return to Glide throughout this program, as its ministry informs the historical events in this hour.
For now, we cut to:

THE PAST:

A train rushes by, seen in grainy black-and-white footage reminiscent of the early years of this century. A
woman can be heard singing softly, unaccompanied, as if comforting a sleeping child on board: *Plenty of
good room, plenty of good room in my Father's kingdom.* A few cars back, we catch a glimpse of a
window, the curtain drawn. Inside, a man's hand sets words to paper:

> I am writing on board a Jim Crow car...a horrible night ride.... Why does the negro
> leave the South?... You feel a large part of that answer on this train...and share for one
> night the longing of the people to reach the line...which separates Dixie from the rest of
> creation.

Everyone Is Welcome

The third hour of THIS FAR BY FAITH begins with the onset of the greatest internal population shift to
have yet occurred in the United States. In 1910, more than 90% of African Americans live in the South.
Between the turn of the century and 1930, nearly two million will make their way north in a mass exodus.
They are "led as if by some mysterious unseen hand which was compelling them on," reports Charles S.
Johnson, an African-American sociologist in Chicago at the time. A group of nearly 150 Southerners,
crossing the Ohio River, a divide "between Dixie and the rest of creation," kneels together and prays.

3-4

---

[i] Treatment written by Sheila Curran Bernard and Lulie Haddad, episode three of THIS FAR BY FAITH, broadcast as
Guide My Feet. © 1998 Blackside, Inc., reprinted with permission.

Sample treatment, *The Milltail Pack*[j]

The Milltail Pack

At the edge of a dirt roadway which runs along a thick wooded area, three red wolves appear as dusk begins to fall. The leader of the pack is an old male in his twilight years with a thick auburn coat and a long nose. Though he's not as fast as he used to be, his gait remains quick, his eyes and ears alert. Close behind are two noticeably smaller wolves. They are siblings, a male and a female just turned three years old. The pack is heading to a corn field just at the end of the road. In the brown dry stalks of last month's corn live mice, rabbits and voles - tasty appetizers for the Milltail Pack.

At nine years old, the aging male is raising, in all probability, his last offspring. He's seen a lot of change over the years, and he's survived to tell the story of how a species on the brink of extinction came to be saved by a handful of dedicated humans and a branch of government. Known to biologists at the Alligator River National Wildlife Refuge in North Carolina as #331, this old male is living proof that predators and people can live together and flourish. The only remaining red wolf that was born in captivity and reintroduced into the wild, his life parallels the timeline of a unique government initiative.

In 1980 the red wolf was declared biologically extinct - in the wild. In answer to this, the US Fish and Wildlife Service implemented the Red Wolf Recovery Plan - an all-out effort to save the species using captive wolves. This was the first re-introductory program of its kind for any carnivore in the world! Against overwhelming odds and after countless setbacks, the program has managed success.

In 1987, a red wolf breeding pair was reintroduced into the Alligator River Wildlife Refuge, and by the next year their first litter of pups was born in the wild. Since then wolves have been introduced on three island sites, three wildlife refuges, a national park, and a number of privately-owned properties in North Carolina, Tennessee, and South Carolina. But it wasn't easy. The recovery plan had to insure genetic diversity, hope the wolves tolerant of people in a captive setting would shy away from them once wild, and enlist public support for reintroduction of a predator in their neighborhoods. And the ultimate goal of the plan, not yet realized, is to have a total population of 220 wild red wolves.

Today there are about 70 wolves living in northeastern North Carolina, and all but one were born in the wild. Number 331 and his brother, 332, were released when they were just under one year old. Running together they sought out a home range that was occupied by a resident male. They killed the wolf and began consorting with his mate, 205. Together the young males shared the area with 331 mating with 205 and 332 taking up with 205's daughter. But 332 was killed by a car leaving 331 the leader of the Milltail Pack. Like gray wolves, red wolves mate for life, but 331 lost his first mate several years ago. He then mated with his step daughter, 394, who was mother to the siblings he takes hunting today. Last year, she died leaving him without a mate and the youngsters without a mother.

The Milltail Pack ranges through farmlands, wooded areas, public roadways and along the banks of Milltail Creek in search of food. They mainly eat white-tailed deer, but their diet also consists of raccoons and small mammals like rabbits and mice. Similar to gray wolves, they tend to shy away from people and stay close to woodlands or farm edges that provide cover. In their home in North Carolina the habitat ranges from farmland to wooded areas including marshy wetlands, and even a military bombing range!

Before becoming extinct in the wild, red wolves populated the southeastern United States, but as man began clear-cutting areas for wood, drainage and farms, wolves and men came into closer contact. Fear and misunderstanding led to indiscriminate killings and bounties. In addition, as coyotes adapted stretching their habitat from western states into the southeast, they interbred with red wolves, threatening the wolves' genetic purity.

The Milltail Pack has lived through the successes and failures of the Red Wolf Recovery Plan and now stands on the threshold of a new debate. Can man use this program as a model for other species and can we learn from our mistakes? Despite the success of such re-introductory programs, there will always be opponents of predators. In 1995, gray wolves were reintroduced into Yellowstone National Park and today their fate is questionable because opponents to the reintroduction have waged a court struggle to have them removed. In North Carolina opponents to the Red Wolf Recovery Plan still threaten to shut down the program with lengthy court battles. Last year 11 Mexican wolves were released in Arizona after 16 years of planning, and today they are all dead - most were shot by angry ranchers. For conservationists and biologists these programs represent a chance for society to learn from our mistakes. Without the existence of top predators, prey animals go unchecked and often overpopulate areas. And not only is it important to save wolves because of their role as predators, but they are a leading symbol of wild nature.

Because red wolves were virtually extinct until 1987, little was known about their behavior. But biologists are learning that their social structure, feeding and breeding habits are similar to gray wolves. Ten years after reintroducing the first red wolves into the wild, their numbers are growing - evidence of their adaptability, strength and stamina. The leader of the Milltail Pack has survived to sire 4 litters and he and his offspring have a unique story to tell.

Wolves have been in the news for the past few years and are a hot topic. But little has been said about the red wolf or this recovery project. Most of the national press has focused on the gray wolves and their reintroduction to Yellowstone. While there has been regional press about the Red Wolf Recovery Plan, this film is the first documentary to offer an in-depth look at these beautiful animals and the circumstances that have brought them back into the wild.

Film Approach

This film offers an opportunity for a rare glimpse into the lives of a fascinating species, and the film's goal is to tell a success story. Using the Milltail Pack we'll chronicle the program from the early days of life in captivity, move to life today in the wild, and finally speculate about the future of the recovery program and these amazing animals. We have access to footage of wolves in captivity, footage of animals being released, and filming in the wild today. {In order for the biologists to monitor the health and movements of released wolves, most of the animals are radio collared which makes it easy for us to locate packs and differentiate between them.}

This film will take the viewer on an odyssey of survival through the eyes of an aging red wolf. Filming will include captive animals at the Alligator River National Wildlife Refuge, wolf capture and tagging, wolf release, and behavior of family groups in the wild. In addition, interviews with biologists who have been working in the program for 11 years as well as area farmers and townspeople will help illustrate how these wolves came to be accepted on both private and refuge land and how they've managed to survive. While the focus of the film is the red wolf, we'll round out the piece with a look at what's happening to the Mexican wolf and the grays in Yellowstone.

---

[i] Treatment written by Holly Stadtler, film broadcast on EXPLORER WILD as *America's Last Red Wolves*. © 2000 Dream Catcher Films, reprinted with permission.

Sample editing outline, *Lalee's Kin*[i]

AUGUST
A NEW SCHOOL YEAR BEGINS

LLW AND KIDS ON PORCH

> Intro kids
>
> Main flunked first grade

BOYS BATH – before school

LOST CLOTHES (night before school)

TELEPHONE GAME

FIRST DAY OF SCHOOL – LW brushes Redman's hair

PARKING LOT ADVICE – LLW and Redman

REGISTRATION – LLW and Redman

SAN'S HOUSE

> Supplies

DON'T NOBODY KNOW

SUNSET

> Praise Jesus

GRANNY CRIES ON PORCH

> No pencils

KIDS GET ON SCHOOL BUS/ARRIVE AT SCHOOL

REGGIE – If kids don't come to school first day we're not going to solve anything

> We have a test Oct. 1 and instruction begins now
>
> Someone has to be Level 1, but we don't want to be it

GRANNY IN SCHOOL

SADIE DILLS

COTTON FIELD

LALEE AND REGGIE RE COTTON PICKING AND PLANTATION MENTALITY

> R- Closed schools

---

[i] © 2002 Maysles Films, Inc., reprinted with permission.

Sample page, script (single column), *The Donner Party*[i]

VOICE 001: It is odd to watch with what feverish ardor Americans pursue prosperity – ever tormented by the shadowy suspicion that they may not have chosen the shortest route to get it. They cleave to the things of this world as if assured that they will never die – and yet rush to snatch any that comes within their reach, as if they expected to stop living before they had relished them. Death steps in in the end and stops them, before they have grown tired of this futile pursuit of that complete felicity which always escapes them.

Alexis de Toqueville

TITLE: THE DONNER PARTY

NARRATOR:　It began in the 1840s, spurred on by financial panic in the East, by outbreaks

of cholera and malaria, and by the ceaseless American hankering to move West.　When the pioneer

movement began, fewer than 20,000 white Americans lived west of the Mississippi River.　[Ten

years later the emigration had swelled to a flood, and] Before it was over, more

than half a million men, women and children had stepped off into the wilderness at places like

Independence, Missouri, and headed out over the long road to Oregon and California.

In places their wagon wheels carved ruts shoulder-deep in the rocky road.

The settlers themselves knew they were making history. "It will be received," one

Emigrant wrote, "as a legend on the borderland of myth." But of all the stories to come out of the

West, none has cut more deeply into the imagination of the American people than the tale

of the Donner Party high in the Sierra Nevada in the winter of 1846.

INTERVIEW HS24: Human endeavor and failure. Blunders, mistakes, ambition, greed – all of the elements. And if you call the rescue of the surviving parties a happy ending, it's a happy ending. But what about those that didn't make it. Terrible, terrible.

Harold Schindler

INTERVIEW JK1: We're curious about people who've experienced hardship, who have gone through terrible ordeals. And certainly the Donner Party, you know, 87 people went through a crisis the like of which few human beings have ever faced. And we're curious about that. It can tell us something

1

---

[i] Written by Ric Burns. © 1992 Steeplechase Films, Inc., reprinted with permission.

Sample page, script (two column), *Lift Every Voice*[1]

SERIES TITLE	*I'LL MAKE ME A WORLD: A CENTURY OF AFRICAN-AMERICAN ARTS*
NAME OF SHOW	*EPISODE 1: LIFT EVERY VOICE*

Lower third:
Melvin Van Peebles
Filmmaker

Van Peebles: People always talk about the—the down side of racism. There's an up side, too. The up side is that nobody thinks you're smart. They don't even know why they don't think you're smart. Don't woke 'em, let 'em slept. Just go ahead and do the deal you have to do. Racism offers great business opportunities if you keep your mouth shut.

clips of Bert Williams –
Nobody

(hearing a few bars of *Nobody*)
When life seems full of clouds and rain
And I am full of nothing and pain
Who soothes my thumping, bumping brain?
NOBODY.

lower third:
Lloyd Brown
Writer

LLOYD BROWN: Bert Williams combined the grace of a Charlie Chaplin, imagery and all, and at the same time with a very rich voice too. And so he—he was...wonderful comedy.

lower third:
James Hatch
Theater Historian

HATCH: He has a...(laughing) song where he's obviously explaining to his wife who the woman was that he was seen with. And the refrain chorus line is "She was a cousin of mine." He has that line, I would say, six or seven times in the song: "She was just a cousin of mine." Every time it's different. Every time it's a new interpretation. (v/o) The man was a genius.

Stills of Bert Williams

NARRATION 1: In the earliest years of the 20th century, Bert Williams was the most successful black performer on the American stage. But each night, he performed behind a mask he hated: blackface.

Lower third:

Ben Vereen
Performer

VEREEN (v/o): Bert Williams didn't want to black up. But socially during that time, he had to. And he realized that. He was a very intelligent man.... We have to hide our identity by putting on this mask, in order to get things said and done. (o/c) But we did it. We did it. And today we don't have to do it. But we cannot forget it.

---

[1] Written by Sheila Curran Bernard; episode one of *I'll Make Me A World.* © 1998 Blackside, Inc., reprinted with permission.

Part III
SHOOTING AND EDITING

12

Shooting

Shooting with the story in mind means being prepared to get all of the visuals you need to tell the story you think you want to tell, and being prepared for those surprises that are likely to make a good documentary even better. Who shoots, how, and with what, depends on a host of variables. Are you shooting on your parents' farm or in the middle of a political campaign in a foreign country? Is the event you're covering something that happens every day, or is it a once-in-a-lifetime opportunity? Are special skills or equipment needed to get the shots you need?

CREW SIZE

The actual configuration of a documentary crew can vary widely. At one end of the spectrum, a filmmaker as renowned as Spike Lee might set out with the kind of crew more likely to shoot a Hollywood feature than an independent documentary. "Normally when you shoot a doc, it's you as the producer, camera, an assistant (if you're shooting film), sound, and maybe a production assistant," says Sam Pollard, who edited and coproduced *When the Levees Broke* with Lee. "But when we flew out of Newark the day after Thanksgiving [in 2005], it was Spike, me, a line producer, three cameramen, four assistants, and six graduate students from NYU. Then, when we got to New Orleans, we got a location manager with his four location people, five vans, five drivers, a camera loader—I mean, it was like an army."

Filming the spectacular footage of birds crossing exotic skylines in *Winged Migration* took five teams of people, according to the film's press material, including 17 pilots and 14 cinematographers and the use of "planes, gliders, helicopters, and balloons." (The DVD's bonus material includes a fascinating look at how this film was made. Most significantly, birds were raised from birth by humans upon whom they imprinted, and their flight is actually in pursuit of the "parent" bird riding, with a cinematographer, in an ultralight airplane. In some cases, birds were transported between locations.)

At the other end of the spectrum are two- and even one-person crews. In general, working alone is not ideal, although there may be situations in which a project or scenes of a project can benefit. In making their film *So Much So Fast*, for example, Steve Ascher and Jeannie Jordan worked as a team, with Steve shooting. But Steve says they discovered that when Jamie Heywood (who'd been diagnosed with ALS) was alone with one or both of his brothers, "it worked out better if it was just me alone. If we were both there, Stephen's focus would get split." So Steve shot these scenes alone, eventually wearing a mic as he engaged the brothers in conversation.

Jon Else, who has served as a cinematographer on hundreds of films and directs the graduate program in documentary at the University of California, Berkeley, says that with "very few exceptions," a minimum of a two-person crew is the way to go. "Working as a one-person crew involves such incredible compromise, you only have so much brain power, you only have so much muscle power," he explains.

Are you under significant time constraints? Maysles's principal filmmaker Susan Froemke had just one day in which to film the making of the cast album for Broadway hit *The Producers*, and her work could not interfere with the album's production. The solution, as she describes in Chapter 21, was to hire a trio of very experienced vérité shooters.

SHOOTING WITH THE STORY IN MIND

You want to go into the field with a clear sense of your film's story and approach so that you can maximize the quality and impact of what you get, and so you'll be better able to recognize and take advantage of those moments you couldn't possibly have anticipated beforehand.

Some films require more visual planning than others. As mentioned, watch the "making of" documentaries on the DVDs for *Winged Migration* and *March of the Penguins*, about the challenges of making those films. Read interviews with Nathanial Kahn as he discusses *My Architect*, and how important it was to him that his footage capture the power of the buildings that his father, a world-renowned architect, had designed. Each film demands its own type of preparation.

Thinking Visually

Will your film be dependent on interviews and narration, or can scenes and sequences be played without sound and still convey story? With live-action filming, unless a member of the core team is shooting, the best way to ensure visual storytelling is to *involve* your cinematographer and not to simply use him or her as a "shooter." Being able to frame images beautifully is not the same thing as being able to frame *meaningful* images beautifully. Boyd Estus, a director of photography whose credits include the Academy Award–winning *The Flight of the Gossamer Condor*, has shot both documentary and drama for venues including the BBC, PBS, Discovery Channel, and National Geographic. When a documentary producer calls him about shooting, Estus always asks to see an outline or treatment in advance, something that gives him an idea of the big picture—not only what's being filmed, but why.

In cases where a crew is filming an event, the sound recordist, too, should be in on the story, in part because he or she is often better able to anticipate, through listening to the conversations of key players who've been miked, where the action is going next. "They often will hear things that nobody else hears," Estus says, adding that when he shoots vérité, he also wears a headset so that he can hear the radio mikes directly. This can pay off in unexpected ways. For example, Estus worked on a series called *Survivor, M.D.*, which followed seven Harvard Medical School students over a period of several years as they became doctors. He was filming a student assisting in a heart operation when the patient, an elderly man she'd grown close to, died. Estus watched as the student walked off by herself, to the back of the operating room.

"By then, I knew her well enough to know she would have trouble [with the loss]," Estus says, and because he was wearing a sound monitor, he could hear that she was crying. He stayed in the distance but continued to film as the senior surgeon approached the student and consoled her, but also reminded her that as a physician, she had to balance her own feelings with the family's need for her professional guidance. She nodded, and together the doctors went to speak with the patient's family. Since the story was about the making of a doctor, the emotion shown by the tears was important, but not as important as the lesson—another step on the road to becoming a physician. The moment feels intimate despite the fact that Estus stayed several feet away (he shot the scene hand-held until a tripod was slipped underneath the camera as it was rolling). "Normally I'm right on top of people, especially for that kind of shooting," he says. "But I didn't want to break the spell. And also, I felt the perspective was appropriate, the two of them meeting." Estus notes that, while at times like this he can be afraid to move a muscle for fear of interrupting the moment, at other times he's proactive in ensuring that he gets the coverage he wants.

What you shoot and how you shoot it involves more than simply documenting an event; it's a way of contributing to the story. "Think about what the scene is supposed to say, as much as you can, both before it and during it," says Steven Ascher, who coauthored *The Filmmaker's Handbook* (with Edward Pincus). He adds that the same applies "to the broader structure, in terms of how you go about deciding what to film, how much of it to film, and whom to film." In many cases, you may be filming a scene or sequence without knowing exactly how it will come out or how the overall story will ultimately be structured. "But you should be asking yourself, what seems important, who's compelling, how might the story be structured?" Ascher says. He notes that first-time filmmakers often have trouble projecting ahead like this. "They haven't done it enough to think about, what is a narrative spine, what is structure, how will scenes get distilled? They tend to overshoot and at the same time not shoot in a focused way that makes themes emerge."

If your crew understands what your storytelling needs are, they can help when the unexpected occurs. When Karin Hayes and Victoria Bruce left Colombia after their first shoot for *The Kidnapping of Ingrid Betancourt*, they left their second camera, a small digital recorder, in the care of their Colombian cinematographer. As they explain in Chapter 17, his own camera had been stolen during the kidnapping, and they wanted to be sure that if anything important happened, such as Betancourt's release, he would be able to film it. Unexpectedly, Betancourt's father died, and the cinematographer's brother covered not only the funeral but also the visit of Betancourt's two children, who'd been sent for safety to live with their father (Betancourt's ex-husband) in France. "That was the only time they were back in Colombia," Bruce noted. "So it was great that we'd left that camera there." The funeral sequence is one of the film's most powerful.

SHOOTING WITH THE EDITING IN MIND

It's important that footage be shot in a way that it can be edited. There needs to be sufficient coverage to give you options, and to let a scene *play*. You are not shooting news, where one shot per scene might be enough. Think of shooting your documentary the way you would shoot a dramatic feature: Within any given scene, you want wide shots, medium shots, close-ups, and cutaways, making sure that shots are long enough and steady enough to use. You want to be able to create visual scenes that give context and other story information. For example, if someone is talking or performing, you want shots of the audience, to let viewers know where the speech or performance is directed and how it's being received. You'll want exteriors of the performance space—is it a vinyl-sided church in the middle of a rural area, or the Kennedy Center in Washington? You'll want identifying markers, if they exist: the marquis, a handwritten sign introducing the speaker, a cutaway to a program. You want to see what people are looking at, the angles at which they see each other, their points of view as they look at the world. (Look at *Murderball* for an excellent example of this; the film was frequently shot from the point of view of those in wheelchairs.)

Note that you're not randomly shooting everything possible; you're making sure that you have visual information that conveys basic narrative information: what, where, how. You want to establish the time, place, and people, looking for visuals that might let you cut back on verbal information. Look for the telling details that reveal character, whether it's the cigarette burning untended or the pile of liquor bottles in the recycling bin. Look for shots that show how people behave in relationship with each other and how skillfully they handle the tools of their work. You might want to look for humor. And as mentioned, you need to be sure that you have a sufficient range of angles, shots, and cutaways that your editor can condense hours of material into a final film that tells a coherent and visually satisfying story.

Cinematographers try to "cover scenes to leave as many storytelling options as possible open," Jon Else says. "I have kind of written on the inside of my eyelids a list of basic storytelling shots that I have to have coming away from a scene, about a half dozen shots." These include the widest possible angle of a landscape or cityscape, a proscenium shot in which all the figures involved in the action are in the frame and large enough that their faces and actions can be seen, several angles on any process being filmed, and close-ups "on every single face of every person, both talking and not talking."

If there's a sign saying, "Joe's Orchard" or "The Henry Ford Motor Company," Else says, you want to get a "nice picture of the sign, preferably one picture with something happening in the foreground or background and one picture without anything happening." If there are time markers such as clocks, you want to get a shot of them. "A lot of it's cliché stuff, and 90 percent of the time you don't use it," he says, "but that one time you need to show that time has passed, the clock is invaluable." And finally, he notes that you want to be sure to shoot simple indicators of direction. "If you're next to a river," for example, "you want to make sure that you get a shot that's close enough that you can see which way the current's going."

For those who shoot in film, the cost of stock and processing seems to mandate careful shot selection. "I used to joke that there should be a dollar counter in the viewfinder instead of a footage counter," says Ascher, who shot *Troublesome Creek* (1996) on film and *So Much So Fast* (2006) on digital video. "In film you're really thinking ahead about each camera move, how can it cut with the others, what will it mean. 'I'm now doing a close shot, I'm now doing a move from character A to character B.' People who learn to shoot with video often shoot more continuously, and it's a real problem. They don't stop the camera, they're not thinking about where shots begin and end, and sometimes that results in uncuttable footage."

CREATING VISUALS

Not all film ideas are inherently visual, especially those that concern complex or technical issues. If you haven't found a visual story through which to explore these issues or if your stories alone don't sufficiently cover the subject, it's likely that you'll try to find general visuals that will at least put some images on screen as your experts and/or narrator speak. For a story on educational policy, for example, you might spend an afternoon filming at a local elementary school; for a story on aging, you might attend a physical therapy session at a local hospital. This material is often described as "wallpaper" because the visuals themselves are generic, in that they're not linked to any particular character or story.

With that said, created visuals are often necessary to a film project, and the more creative you can be with them, the better. In developing a film on the controversial diagnosis of multiple personality disorder, for example, filmmaker Holly Stadtler and her coproducer came up with a variety of visuals. To demonstrate the concept of dissociation, they filmed a child in her bedroom, on the bed, playing near the bed, standing, sitting, and then combined these images in the editing room. The result is a portrait of the child surrounded by "alternate" versions of herself engaged in a range of behaviors. Stadtler also mounted Styrofoam heads (wig forms) on turntables and had them lit dramatically. "I wanted to have some footage I could cut to that wasn't specific and wasn't someone just sitting in a park or something," she says. To further explore dissociation and compare it to the common phenomenon of "highway hypnosis"—losing track of where you've been while you're driving—they combined point-of-view shooting from within a car (including a car going through a tunnel) to a more dizzying "drive" through corrugated steel pipe, shot with a lipstick camera.

Demonstrations may also be devised to advance your story or themes. Michael Moore set up a sequence in which he opened a bank account in order to receive a free gun in *Bowling for Columbine*. For the series *The Ring of Truth*, we arranged a number of demonstrations of scientific concepts, from a technician weighing the dot of an "i" to a surveyor making a rough map of Monticello, Thomas Jefferson's homestead in Charlottesville, Virginia.

Morgan Spurlock's *Super Size Me* is built around a demonstration, a 30-day diet that only occurred for the sake of the film. Spurlock interweaves this with a range of shooting styles. He travels to several different schools and school districts to investigate approaches to diet and physical education, for example. He films a man before and during gastric bypass surgery. He interviews people on the street, asks a family in front of the White House if they can recite the pledge of allegiance, and finds a man who's fanatical about Big Macs. All of these scenes had to be planned, and each element of the film had to be weighed against the other elements. It costs money to shoot, so you don't want to waste time filming scenes or sequences that duplicate each other, whether literally or emotionally, because if they do, as discussed in the following chapter, they're likely to be cut.

Visual Storytelling in the Wild

Creating visual stories out of nature and wildlife footage can be very expensive and time-consuming, but the results, as evidenced by the blockbuster hits *March of the Penguins* and *Winged Migration*, can be spectacular. These productions took considerable time, money, and technology. But what about the relatively lower-budget natural history documentaries that are popular on television?

Filmmaker Holly Stadtler produced *America's Last Red Wolves*, a half-hour film for the series *National Geographic Explorer*. Her approach to wildlife films comes, in part, from her experience filming a documentary about the making of *The Leopard Son*, a Discovery Channel feature produced several years ago by noted naturalist Hugo Van Lawick. "*The Leopard Son* started out being called *Big Cats*," she says, "a story about lions, cheetahs, and leopards in the Serengeti." Filmed on 35 mm over a period of a year, the story evolved on location and in the editing room; the final film focuses on leopards, and the real-life drama of a young leopard coming of age. Stadtler spent several weeks on the Serengeti with the production crew and saw how Van Lawick captured natural behavior by "getting the animals used to his presence, staying with it and persevering, and not manipulating things in the environment. And so I became this purist," she says. "'This is the way to do it.'"

With the growth of cable and the decrease in the amount of money available for production, however, filmmakers must often find ways to make quality wildlife films that don't require the time needed to fully habituate animals to a film crew's presence. This can be a tricky business due to ethical issues involved in wildlife shooting. Concern has long been raised over such practices as tying carcasses down so that animals will come to feed at predictable spots, for example. Stadtler also notes that some people object to filmmakers using vehicle lights at night because it can affect the outcome of a kill. "What I try to do is find a happy medium," she says. "For instance, there's no way you can get 25 feet from wolves feeding in the wild—they're going to take the carcass and go—or that you could get that close to a den site. We had a lot of discussion about setting up remote cameras that could be tripped by sensors, which I had done on *Troubled Waters* (a one-hour film for TBS), but you get a shot or two and the animal leaves."

Red wolves were once extinct in the wild; they were bred in captivity by the U.S. Fish and Wildlife Service and then reintroduced into the wild at the Alligator River National Wildlife Refuge in North Carolina, beginning in the mid-1980s. Some wolves remain in captivity, however, and Stadtler took advantage of this to get the close shots she needed. She and the crew masked the fencing behind the wolves; the cameraman stood about 25 feet away from the wolves on the other side, poking his lens through the fence and filming as a deer carcass was put out for the animals. "That's how we got some beautiful images, close up, of wolves," Stadtler says. "The only other way we could have done that is if we had, in essence, habituated the wolves in the wild to our presence, which would have required months of being there—and even then, I'm not sure how close they would have allowed our camera people."

TONE AND STYLE

Visual storytelling goes well beyond *what* you shoot: How you shoot, how you light, and how you treat the material in postproduction are also critical. Tone (Does the light convey something harsh and cold or warm and familiar?), point of view (From whose point of view is a scene shot? Is it from a first-person point of view, or is it omniscient? Is the camera shooting up at the subject or looking down?), and context (Does the subject fill the frame, or does he or she appear small and overwhelmed by the surroundings?) are all important considerations. Knowing at least some of the answers in advance can help you plan your production needs, including lights, lenses, and filters; whether or not to use special equipment such as dollies and cranes; and how specialized (and experienced) you might need your production crew to be.

SHOOTING FROM THE HIP

It can takes months, if not years, to raise enough money to do films the "right" way. Unless you're a name filmmaker, chances are that the path between you and that kind of movie will be littered, as discussed in previous chapters, with proposals, rejections, more proposals, more rejections, and the occasional but still-too-small grant. At least that's the way it is in the United States, where a relatively quick time line for a higher-budget independent project to move from idea to broadcast can be three to five years. Some very worthy films and series have taken considerably longer, and some equally worthy projects have never made the final hurdle to production. (This isn't full-time attention; it's not unusual for projects to go in fits and starts as producers intersperse development on one or more programs with additional, paying work on other films.)

So what do independents do if the story won't wait but early funding is likely to be difficult to raise? The answer depends in part on the filmmakers. Those who have significant experience and some resources may simply develop the film outline and start shooting. Their financial investment is limited to their time and out-of-pocket expenses such as equipment rental and travel, but since they themselves are experienced personnel, the resulting film is likely to be professional in quality. Those without significant shooting experience may choose to teach themselves quickly or do what they can and hire professionals to help. Two examples of this kind of filmmaking can be found in this book. In Chapter 17, Victoria Bruce and Karin Hayes talk about starting *The Kidnapping of Ingrid Betancourt* on short notice and with limited funding. The resulting film, completed in less than a year, won the Audience Award at Slamdance for Best Documentary Feature and was purchased and aired by HBO Cinemax. In Chapter 24, Per Saari talks about recruiting friends to help him explore the life and death of his 30-year-old brother Hans, an extreme skier. The finished 45-minute film, which has played in a number of festivals, takes audiences on a memorable journey across landscapes and time. Both of these films demonstrate that a powerful story, told well, can overcome some cinematic rough edges. (The converse is not true: A weak story shot spectacularly well is still weak story.)

Some films, as described, demand very high production values. *My Architect* required a very particular caliber of photography to bring architect Louis Kahn's buildings to life. *Grizzly Man* succeeds not only because Timothy Treadwell was such a fascinating person, but also because the footage he shot is of such high quality. *March of the Penguins* is visually stunning, and while a compelling story could be told about the incredible life cycle of emperor penguins, it wouldn't, in my view, have been an international hit were it not for the extraordinary images captured by Laurent Chalet and Jerôme Maison. But as mentioned, not all films need or even want such polish—sometimes a grittier feel gives a film a certain intimacy.

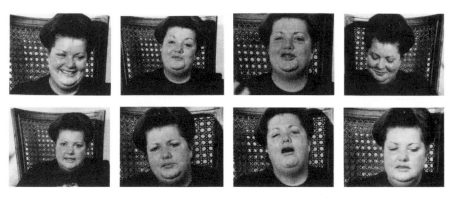

Betty, from *Betty Tells Her Story*. Photos courtesy of Liane Brandon.

INTERVIEWS

Before shooting, look at films that contain interviews and decide what you like or don't like about an approach and what you want to do in your own film. Do you plan to appear on camera along with your interviewees, as Judith Helfand did in *Blue Vinyl*? Do you want your interviewees to appear to be addressing the audience directly? Do you want to take a less formal approach to interviewing, asking your subjects questions as they go about their lives or filming them as they discuss specific subjects with each other?

Your answers to these questions will affect how you conduct and shoot your interviews. If you're not going to appear on camera, and your questions won't be heard as voice-over, you'll need to frame the question in a way that elicits a full answer, not just, "Yes. Sure. Oh, yes, I agree with that." You might want to ask the person being interviewed to incorporate part of your question in his or her answer, as in, "When did you know there was trouble?" Answer: "I knew there was trouble when..." In any case, you'll need to listen carefully as the interview is under way to make sure that you're getting something that will work as the beginning of a sentence, thought, or paragraph. If necessary, ask the question again, maybe in a different way.

Go into the interview knowing the handful of specific story points the interview needs to cover, and then include other material that would be nice to have or questions that are essentially fishing—you're not sure what you're going to get, but the answers could be interesting. Note that if you've cast the person you're interviewing in advance, you probably already know what ground the interviewee can best cover. It's rarely productive to ask everyone in a film the same 20 questions.

Conducting Interviews

Everyone approaches interviewing differently. Some people work to put the subjects at ease, starting with more "comfortable" questions before easing into material that's more touchy. As mentioned, filmmakers whose style is more confrontational may show up with the cameras rolling. Sometimes you're asking someone to relate an event he or she has told many times, and the story's taken on a polished quality that you want it to lose; it may take getting the person riled up, or challenging something about the story, to accomplish that.

Another strategy for interviewing, notes Boyd Estus, "is for the person asking the questions not to look at the interviewee as a source of information but to get them involved in a conversation, which often involves playing devil's advocate. 'I really don't understand why this is better than that. Can you explain that to me?' So the person's engaged, as opposed to spouting a pat answer."

The Interview Setup

Only rarely is an interviewee asked to speak directly into the camera, in part because few "regular" people can do it comfortably. (Filmmaker Errol Morris achieves this effect through an elaborate setup he devised, called an *Interrotron*™, in which the interviewee speaks to an image of Morris on a screen placed over the camera lens.) Most filmmakers, instead, sit opposite the person (or people) being interviewed and just slightly to the left or right of the camera lens. The person looks at the interviewer, and so appears to be looking just slightly off camera. Although some cinematographers work further away, Boyd Estus likes to position the camera fairly close to the interview subject, within five feet or so. "It does two things," Estus says. "If the person moves, they change size in the frame, which makes it more three-dimensional, whereas if you're on a long lens they're plastered against the background." More importantly, he says, this puts the interviewer in comfortable range of the questioner.

This kind of intimacy may also be enhanced by conducting the interview over a table. If both parties lean forward, they're very close, and their hand gestures will be in the frame. Estus notes that wooden chairs with arms (often found in academic institutions) can be especially good, because the arms tend to be higher than normal. "The gesture's in front of your face, and if you're leaning forward you look more energetic." You don't want the chair's frame or headrest to show behind the person, and as a rule, try to avoid chairs that swivel or rock.

Another decision to make is whether the interviewee should be looking slightly to the left or to the right. If, for example, you know that you want two people to be "answering" each other on film, you might want them to be facing different directions. This isn't always possible to do, but if it's a style you like, you'll need to plan for it in advance. You and your crew also need to think about the other visual content in the frame. "Part of the job is to sell the person so that the audience really wants to hear what they say," says Estus. "My approach is to try to make an environmental portrait, so that the setting the person is in and the way they look tells you something about them and the subject matter. In wide screen (16:9) television that's much more important because no matter how tight you are on the head, there's half the screen hanging there empty, and a wall of books doesn't tell you anything."

Additional decisions, stemming from the style of film and approach to storytelling, include how you light the interviews and whether you strive for some kind of consistency in look throughout the film (or series). How do you want the interviewee to come across? There are ways to light that will flatter someone's face and minimize the distractions that could leave viewers focusing on the appearance of an interviewee, rather than his or her words. What are your subjects wearing? For more formal interview setups, some producers ask subjects to bring a few clothing options. (For some films, a stylistic decision might be made to ask interviewees to dress one way or another; Estus did a series with gothic themes in which the interviewees were asked to wear black.)

The visual context of an interview and the visual cues contained within it can be very important to the storytelling. How tightly do you frame the interview? Some cinematographers will stay wider for expositional information and move in closer as the interview gets more intimate and/or emotional. What do the interview setting and subject's clothing convey? In *The Thin Blue Line*, Randall Adams and David Harris are interviewed in a setting that suggests confinement, and in fact both turn out to be in prison. Law enforcement people are all filmed indoors, in suits and ties. David Harris's friends are filmed outdoors, in casual clothing. Because Morris uses no lower thirds (on screen titles) to identify speakers by name, these visual cues serve as a form of identification.

If you've filmed someone involved in his or her work or at home, you probably have footage that advances our understanding of the character (we can see that she is confident as she works very complex machinery, or that he is devoted to his children) even as we hear who the person is. But it's still common to see typical and uninformative introductory shots of the interviewee—"Walking into the Building" or "Entering the Office" or "Working at the Computer." Even some films that are otherwise excellent resort to these shots. In hindsight, there are almost always better alternatives.

Interview Styles

Interviews need to have an energy and immediacy about them, as well as a credibility. They also need to serve the story being told. Watch a range of interviews and you'll see that they can be very different. Is the interviewee talking about a subject from a distance, or is he or she speaking as if the event is ongoing? It's not only experts who talk about subjects; people often shape stories after the fact, especially if they've told them before, and it creates a kind of distance between the storyteller and the story, which is sometimes desired, but not always.

Filmmaker Liane Brandon discovered this when she made *Betty Tells Her Story* (1972). Brandon met Betty when both were consulting for the Massachusetts Department of Education. During a coffee break, Betty had told her a story about buying a dress and then losing it before she had a chance to wear it. The story stuck with Brandon; the women's movement was in its infancy, "and we were just beginning to think about women and clothing and culture in addition to the larger equal rights issues," she says. At first, Brandon thought of turning the story into a short drama, but soon realized that what intrigued her was as much the storyteller as the story.

On a teacher's salary, Brandon could only afford three 10-minute magazines of black-and-white film. "I borrowed Ricky Leacock's camera, and John Terry, who worked with Ricky at M.I.T., volunteered to do sound," she says. At Betty's house, Brandon set up the camera and lights and then asked Betty to simply tell her story. "The first version that you see in the film is the first take that we did. I never told her how long a magazine was, but somehow she ended the story just before we ran out of film." It was basically the story as Betty had first told it to Brandon; a witty anecdote about a dress she'd found that was just perfect—and then she never got to wear it.

To be sure she had what she needed, Brandon asked Betty to tell the story again, which she did. It was essentially the same as the first take, "but in the middle of it a truck stopped in front of her house," Brandon says, "and the horn went off, and it wiped out a couple of minutes of audio. I was really upset, but I knew I had one more magazine left."

They all took a break. Brandon worried that she was imposing on Betty, who'd never been on camera before, "but was being a really good sport." Out of curiosity, the filmmaker asked Betty how she felt when the events were taking place. "Betty's eyes opened wide and she said something like, 'I don't think I ever thought about what I was feeling; I mostly think about how I remember the story.' You know how people change and shape stories to make them good stories? Especially good storytellers."

With the cameras rolling again, Brandon asked Betty to try telling the story as she felt about it while it was happening, rather than as she remembered it. "Everything changed: body language, eye contact," Brandon says. "The minute she started telling this story, I got chills up and down my back. I was very surprised by the feelings that she talked about; I don't think she'd ever told or even thought about the story that way." Told from within rather than without, the story is no longer a humorous anecdote; it's the painful memory of a plain, overweight woman who found a dress that made her feel beautiful, then lost it before she ever had a chance to wear it.

This was before people routinely exposed themselves on national television, Brandon notes. As a filmmaker, she didn't know what to do with two very different versions, filmed in three takes. "I thought one of those takes would have to be the story, because I'd never heard of a film where you show more than one take," she says. She showed the first version to some college students, who thought it was "cute." She showed the third version to another group, who said, essentially, "Bummer. Get a life, lady."

Neither story worked alone. "I tried split-screening them, I tried intercutting them, I tried everything and nothing worked, and so I just let them sit. For a film that has almost no cuts, it took longer to edit than lots of films that have lots of cuts," she says. She finally got rid of the middle version and ran the first and third consecutively, with some black leader in between that reads, *Later that day, the filmmaker asked Betty to tell her story again.* The contrast between the two takes is what gives the film its power, revealing information about the stories we tell ourselves, the selves we present to the world, and the different ways there are to tell a story. For filmmakers (and others), it's a fascinating look at the way in which a shift in interview style can lead to a very different response.

13

Editing

Many of the storytelling issues covered elsewhere in the book come into play again in the editing room. On the majority of films, story and structure do not truly come together until the editor begins to assemble and pare down filmed material. Several versions of the film may be cut before the best point of attack is identified; you may be cutting toward one ending for weeks before you realize that, in fact, the film ends on an even earlier and stronger note.

Although every project is different, the basic editing process is that you screen everything and make a long assembly of your footage, which is then honed into a rough cut, a fine cut, a picture lock, and finally, a script lock. The assembly includes the material you've shot to date as well as archival material, if any. (Often, you're working not with original archival footage but with "slop" dubs, such as preview reels or stills you might have shot quickly in the editing room. Later, when you know what images will stay in the film, you negotiate for rights to use this material, order broadcast-quality duplications, or arrange for broadcast-quality filming of still material and artifacts.)

As the editing progresses, you work toward a rough cut. This is a draft of your film that is significantly longer than the final show will be. But your general story and structure are in place, and you have some, if not all, of your elements on hand. The rough cut stage is often the best time to reassess major issues of story and structure and experiment with alternatives; this becomes more difficult as the film is fine tuned. By *fine cut*, the film is almost to time. (For example, a film that will end up being 57 minutes long might be 63 minutes at the fine cut stage.) Major problems, hopefully, have been worked out. If there is narration, this is the time to begin polishing it. And for the movie as a whole, this is the time to make sure the facts are accurate. *Picture lock* means that all of the images are in place and to time. *Script lock* means that any outstanding issues of narration or voice-over are resolved and that the material can be recorded and laid in without further changes.

Jeanne Jordan and family in 1960, from *Troublesome Creek: A Midwestern.* Photo courtesy of the filmmakers.

GETTING TO ROUGH CUT

The interaction between producer, director, writer, and editor (or some combination of these) differs with each project. Some teams watch the rushes (the raw footage) all together and discuss which interview bites work, which scenes are strong, and how material might be assembled. Some editors screen the footage alone because they want to evaluate the material without being influenced by the producer's ideas of what worked or didn't work on location. "I really like to just look," says Jeanne Jordan, an accomplished editor. "I don't want people to even tell me 'This was a difficult interview' or 'I didn't get what I wanted.' "

As you screen the footage, you're watching for moments that affect you in some way, whether emotionally or intellectually. Look for scenes and sequences that can play on their own, interview bites that seem strong and clear, material that has the potential to reveal themes and issues you want to raise, and the special moments that you hope audiences will discuss with each other at work the next day. "I'm looking for emotion, that's always my first thing," says Sam Pollard, who works frequently as an editor. "Then I'm looking for some tension and opposition, because that's going to always make those sequences work the best. And if I feel none of those elements are in there, then I figure I've got to convey another type of feeling. Maybe this is a moment where you just sit back and listen to some music; maybe it's a moment to be somewhat reflective. You've got to know what the material says." Each person will come away from a first screening with his or her own favorite moments; this memory of what was strong in the raw footage will be useful as you shape and trim the material into a coherent story, all the while working to retain the energy it held in its raw state.

Some editors work off a written outline of scenes and sequences, especially if the film consists primarily of live action, such as cinéma vérité. If there is a significant amount of interview material, however, whether or not there is to be narration, the producer may take transcripts of the interviews and cut and paste selected bites into a "paper edit." If the project was shot to a script or a script-in-progress, that working script will be adjusted to reflect the actual material on hand. In either case, rough narration can be written to seam together disparate elements, make a transition clear, or hold a place for a sequence that's still to be shot. In many editing rooms, "scratch" narration is recorded and cut in against the picture, to better evaluate its effectiveness.

As previously discussed, what works on paper won't necessarily work on film. The juxtaposition of two interview bites and two filmed sequences might read very well, but there may be something about the way a phrase is spoken or the scene plays out that makes it less than powerful on screen. This doesn't mean that you shouldn't do paper cuts; they can be a faster and easier way to "see" an edit before realizing the changes physically. But since a good portion of the paper editing won't work on film, it's also useful to know why you're suggesting a particular change, in addition to what it will be. Perhaps you pulled a bite because it conveyed two specific points; if your choice doesn't work, the editor might be able to satisfy those points in a different way, either through a different bite, a combination of bites, or perhaps through a scene that he or she has just edited that makes the interview bite unnecessary.

The editor, meanwhile, may be assembling scenes, whether from live action or archival footage, shaping them individually, and putting together the strongest beginning, middle, and end possible before sequencing them into the overall film. The editing process tends to be very collaborative. A producer or director coming into the editing room to watch a cut in progress can often see links and transitions that the editor may not have seen, or he or she may see something in what the editor has assembled that will spark a realization that additional material—a piece of artwork, a fragment of music, a different interview excerpt—is needed. It's a give-and-take process, with everyone in the editing room putting themselves in the role of viewers as well as storytellers. Ultimately, there has to be a single person who makes decisions, usually either the producer or the director. But the give and take, especially when the discussion is not only about a specific scene or shot but also what it adds to the overall storytelling, can be very productive.

Transcripts

If you've conducted interviews, you should get them transcribed, accurately and thoroughly. Not a summary ("Dr. Fisher talking about gravitational forces . . . "), but an exact transcription of what is said, including the "um, um, he said, he said, um, well, let me back up by saying that what gravity is not, is . . ." This will save you a lot of time later, because you're likely to go back to these transcripts repeatedly during the editing process in search of story solutions, and an inaccurate or incomplete transcript can mean that you assemble a scene based on what you think someone said, only to find out that it's close but not what you need, or that it's great but the answer took forever. Some filmmakers will also transcribe scenes that have a lot of dialogue, such as a meeting, press conference, or conversation.

In the case of foreign language interviews, filmmakers in the field often rely on quick translations to get a sense of what's being spoken. In the editing room, particularly if no one on the team is fluent in the interview language, it's good to get an accurate and detailed translation as soon as you can, but no later than rough cut. You don't want to fine-tune a film to interview material that doesn't say what you think it says.

When viewing the interviews, make notes on the transcripts to help you remember what someone's energy level is like, if there are problems such as flies or a microphone in the frame, or whether someone sneezes. Some portions of the interview may be usable but only as voice-over; others may be useful as information only. Better to write it down once than to go back to the same bite three times in the course of the editing session because you forgot that there was a reason you didn't use it in the first place. (You're also writing down time code that corresponds to the transcript, so you can find material quickly.)

Another reason to transcribe interviews is that it's unfortunately very easy to cut someone's words up, assemble them with other interviews, and eventually lose track of what the original answer was. I always try to make a point of rereading the transcripts as the editing nears completion (or if I'm hired to help on a project late in the editing stage), for three reasons: to make sure the interviewee is not being misrepresented; to make sure that some terrific material wasn't overlooked earlier when the story was somewhat different; and to look for color and details that might be helpful to narration, if there is narration.

Editing Interviews

Chapter 6 discussed the issue of cutting interview material down for time. When these cuts are made, the editor often covers them with cutaways. For example, an interview with a scientist about cloning might use cutaways of the scientist at work, or archival footage of Dolly, the cloned sheep, or cutaways to graphics illustrating the scientist's point. It has also become somewhat more accepted to simply cut the footage and allow the viewer to see the image jump—one minute the speaker is looking to the left, the next he is looking down, but still talking; this is known as a *jump cut*. Sometimes an editor will soften this cut with a slight dissolve, or a fade in and out of black, but the cut is still apparent.

Another style of jump cutting is to include a few quick images that inform the interview but do not imply a seamless whole. In interviews with former Alabama governor George Wallace for the documentary *4 Little Girls*, editor and coproducer Sam Pollard made a series of evocative jump cuts to shots of Wallace with a cigar: lighting it, inhaling, blowing out smoke, looking away. Pollard says he was inspired by Oliver Stone's use of jump cuts in *JFK*. "Stone conveyed so much information through the way he cut it that I wanted to try to emulate that," he says.

Juxtaposition

The juxtaposition of two shots, or two sequences, adds meaning that is not necessarily contained in either of the elements alone. This works to your advantage, but it's also something to guard against if the juxtaposition creates a false impression. If you cut from someone saying, "Well, who was responsible for it?" to a shot of Mr. Smith, you are creating the impression that Mr. Smith was responsible, whether you meant to or not.

Entering Late, Exiting Early

As you edit, try to enter a scene at the last possible moment and leave at the earliest possible moment. This doesn't mean chopping the heart out of a scene or losing its context, but it does mean figuring out what is the most meaningful part of that scene, and what is just treading water on screen. Suppose you've filmed a sequence in which a mother goes to the grocery store, chats with a neighbor or two, fusses with the butcher over a choice cut of meat, waits in line at the checkout counter, drives home, prepares a meal, calls her college-age daughter to the table, and then watches with dismay as her daughter storms off, angry that her mother has not respected the fact that she is a vegetarian—a fact that the mother says she didn't know.

Where you enter and exit this scene depends on what the scene is about. Is it about the mother going to tremendous lengths to make her daughter feel welcome at home, perhaps because of a recent divorce or the daughter's expulsion from school? Or is it about a chasm between mother and daughter and their inability to communicate even basic information? If it's the former, the scenes in the grocery store help to establish the mother's efforts to please; if the latter, the grocery store scenes aren't really relevant. You could convey their lack of communication with the following shots: the mother puts the steak on the table; the daughter refuses to eat it and storms away; the mother is left looking at the steak.

Where do you end the scene? Again, it depends on where your story is going. If the story is about the fuss the woman made to please her daughter, you might end it with the reversal: the daughter rejects the food and storms away from the table. But if it's about the communication between mother and daughter, you might want to go a bit further and see what happens next. Will the mother try to find some other way to reach the daughter, perhaps by cooking a vegetarian meal?

Again, you don't want to cut scenes to their tightest in terms of the action; you want to focus them so that their meaning and their emphasis in your film's narrative are clear.

Anticipate Confusion

In general, audiences are willing to do quite a bit of work to figure out what the story is and where you're going with it—that's part of what makes viewing a good documentary an active rather than passive experience—but eventually, if they become too lost, they'll give up. A good storyteller anticipates the audience's confusion and meets it in subtle and creative ways, skillfully weaving information in where and when it's needed and not before. It may take some effort to bring a general audience up to speed on what those gadgets actually do or how certain laws of physics work. But armed with that information and an understanding of how it furthers or frustrates the efforts of the protagonist to reach a goal, solve a mystery, unlock a secret, or prove a theorem, the audience can be one step ahead of the story. Those moments when the audience "gets it" just before you, as the storyteller, give it to them, are enormously satisfying.

Just as you want to present information at the moment it's most needed, you also want to be careful not to clutter a story with too much detail. Many film stories get diluted by details that the filmmakers are convinced are "important," although they are not directly relevant to the story at hand. If you're telling the story about a candidate's political campaign, for example, you might not want to spend a lot of time looking at his business career. If there's something about his career that he's promoting on the campaign trail—he wants to bring his cost-cutting strategies to the job of managing a state budget, for example—then it might be relevant. Otherwise, it's taking up space that you need for your story.

Be careful, though, that you don't "cherry pick" your information, selectively using only those details that support your argument or "take" on a story and ignoring those that contradict you. It's possible to be factually accurate and still create an overall story that is fundamentally dishonest. Choosing some details from a person's life as a means of focusing a story is not the same thing as selectively leaving out information you don't want the audience to know. Ultimately you'll be found out, and it weakens your film and credibility.

ROUGH CUT TO FINE CUT

As the film moves toward completion, footage is dropped and hard decisions must be made. Is the story working as filmed, or is new material needed? Does the story that was set up at the film's beginning pay off at the end? Is it being told for maximum audience involvement? Is this the kind of film that people will talk about? Will it keep an audience watching? If the filmmaker hopes to convey important but difficult concepts, are those concepts being communicated accurately and well? To get the film to a broadcast length, would it be better to delete an entire scene or subplot, or should time be shaved off a number of scenes?

One way to begin answering these questions is by showing the film to an impartial audience. Often this is done at rough cut and, schedules and budgets permitting, again at fine cut. You want to invite people who don't know the story and aren't necessarily interested in it, as well as people who know the story better than you do. If, in previewing your film, you discover that the message you think you're sending is not the message being received, there's a problem. As simple as this seems, it's not uncommon for filmmakers to simply decide there must be something wrong with the audience. "I've said it clearly; I don't know why they're not getting it." Or they fear that if they "pander" to an audience, they will be toning down their "message." It doesn't work that way. If one person doesn't get your film, maybe it's just not that person's cup of tea. If two people don't get it, fine. But if a significant portion of an audience has missed your point, your point isn't being made.

Screening Tips

You want to invite a manageable number of filmmaker colleagues, scholars, and a general audience of "others" to these screenings. If you have a very small screening room, it may be necessary to show the film more than once to get an adequate cross-section of reactions. Before the screening starts, make sure everyone has paper and pencils for note taking. You or an appointed moderator should explain what stage your film is at, mentioning, for example, that it's running several minutes long, that narration is provisional, and the footage has numbers and other information printed on it that will be gone by the time it reaches broadcast or plays at an upcoming festival. In other words, it's a work-in-progress, and their input and help are extremely valuable to you. Make it clear that you will be asking for their reactions, both positive and negative. Ask them to please stay in the room for a few minutes immediately after the film ends. Then dim the lights, but not so low that people can't see to scribble occasionally in the dark. As the film plays, notice the audience's reactions. When do they seem intent on the story? When is there a lot of shuffling and coughing? Is there laughter? Are there tears?

After the film ends, ask people to jot down their first impressions, anonymously if they'd prefer. Then start the discussion, with you or the moderator asking for broad impressions—what worked, what didn't, what was surprising or confusing or fascinating. After a while, move on to specific questions agreed on by the production team, such as, "Were you confused by the transition to France?" "If you had to cut eight minutes out of this film, what would you cut?" "Did you understand that Dan was more concerned about Marcie's health than about his job?" Concrete responses can be very helpful.

Two important points. First, during a feedback session, the members of the filmmaking team should be quiet. Don't answer questions, offer explanations, or defend any aspect of the film-making. You are there to receive information, period. It will waste the opportunity afforded by this valuable audience if you take 15 minutes to explain why it was important to keep the sequence with the demolition derby in, or to explain the backstory that left this audience mystified. Even if it kills you to sit there and listen to people debate subjects that you know the answer to, restrain yourself. You're not there to educate this audience on the topic or show them that you do know more than was up on the screen; you're there to get a good sense of what actually was on screen and where it needs work.

Second, take any and all suggestions, say thanks, and keep going. You know, and your entire production team knows, that you can't possibly afford to shoot another four interviews, as the guy in the corner suggests, or that cutting out the trial sequence would make your entire film irrelevant. After this audience goes home, however, consider why these suggestions were made. Non-filmmakers don't always know how to articulate a problem, and they can't be expected to know how to fix it. You can and do. If your audience thinks that you're missing significant interviews, is there information that those interviews would add that you could convey in some other way? If you believe the trial sequence is critical and they think it's disposable, what's wrong with it? Is it edited badly? Is it in the wrong place? Is the narration not effectively setting it up so the audience can see its relevance?

You don't have to take anything that anyone says as marching orders. But you do need to pay attention to which elements of your film are working and which will send your audience racing for the remote or the door.

With that said, it's your film. Know when to trust your gut. Understand that there will be a degree of criticism that is not about your filmmaking but about your ideology. Someone doesn't understand why you would even give the skinheads a chance to speak. Someone else thinks it's invasive to stay focused on the woman sobbing because her son has blown his mind on inhalants. This is useful information to have, because it anticipates some of the criticism the final film might receive. But if the issue is not one of fact, or clarity, but of style, the choice is yours to make. Hear that people don't like it, but decide for yourself what makes you and your team comfortable.

The same is true of scholarship. Tell an accurate story, but don't feel compelled to tell everything. It's sometimes difficult for scholars who care deeply about their subjects to see that the entire section on primate behavior is only six minutes long or that you decided not to include a certain letter that Albert Einstein wrote. Accept the criticism and really consider whether or not it would enrich the story you have chosen to tell on film. If not, file this information away for use later in the companion book or website, if you're creating these, or for the teachers' guides and other educational and community engagement components of the project. Your film is successful if it appeals to a wide audience with a strong story and motivates part of that audience to go to the library or the web for more information.

FINE CUT TO PICTURE LOCK

The process as you get down to the wire is more of the same, looking backward as well as forward. It's often very helpful at this stage to go back and reread initial outlines and treatments to see if you've lost a story thread along the way that might prove useful. You might also reread transcripts to see if the changes that you've made to the structure are better served by interview bites you didn't pull because you were looking at a very different film back then. It's even useful to look back into research files, to make sure there aren't details and other tidbits that might speak volumes. And, of course, you are by now immersed in the task of making sure that everything that will end up on screen has been fact checked, not once but twice.

Fact Checking

Fact checking means going through your script line by line, finding the information that needs to be verified through at least two credible sources. If you can't confirm a fact—and it happens—find a way to write around it. Maybe you don't need to say that 25,000 bikers rode into town. If your sources all agree that it was "over 20,000," then say that instead.

What needs to be checked? Pretty much everything:

- "Brilliant and fearless, Admiral Marks now seized command of the troops." *Brilliant* and *fearless* both need corroboration, as does *seized command*. You don't want to find out after broadcast that Marks was widely considered a coward, or that command was thrust upon him when the admiral before him came down with food poisoning.
- "The congresswoman was exhausted and frustrated, convinced now that the bill she'd authored would not be

passed." *Exhausted* and *frustrated* need to be confirmed, and you should have solid evidence that at this point, she truly was convinced of the bill's failure, and that she had *authored* it and not simply supported it. (Confirming an emotional state depends on reliable reports from reliable eyewitnesses, recorded as close to the event as possible.)

You need to fact check interview and sync material as well as narration. For example, an auto manufacturer says, "Forty percent of the tires we got in had the problem. They all had to go back." He's the expert, but you find out that in fact, 25 percent of the tires were sent back because of the problem. You can't hide behind the argument that "He said it, I didn't." As the filmmaker, you are incorporating the statement into your film and, therefore, it will be *your* statement as well. In this case, the line has to go. Of course, if the falsehood is deliberate, and that's part of your story, or if it's clearly a lie and therefore reveals character, you don't need to cut it. But when it is presented as significant evidence to support the argument you're making, then it must be accurate. However, there is also some room to maneuver. For example, if you've confirmed that 38 percent of registered voters in Millville voted for a rise in property tax, and the mayor says, "I don't know, about a third of the voters wanted it," that's probably close enough to use.

FILM LENGTH

If you're creating a film for which you have a specific venue in mind, length is something you want to plan for from the beginning. A theatrically-released film will tend to run around 80 to 90 minutes or longer. A film for broadcast has to meet the length requirements of the programmer, leaving time as needed for series credits, packaging, and, in some cases, commercial breaks. The subject and story, too, will suggest appropriate length. When I'm helping people to develop ideas, one of the questions we ask ourselves is, "How much time would it take to tell this well?" If a subject seems to demand three hours, do we reasonably think we could raise money to produce it (and convince programmers to give us a three-hour television slot), or do we want to narrow the focus and try to create an hour-long film that might appeal to the commissioning editors of an existing series?

It's usually better to resist the temptation to leave your film long. Filmmaking is about making choices, and among the most important choices you face is what to include and what to leave out. The final length of Per Saari's film, *Why He Skied*, an independent project created without a specific venue in mind, was determined "just by the cut," he says. "It felt like it was done; it always hovered around 45, 47 minutes." If your story feels complete in 45 minutes, padding it with extra footage won't make it a longer story, it makes it a 45-minute story that took an hour to tell.

PROBLEM SOLVING

Every film has its own problems, but the following ones seem fairly common:

No Story

You have scenes and sequences that are interesting but aren't adding up to a coherent whole. One reason for this may be that there really wasn't a clear story to begin with. What you can do at this point is take a step back and return to the earlier stages of the process. Knowing what you know now, try to write up an outline that identifies what the story is, what the train is, *whose* story it is, what the key moments are that you're driving toward, how the story is resolved, and the key points you hope the audience will take away from the film. Then look at your material with this information in mind and see if you have what you need. You may need pick-up material to fill in the gaps, but you also may be surprised to find that you *are* heading in the right direction, and just need to do a bit of housekeeping.

For example, you may have to drop favorite scenes because they don't serve the story that you now realize you're telling. If a shot or a scene or even a sequence is a distraction rather than an addition, it's got to go, no matter how expensive it was to shoot or how difficult it was to get. You can spend some time trying to fiddle with it, see if you can possibly make it work, but, ultimately, if the material is beside the point, it goes. The same standard should be applied to interview material. If you didn't plan ahead but instead simply shot a few available experts, it's very possible that there will be redundancy and somebody's interview will be dropped. (If you end up cutting people out of a show, do them the courtesy of letting them know before the program is aired.)

You Start One Story and End Another

A related problem is that the film starts one story and then drifts onto a different track. As discussed in earlier chapters, outlining the film story can help, along with an openness to changing your initial concept of the film, given the natural direction it has ended up taking. Otherwise, you need to accept that the film you now wish you'd shot just isn't covered in the footage and either go back out to get what you need for the story you want to tell or make a different story out of what you have.

Be careful, however, when bending material to tell a story other than the one for which it was originally shot. Be especially careful in situations in which the editing team is separate from the production team, and the link between subject and original storyteller has been lost. It's possible to tell a great story that fundamentally misrepresents the material that was filmed. It's also possible to tell a different but still highly accurate story, especially if you take the time to explore your material with the new story in mind and can conduct additional interviews or shoot pick-up footage as necessary. It's a lot of work. Getting usable and accurate material out of footage that was shot for a different reason is time-consuming and often frustrating, and in some cases, dishonest. Footage of Sally's graduation party should not be substituted for the engagement party you didn't film. Find a way to use the party footage to make a more generic point, if need be.

Too Many Characters or Story Threads

You didn't want to give up the incredible research you did or the wonderful people you found, so now you find yourself telling the stories of eight people, all with different goals but perhaps a common thread—maybe they're all recent college graduates look-ing for work in the United States. But your film is only an hour long and everybody is getting short shrift, or audiences can't keep track of which person was having trouble with his neighbors and who was being investigated by the Immigration and Naturaliza-tion Service and which one was going to move her business to

Seattle. You may need to make choices as to which people best embody the themes you are trying to convey or the policy issues or areas of discrimination you want the audience to know about.

You can also get distracted by too many details within an overall story. No matter what style film you're making, you need to keep track of the one primary story you're telling, folding in additional threads (or subplots, backstory, etc.) as they serve that one story.

Too Many Beginnings or Endings

The film opens with a look at the farming industry and the cultivation of wheat. The narration offers some information as to what's being presented, and the audience thinks, "Oh, it's a documentary about farming." Then it seems to start again with a look at the processing of wheat into bread. "Oh, it's a film about food as big business." But then it starts again, and gradually it becomes clear that your film is really a look at the health issue of wheat intolerance or sensitivity. An unfocused opening is a fairly common problem, so it's good to watch out for it, asking yourself as the story unfolds, "What do I think this story is about at this point?" The primary story you're going to tell should start soon after your film begins, and it should be possible, from the way that story is launched, to anticipate—not to know, but to anticipate and be curious about—how it will end. In this case, the remaining details of wheat farming and the baking industry can be folded into that overall story.

Where you end your film is also very important. Appearing to end it, and then ending it again, and then ending it again can dilute a film's overall power; furthermore, there's generally just one ending that will truly bring a satisfactory resolution to the story you set out to tell. Resolution does not mean things are resolved; it means that you've reached a conclusion that satisfies the questions and issues initially raised in your film's opening moments.

Not Enough Breathing Room

In the rush to cut a film down to time, to get everything tight, and to make every point, it's possible to trim interviews or scenes into oblivion. The production team doesn't necessarily notice; they've been looking at this guy day after day and week after week, so they know what he's going to say, they've heard it before, and the joke is no longer funny. Or they realize that they can say in two lines of narration what that scene takes nearly two minutes to convey. It's important to resist this—you need the energy that real people bring to a film and the enthusiasm they bring to their storytelling. While radio and television news reports may cut interviews or scenes into fragments, you generally want to let material play for a reasonable period of time.

It's often better to offer a little less information or a smaller number of scenes than to include everything and give all of it short shrift. Filmmaker Jon Else discusses this in terms of "the parable of the peach pits," which the producers came up with on the first season of *Eyes on the Prize.* "There are various versions of it, but it boils down to the idea that there's a wise king who has no heirs, and he says that he'll give his kingdom to whoever among his subjects can fit the most satisfying collection of peaches into a box that is a given size, say, 57 minutes on a side," Else says.

"It's a long shaggy dog story, but people start trying to put peaches in the box. They kind of squish them, to fit one more in, and then some fellow gets the bright idea that without letting the king see, he'll shave a little bit off the back of one of the peaches. So he shaves a little bit off and manages to get 13 peaches in instead of 12, and then he sees that if he shaves a little bit off another one he can get 14 peaches in, and he's shaving away at these peaches and cutting little chunks off them and before long, what he has is a box full of peach pits."

The moral, says Else, is that in making films "we often try to cram so many different episodes and so many different pieces of incident and character and policy in, that in the process we wreck them all." At the end of the parable of the peach pits, the winner is the person who finds "a few perfectly ripe, naturally soft peaches that perfectly fit into this box without violating any individual peach." Less can be more.

Insufficient Casting

You may discover, in editing, that an important voice is missing, or that someone you've interviewed is filling a storytelling role that would be better filled by someone else. If possible, you might shoot an additional interview, trying to match its tone and look to your film's style. Otherwise, you need to find another way to bring this point of view forward, such as through archival voices or the way a scene is edited. It's also possible, as your story becomes more focused, that you've neglected to ask someone important story-related questions. Depending on how significant the problem is (and the size of your budget), you can either do another interview with that person, intending to either replace one with the other or somehow use both (although cutting directly between them may prove difficult), or you can work to match the audio enough so that you can use the pick-up material as voice-over.

Occasionally, an entirely new sentence can be crafted from someone's existing interview, a sentence the person never uttered but one that you think he or she would agree with. If you really want to do this, and it's your only option, you must run this new sentence past the person and secure permission to use it

GETTING UNSTUCK

Even the best creative minds get tired. You try six ways of cutting something and it still doesn't work, or the editor thinks it works one way, the director hates it, and the producer is thinking that now might be a good time to get that law degree. Assuming that you have at least something strung together in sequence, take a step back and try throwing all of the pieces up in the air. This is easier done at rough cut than fine cut, but it's a useful exercise in any case. You've got a story and structure that maybe aren't great, but they're fine. Open the door, for a short period, and let everyone throw out the craziest ideas they can think of, without anybody becoming scornful or arguing about why it won't work and that it's already been tried. "What if we started where the film now ends? What if we held off on the fireman's story until after his wife is in the accident? What if we told the story from the child's point of view, and not his parents'?"

Just throw it all out there and then try a few things. Maybe none of them will work. But in the difference between what was boring and safe and what is outrageous and stupid, you might see new opportunities. In other words, two wrong answers may lead you toward one that's right. You can't do this indefinitely, and at some point whoever's in charge has to make the final call. But what you end up with might be really interesting.

BE YOUR FIRST AUDIENCE

A mark of a good storyteller is the ability to look with fresh eyes—the audience's eyes—at material each time a new cut is available, and to honestly assess its weaknesses. If you see problems, don't ignore them. Audiences are uncanny in their ability to see that one flaw you thought you could gloss over or the transition whose absence you thought you'd masked with some fancy music and images. At the same time, you can't cut a film or tell a story with a critic on your shoulder. Don't second-guess yourself; that's not what this process is about. Instead, ask yourself every step of the way, "Is this interesting? Would I keep watching? What do I care about here? Who am I worried for? Am I confused? Where do I need more information?"

Chances are, if it works for you—the editor, producer, director—it will work for the audience.

14

Writing Narration and Voice-Over

Narration is not the worst thing to happen to a documentary, but bad narration might be, which might explain why so many filmmakers want to avoid it at all costs. We've all seen films that were talky, preachy, hyperventilated, and dull. But there's also narration—including extensive voice-over commentary, such as that spoken by one of the film's subjects or by the filmmaker—that makes films funny, sarcastic, spare, poetic, and elegant. *Enron: The Smartest Guys in the Room, Super Size Me, Grizzly Man*, and *Born into Brothels*, among many recent films, have effective narration. *Enron's* narration is the most traditional, in that it's spoken by an unseen person, the actor Peter Coyote, who has no identity in the film other than to provide information that moves the story along. *Super Size Me*, narrated in voice-over and on screen by filmmaker Morgan Spurlock, is packed with what would be considered traditional narration: facts and figures about nutrition, health, the food industry, and more. *Grizzly Man* is narrated in the first person by filmmaker Werner Herzog, whose voice-over tells of his journey to explore the legacy and death of naturalist Timothy Treadwell. *Born into Brothels*, while narrated by Zana Briski, does not refer to her role as the film's producer and director (with Ross Kauffman), but to her involvement in the story, as a photographer helping a group of children in the brothels of Calcutta.

Narration or voice-over, if done well, can be one of the best and most efficient ways to move your story along, not because it *tells* the story but because it draws the audience into and through it. Narration provides information that's not otherwise available but is essential if audiences are to fully experience your film. "When documentary makers dive into fairly complicated historical policy or legal and legislative issues," notes Jon Else, "narration is your friend. It may mean that you have only two or three lines of narration in a film, but something that might take 10 minutes of tortured interview or tortured vérité footage can be often disposed of better in 15 seconds of a well-written line of narration."

POINT OF VIEW

When crafting narration, it's important to choose the point of view from which to tell the story, for example:

- First-person narration is when the narrator speaks of him- or herself. *I needed to find out.* This point of view is generally limited to what the narrator knows at a given point in the story.
- Second-person narration may be found more often in print than on screen. It has the narrator addressing the audience as "you," as in *He asks if you want a soda, and you say yes.*
- Third-person omniscient is the most commonly used form of narration; it is written using "he" or "she," and the narrator can slip in and out of anyone's thoughts or actions. For example, *The mayor was well aware of Smith's plans. And from his campaign headquarters, Smith knew that the mayor's response, when it came, would be fierce.* Most often, this narration is described as "objective," meaning that it is limited to factual information that can be observed or verified. However, as discussed in the first chapter, it still has a point of view, no matter how balanced or neutral it seeks to be.
- Third-person subjective uses the "he" or "she" form, but is limited to the same point of view as first-person narration. In other words, I might describe the writing of this chapter as *She sits at her desk and types, wondering if she'll meet her deadline.*

Beyond the narrator's point of view, there is also a point of view in the words being spoken. Even if you've chosen an omniscient narrator, you want to be careful not to jump back and forth between points of view, but instead situate the viewer. For example, if you begin to narrate a Revolutionary War battle from the point of view of the advancing British, you don't want to suddenly switch to the American side without signaling to the audience that you've done so. In other words, the following (imagined) scene is confusing: *British forces prepared their charge as the Americans assembled near Boone Hill. General Washington ordered his men, a ragtag group of 300, to stand firm. The soldiers advanced, a force of nearly 2,000 in territory that offered little resistance.*

Told from the American point of view, the scene might go like this: *The Americans were assembled near Boone Hill when they got word that British forces were advancing. General Washington ordered his men, a ragtag group of 300, to stand firm, as nearly 2,000 British soldiers advanced toward them.*

From the British point of view, it might go this way: *British forces prepared to charge on the Americans who were assembled nearby. A force of nearly 2,000 men, they had little difficulty with the terrain as they approached Boone Hill, where General Washington was waiting with a rag-tag force of about 300.*

Obviously, your writing should fit the visuals. But it's very easy in a case like this to quickly lose track of who's fighting whom, who's advancing where. One way to help, as the filmmaker, is to maintain a consistent point of view.

VARIETY IN NARRATION

At times, filmmakers "narrate" films without speaking, through the use of text on screen. This usually means using either title cards (text on a neutral background) or lower thirds (text over a scene) to add information that's not otherwise evident. This technique is generally used in films that are strongly vérité (action unfolds on screen) and is always used sparingly. Filmmakers who use title cards generally use them to set up the film and then, on occasion, to establish time and place or to bridge sequences.

For example, the documentary *Spellbound*, about a group of children who compete in the National Spelling Bee, sets up the story with a brief series of cards that immediately follow the film's title. The cards come on in the following order (numbers are added here for clarity and do not appear in the film): 1, joined by 2, both off; 3, joined by 4, both off; 5, joined by 6, both off:

1. *Across the country, 9,000,000 children compete in school and city spelling bees.*
2. *Only 249 qualify for the Nationals in Washington, D.C.*
3. *Over two days of competition 248 will misspell a word.*
4. *One will be named champion.*
5. *This is the story of eight American children*
6. *who, one spring, set out to win the National Spelling Bee.*

These effectively set up the story to come; later, text on screen briefly introduces the protagonists, for example: *Perryton, Texas* (over an establishing shot of the town) is followed shortly after by *Angela* (over an establishing shot of Angela).

When to narrate, how to narrate, who should narrate—these are important storytelling decisions, driven in part by the content of the film and the style and tone adopted by the filmmakers. Compare the narration in *Enron* with the lack of narration in a film like *Spellbound. Enron,* based on the reporting of *Fortune* magazine's Bethany McLean and Peter Elkind, seeks to give general audiences an understanding of a corporate financial scandal that was enormously complex. The narration is relatively spare, but it helps the filmmakers weave together a complicated body of evidence derived from interviews, news reports, audiotapes, video coverage of hearings, and more. In contrast, *Spellbound* does not set out to provide a wealth of complex factual data, but instead seeks to let viewers inside the homes and lives of selected children as they prepare for a national competition, and then follows them there to see how they do.

As mentioned, Werner Herzog's voice-over in *Grizzly Man* is an important part of the film's story. The film begins with an intriguing excerpt of Treadwell's footage. Then, like the title cards at the start of *Spellbound,* the first words we hear from Herzog set up the premise of the film to come:

All these majestic creatures were filmed by Timothy Treadwell, who lived among wild grizzlies for 13 summers. He went to remote areas of the Alaskan peninsula believing that he was needed there to protect these animals and educate the public. During his last five years out there, he took along a video camera and shot over 100 hours of footage. What Treadwell intended was to show these bears in their natural habitat. Having myself filmed in the wilderness of jungle, I found that beyond a wildlife film, in his material lay dormant a story of astonishing beauty and depth. I discovered a film of human ecstasies and darkest inner turmoil. As if there was a desire in him to leave the confinements of his humanness and bond with the bears, Treadwell reached out, seeking a primordial encounter. But in doing so, he crossed an invisible borderline . . . .

Herzog plays a number of roles as the film's narrator. Sometimes he provides basic exposition: *Timothy grew up with four siblings in Long Island . . .* or lends his expertise as a filmmaker: *Now the scene seems to be over. But as a filmmaker, sometimes things fall into your lap which you couldn't expect, never even dream of.* Perhaps most interesting are Herzog's challenges to Treadwell. At times, these are simple statements of contradiction, for example: *Treadwell saw himself as the guardian of this land and stylized himself as Prince Valiant, fighting the bad guys with their schemes to do harm to the bears. But all this land is a federally protected reserve . . . .* But Herzog also argues directly with the Treadwell we see on screen, as when Treadwell mourns the killing (by other animals) of a bear cub and then a baby fox. Treadwell says, in his footage: "I love you and I don't understand. It's a painful world." In voice-over, Herzog responds: *Here I differ with Treadwell. He seemed to ignore the fact that in nature there are predators. I believe the common denominator of the universe is not harmony, but chaos, hostility, and murder.*

WHEN IS THE NARRATION WRITTEN?

When you write narration varies from project to project. A film adapted from a book might begin with the text. Sometimes a narrative device doesn't suggest itself until well into the editing, as happened when the producers decided to use voice-over excerpts of an old diary as the narrative spine in *Yosemite: The Fate of Heaven.*

In general, if you are using narration to seam together visual images, interviews, and perhaps archival material, the final narration (or voice-over) won't come together until you're editing. You may assemble other elements first, such as filmed footage, archival material, or interview bites, and then rough out narration as needed to help move the story along. Sometimes you need to write "into" a talking head, which means that your words are needed as a kind of setup, to make the meaning of the upcoming interview bite more clear. Sometimes you need narration to set the stage for a scene that can then play out on camera without interruption, or to make a transition from one sequence to the next.

With personal essays, the narration reveals both the story and the storyteller. In Chapter 24, filmmaker Per Saari talks about his struggle to write voice-over for his short film, *Why He Skied*. "It was really difficult to make it concise and to come up with a conclusion that made sense," Saari says, adding that he reworked his voice-over and rerecorded it "probably a hundred times."

WHO WRITES THE NARRATION?

Film writing is a different skill than magazine or book writing. While some prose writers make the transition successfully, not all do. Writing to picture—writing words that will be heard rather than read—and structuring a film story within the confines of the time allotted, whether 30 minutes or eight hours, are specialized skills. Just as a great poet might be a terrible screenwriter, a great print journalist might not write a good movie.

On many documentary projects, the film's producer is also the writer. But there are no hard and fast rules. Some projects involve a writer from the beginning; others bring a writer on board at the assembly or rough cut stage. Some directors write. Some editors write or at least draft out scratch narration that is then polished by, or with the help of, a writer.

If you are going to bring in an "outside" writer (as opposed to involving the producer or director in that role), it's best to do so as early in the production process as possible. This might mean, for example, that the writer consults on and off until editing is under way, at which point he or she works on a more regular basis. An experienced film writer can point out potential structural weaknesses in an outline or treatment and help develop a "must have" list for production. At the assembly stage, a writer can help develop an editing script, focusing not just on narration but on the structure of the storytelling itself. A writer, ideally, knows all of the storytelling elements well and plays a significant role in using them to tell the strongest story possible.

Juan Carlos Lecompte and cardboard figure of his wife, from *The Kidnapping of Ingrid Betancourt*. Photo by Ana Maria Garcia Rojas, courtesy of the filmmakers.

Bringing a writer on at the end simply to polish narration can work if the film is in good shape, but it can be frustrating for everyone if improving the narration doesn't solve a problem that might better have been addressed earlier on by making different story or structure choices. By the time you're polishing narration, most of your editing resources are gone, and it can be very hard on everyone to have to pull things apart and look at the film with fresh eyes.

It's also true that if you plan to hire an actor or other celebrity to narrate your film (such as Peter Coyote for *Enron* or Morgan Freeman for *March of the Penguins*), you may not know exactly who will be narrating until quite late in the process. At that point, you may need to fine-tune the narration, to some extent, to suit their unique voices and identities.

WRITING TO PICTURE

The camera pans across a sepia-toned still photograph of a wagon train on a dusty road. To the side, an old farmer stands, watching as the wagons pass. The shot ends on a hand-painted sign tacked to the back of one of the last wagons: *Califna or Bust*. As you watch this shot on screen, which line of narration would be more useful to you?

- *The wagons set out along the dusty road.*
- *On August 4th they set out; four men, five women, and eight children determined to find gold.*

Which narration breathes life into the photograph, and which just states the obvious? Narration should add information to picture, not simply describe it. Above all, narration should advance the story.

Here's a second example, from a film that follows a group of college friends as they face their first year in the job market. In a live-action scene set in a private home, a group of young women sits down to a fancy dinner. One of them, dressed in an expensive-looking suit, sets a roasted turkey on the table. Which narration is useful?

- *Donna is the most vivacious of the group, and the most fashion-conscious.*
- *Donna, who graduated with high honors from Harvard Law School, hopes to pursue a career in advertising.*

Obviously, what you say depends on what the audience needs to learn. But we can tell from watching the scene that Donna is vivacious and well-dressed. We can't tell from looking at her that she went to Harvard Law School. That narration adds to picture.

Here is another approach that people sometimes use, believing that it will create a sense of tension:

- *Donna, the organizer of this gathering, would soon learn that her life would change in ways she couldn't imagine.*

What exactly does this add? Are you on the edge of your seat wondering how Donna's life will change? No. This sounds like it's intended to build tension, but it's just words. Tension comes from the story, not a narrator's hints.

Just as you should write to picture, you should never write against picture. A common mistake people make is to write in a way that sets the film up to go in one direction, when in fact the images are going somewhere else. Here's an example. We see a group of executives sitting around a table, talking. Narration: *The board decided to hire a consultant, Jane Johnson.* Cut to a woman talking. Wouldn't you assume it's Jane Johnson? If it's not, it's going to take a moment to readjust your thinking, to figure out, well, if it's *not* Johnson, who is it? By then, you'll have missed at least part of what this woman has said.

Suppose the woman that we cut to is on the board of directors, and she's explaining why they're hiring Jane Johnson. The edit makes sense. But the narration gets in the way. Try again. We see a group of executives sitting around a table, talking. Narration: *The board decided that a consultant was needed.* Cut to the woman from the board, who explains, "We were spinning our wheels. And so . . . ." It's a minor difference but an important one.

Words and picture should work together, each adding to the buildup of your story. Words should also accurately identify the picture. This can be frustrating to filmmakers when the visual record is limited. Suppose, for example, that you are telling the story of a man and woman who met in Ohio at a USO dance, the night before he was shipped off to fight in the Second World War. But the family only has photographs that were taken five years later, after the man returned from the war and the couple, now married, had a child. No footage exists of that particular USO dance or even of the club in which it was held. Can you use footage of another USO dance, from another state and another year?

Of course you can, but your narration should avoid creating the false impression that the audience is seeing the real thing. For example, suppose the editor cuts in footage of a USO dance held two years later in a different state. The narration says, *On February 2, 1942, at a USO dance in Columbus, Ohio, Tim finally met the girl of his dreams.* The audience may think, "Gee, isn't that amazing, there was a film crew there to capture it." I think it stretches credibility, and if the audience assumes that this couldn't possibly be the USO dance on the night in the city, they will see your footage for what it is—wallpaper. From that point on, the archival value of the footage is diminished, and the rest of your material becomes a bit suspect, deservedly or not.

There is an alternative, using the same scene, same footage. Open the narration wider, as in this example, *USO dances were held in gymnasiums and hospitals, canteens and clubs throughout the U.S., and it was at a dance like this that Tim met the girl of his dreams.* You're not writing as closely to that one particular image; at the same time, you're offering a valuable reminder that your characters are just two people caught up in a time and a situation that's bigger than both of them. The footage is no longer generic wallpaper, but illustrative of an era.

Writing to picture also means that the words you choose work in tandem with the visuals. Here's an example. You are making a film about a team of cyclists competing in the Tour de France. You need to introduce Ralph Martinez, riding for the Americans. In the scene you're narrating, it's early morning and the cyclists are gathered in a village square, drinking coffee or juice, eating pastries, and psyching themselves up for a day on the Tour. The specific shot starts close on a croissant. A hand wearing a bicycling glove reaches in and picks up the pastry; the shot widens and pulls back as we follow the pastry up to a rider's mouth, and see that it is a young man (Ralph) perched on his bike, sipping coffee as he laughs and talks with teammates. Some narration options:

- *Pastry and coffee start the day for Ralph Martinez and his American teammates.* Too "on the nose"—we can see the pastry and coffee for ourselves.
- *Ralph Martinez, getting ready for his third tour, is riding with the American team.* This won't work, because the words "Ralph Martinez" will fall too soon, probably when we're still looking at a big glob of jam on a croissant. You want your narration to roughly mirror the picture and to arrive at Ralph when the visuals do.
- *Riding with the Americans is Ralph Martinez, in his third Tour de France.* This might work—it's hard to tell until you see and hear it against picture! Note that you don't need to say "team" because it can be assumed. Chances are that by this point in the film you also won't need to say "de France." You want to be as economical in word use as possible. Better to have a moment for natural sound than to keep yammering away at the viewers.

Writing to picture can be difficult, especially for those who resist rewriting. While a film is being edited, nearly everything is subject to change. A scene needs to be cut down to give another scene more time. An archival shot needs to be changed because the rights to it aren't available. A sequence is moved from the last half of the film to the first half and therefore needs to be set up differently. From the assembly through to script lock, narration is a moving target. You must be willing to make changes. When enough changes pile up, the editor or someone else on the production team will record a new scratch narration track and lay it against picture. As you'll discover, at least some of these revisions will need further revising. Eventually, though, the script will be locked, the picture will be locked, and the narration will be finished.

WRITING NARRATION TO BE SPOKEN

Narration scripts are, by design, written to be spoken out loud. Every word counts. Important words should stand out in a sentence or paragraph. Sentences should be short and written in an active voice. Phrases should be reviewed to ensure that they don't create a confusing impression, such as *Mark left Philip. Underneath the house, a skunk was waiting*. Reading it, the meaning is clear. Hearing it, you wonder if Mark left Philip underneath the house, or if the skunk is going to catch Mark unaware. *The remains were sent to the local anthropology lab. There, they believed Dr. Smith could provide vital information*. The remains believe something about Dr. Smith?

You also need to avoid tongue twisters and quotation marks; audiences can't hear the irony when a narrator says, *Eleanor was "sorry," but no one believed her*. On paper, a reader could reasonably figure that Eleanor had made an apology but it was taken as false. To the listener, it sounds like the narrator has determined that Eleanor is in fact sorry, but no one believes her. There's a small but important distinction. (For the same reason, you need to be wary of words that sound alike but have different meanings, and of conjunctions, such as "shouldn't," which may be misheard as "should.")

The solution is very simple. Read your narration out loud, even as you're writing it. You will find it far easier to hear the rhythm, feel where the strong words are falling, and get a sense of what's hard to say or where words are superfluous. Then read it aloud again (and again, and again) against picture. There are a few ways of doing this, and you'll use them all. You can read to picture on the fly, although it's tough to look at the screen and your script simultaneously. You can have someone read aloud as you watch. Time permitting, the most effective way to check narration against picture is to have someone on the production crew record a temporary ("scratch") narration track, which is edited into the film.

If you are the film's final narrator, at some point you'll have to record the actual voice-over. "It's a difficult thing to pull off without seeming either like you're a newscaster or like you're just talking in an interview," says Per Saari. "There's a unique tone that you have to achieve, and it was a real struggle to accomplish that." As you watch documentaries, pay attention to the narrator's tone. Morgan Spurlock's upbeat energy pumps up the narration of *Super Size Me*. Al Gore brings two separate tones to his voice-over in *An Inconvenient Truth*: one is the public voice that lectures on climate change, and the other is a more private, intimate voice in which he talks about his life and family. Actors hired to record voice-over for films tend to aim for clarity and neutrality in their tone.

SOME GENERAL GUIDELINES FOR NARRATION

Reapply the Rules of Grammar

As with proposal writing, narration writing must be grammatical. Common problems include the following:

- Dangling and misplaced modifiers. *Three sheets to the wind, the police officers stared up at Rodney as he stood on the window ledge*. It's Rodney who's drunk, not the police officers. The line should read *Three sheets to the wind, Rodney stood on the window ledge as police officers stared up at him*. But what if you're writing to picture? What if you see the police officers first, and then Rodney? You reveal the information as you see it. *The officers stared up at Rodney, teetering on a ledge, three sheets to the wind*.
- Dangling participles. This is when you start a sentence with a verb and go to another verb without inserting a subject. *Having been recently fired, getting a job was a priority for him*.

Instead, try: *Having been recently fired, he made getting a job a priority.* Or, *He'd recently been fired, so getting a job was a priority.*

- Confusing use of pronouns. *When she was just six, her beloved horse, Yum Yum, died.* Was the horse six, or was it the "she" that we're talking about? A simple solution is something like, *Jennifer was just six when her beloved horse, Yum Yum, died.*
- Lack of parallel form. Avoid statements such as *Four men in Texas, three in Ohio, and one in San Francisco.* That's two states and a city. Either three cities or three states should be used to make the construction parallel. In this case, since there's the possibility of having to list eight cities in total, I'd say, *Four men in Texas, three in Ohio, and one in California.* Here's another example of bad form: *He liked running, fishing, and to build model airplanes.* Try this instead: *He liked running, fishing, and building model airplanes.*
- Incorrect use of *fewer* and *less. Fewer* is for things that can be counted, like students: *There were fewer students this year than last. Less* is for quantities and measures that can't be counted: *There's less support for the new tax law.*
- Inexact use of words. *Since*—It can be a measure of time: *Since the 1980s*; or it can indicate cause: *Since no one bothered to show up, the meeting was canceled.*) *As* and *like*—In general, *as* refers to a similarity: *She dances as if moved by the wind. Like* refers to similarities between nouns: *He hopes to pass regulations here like those already being enforced in Cleveland.* Finally, *and* and *but*—While both are used as conjunctions, *and* is for clauses with similar weight or similar meaning: *The students staged a local sit-in on Saturday, and on Monday they attended a city-wide rally. But* is used when you want to imply a difference in emphasis or a contrast: *The students staged a local sit-in on Saturday, but on Monday they attended a city-wide rally.* The implication is that the rally has greater weight in your story.
- Non sequiturs. These are statements or phrases that follow each other but don't have any logical connection. *Investigators call on a team of forensic scientists to establish the victim's time of death and bring his killer to justice.* There's no indication here of a link between knowing the cause of death and bringing the killer to justice.

The list of common mistakes goes on. Some excellent style books are available, including *The Elements of Style*, a classic by William Strunk, Jr., and E. B. White; *The Associated Press Stylebook and Libel Manual*, edited by Norm Goldstein, and *The New York Times Manual of Style and Usage*, by Allan M. Siegal and William G. Connolly. In addition, there are likely to be people on your staff who are good at grammar, know all the rules by heart, and actually enjoy diagramming sentences. Ask one of them to review your narration before you lock it.

Use Anticipation

Narration needs to follow the arc of the story, not lead it. In the film's opening minutes, you want to set up the questions that will drive your story forward. You then want to anticipate the audience's needs and almost intuitively seed information in, just as—or just after—the question or confusion begins to flicker in the viewer's mind. Pay attention as you watch a well-made film, and you'll notice this happening. You turn to a friend and say, "I don't understand; I thought she couldn't run for governor." and seconds later, the narration answers your question: *A loophole in electoral law had worked to her advantage.*

Avoid Stereotyping

Use the most gender-neutral terms available (e.g., *firefighter* rather than *fireman, police officer* rather than *policeman*). This is important for two reasons. It more accurately represents the world in which we live, and it's a step toward acknowledging (and involving) an audience of diverse backgrounds.

Avoiding stereotyping also means being careful of "code" words (saying "suburban" when you mean white or middle class, for example) and watching out for an overlay of judgment based on stereotypes, such as *She was pushing 40, but still attractive.* Whose point of view does a statement like this reflect? "Pushing 40" implies that this is an unbelievably ancient age, and the "but" is a dead giveaway that nobody on the production team could imagine anyone over 25 being worth a second glance. Stereotypes— dumb jock, dumb blonde, little old lady, "not your grandmother's store"—have no place in documentary narration. Mothers-in-law run corporations and countries; "geezers" set foreign policy or rob banks.

Watch Out for Anachronisms

If you are telling narration from a point of view within a story, stay within the boundaries of that point of view. This means respecting the limitations of your character's frame of reference, including time and place. An example of narration that fails to do this comes from *When Dinosaurs Roamed America*, an animated series from the Discovery Channel. Narrator John Goodman is speaking from the point of view of a dinosaur, trying to size up a new beast he's encountered. *The raptor's never seen a dinosaur like this before*, Goodman says. *Is it a predator, or is it prey? No other creature in the world looks like a half-plucked turkey and walks like a potbellied bear. Still, an oddball can be dangerous.* This narration has the dinosaur comparing what he sees to animals he has no knowledge of, since they won't exist for several million years. For the audience, the comparison may be valuable, but its use here pulls us out of the story. To use the comparison, the producers should have acknowledged the leap in time by moving—even briefly—outside the raptor's point of view. For example, *The raptor's never seen a dinosaur like this before. Scientists today say it probably looked like a cross between a plucked turkey and a potbellied bear. To the raptor, it just looks odd—and oddballs can be dangerous.*

You also want to be careful, when speaking of the past, not to impose your 21st-century values, assumptions, and knowledge. In an interesting way, renowned historian Simon Schama does this (albeit successfully) in his *A History of Britain*. Here is his somewhat breathless description of the pairing of Henry of Anjou (soon to become King Henry II)—"the most hyperactive king in British history"—and his "Guinevere," Eleanor of Aquitaine:

> *But the match was a gamble. He was 19; she was pushing 30. He was relatively inexperienced; Eleanor had seen as much of the ways of the world as it could possibly offer. Henry found himself at the altar in 1152 beside an older woman, described as a graceful, dark-eyed beauty, disconcertingly articulate, strong-minded, and jocular, hardly the frail damsel in the tower. One likes to think that for her part, Eleanor saw not just the usual feudal spur-clanking bonehead, but beyond the stocky frame and barrel chest, someone who was an intriguing peculiarity.*

Look at the point of view in the paragraph above:

- There are two references to Eleanor's age, in terms that imply that this carried the same weight 850 years ago that it does today. It would need to be fact checked and presumably was.
- "Disconcertingly articulate"—disconcerting to whom? What is the cultural or political value that this runs counter to? We have to take Schama on faith that there was a problem with a woman of significant power having a brain in her head and the ability to speak her mind; no context for it is given here.
- "Hardly the frail damsel in the tower" implies the groom's point of view, when in fact it's the narrator's. Schama noted earlier in the film that "this was the age of chivalry, when the myth of Arthur and Camelot was at its most popular," adding that Henry's parents were grooming him to become "a new King Arthur—and to do this of course, he would need a Guinevere." It may or may not have occurred to Henry to size up his bride with Guinevere in mind; the evidence in the film, however, makes this solely Schama's point of view.
- "One likes to think that . . ." furthers the impression that the point of view here is the narrator's and that in fact it is Schama who likes to think that Eleanor saw more than "the usual feudal, spur-clanking bonehead." Would this have been Eleanor's presumption of a man deemed suitable for her to wed? It's possible; it's just difficult to tell here.

This narration does move the story forward at a fast clip and bring characters to life. But Schama can get away with this, in my view, because of his considerable expertise; he carries a certain weight when he makes sweeping and very modern-sounding statements. It's one of those "don't try this at home" situations—or if you must try it, do so with professional (scholarly) guidance. Otherwise, it's very easy to slip up and inaccurately impose 21st-century assumptions on the past—about life, work, gender roles, class, race, all sorts of things.

Limit the Number of Ideas in Each Block of Narration

Your narration should convey only the story points needed to get to the next sync material; if you go too far or include too many points, your audience will lose track of the information and will be distracted or confused by what follows. For example, here's a piece of narration from *Not a Rhyme Time*, a program from the *I'll Make Me a World* series: *In the spring of 1967, Amiri Baraka was scheduled to address the Black Writers' Conference at Fisk University in Nashville, Tennessee. Gwendolyn Brooks was also on the program.*

The tension comes from the fact that (as we already know from the program) Baraka represents the new school, the Black Arts Movement, and Brooks—a Pulitzer Prize–winning author who publishes with a large, mainstream publisher—represents the "establishment." The interaction of the two will help to spark Brooks's transformation, which is the focus of the story.

Look at what happens if we go too far and turn the corner with this narration: *In the spring of 1967, Amiri Baraka was scheduled to address the Black Writers' Conference at Fisk University in Nashville, Tennessee. Gwendolyn Brooks was also on the program. She had prepared to read her poem, "The Life of Lincoln West."* The paragraph now sets us up to learn more about this one poem and away from the anticipated meeting of Brooks and Baraka.

Foreshadow Important Information

The American troops battling the British in the Revolutionary War were promised in July of 1776, when the fighting broke out, that they would all be discharged by December 31. Don't wait to tell the audience this until it's December 31 in your film's chronology. Tell them in July, when they won't think it matters; remind them in September, when the war is dragging on. That way, when winter sets in, it will be on their minds—just as it must have been on General Washington's mind—when the troops are tired and demoralized, and there's no way that Washington can keep his word.

Understand the Different Roles Played by Narration and Sync Material

It's all too common for filmmakers to use talking heads to do work that is better done by narration, and vice versa. Sometimes, this happens because the casting is weak; everybody talks about everything, nothing is differentiated, and they all might as well be narrating.

Ideally, your interviewees should be advancing the story through the lens of their own expertise, experience, and point of view. This is information that is more valuable, in some ways, than narration, and it's certainly more personable. Using these characters to convey information that narration could convey just as well is something of a waste. Conversely, if you replace too many of your talking heads or too much of what they say with narration, you risk pulling the heart and soul out of your film. Even people who are resistant to talking heads would prefer a good visit with an enjoyable character to narration.

Except in films where the filmmaker's investigation, at least in part, drives the film, narration is generally not the best way to contradict an interviewee. The subject says, "No one knew about those documents," and a disembodied voice interrupts, *No one knew? It seemed unlikely.* So how do you contradict people on screen? You find another interviewee to offer a rebuttal, or you film scenes that contain evidence contradicting the interviewee's statement. Let the individuals, facts, and story speak for themselves, and trust that audience members can decide the truth for themselves.

Use Words Sparingly and Specifically

Screen time is a precious commodity, and you want your narration to be as spare as possible. Don't waste good airtime on words that are little more than filler, such as *Salinas. A town of working people, it hardly seems the place for a murder. But on January 14, 1998, the owners of a house discovered something that would change that impression forever.* A quick check shows that Salinas is a city of around 123,000 people, and that in the 20 years before the homeowners discovered a body buried beneath their house, a total of 218 people had been killed in Salinas, including 18 in 1997. The narration pumped emotion into the story, but it's not useful or even accurate.

The perceived need for hype—most often on commercial television—often seems to lead to imprecise writing. *In rural Michigan, a search for a missing man ends in cold-blooded murder.* Well, actually, it doesn't. If the search ended in cold-blooded murder, then someone involved in the search would have ended up dead. What happened is that a missing person case is revealed to be a murder case—the search for the missing man leads to a corpse. Why not say that?

Using words sparingly also means choosing the best word to describe what you mean, being careful of nuances. Does a teenager walk across the room or saunter? Does a CEO say that he doesn't have numbers for the fourth quarter, or does he admit that fact? Has the world leader made an impassioned speech or launched into a tirade? Was a nation's capital liberated, or did it fall? Was it a conflagration—a term that has specific meaning among firefighters—or simply a bad fire? Choose your words carefully, and be sure the meaning you want is not only the most exciting, but also the most accurate.

Along these lines, try to avoid the slogans of others, whether you agree with them or not. For example, rather than adopt the phrases "pro-life" or "pro-choice," state that someone is either for or against abortion rights.

Use Telling Details

A well-placed detail can convey a tremendous amount of story information. If there were any doubts about the need for a campaign to register voters in Selma, Alabama, they were dispelled in *Eyes on the Prize* by this fact: *More than half of Dallas County citizens were black, but less than 1 percent were registered* [to vote]. Details can set a stage where visuals are insufficient, as in *The Civil War* series: *Sherman began his march. Sixty-two thousand men in blue were on the move in two great columns. Their supply train stretched 25 miles. A slave watching the army stream past wondered aloud if anybody was left up north.* And details can convey tone and wit, as in *Troublesome Creek: A Midwestern*, narrated by filmmaker Jeanne Jordan: *Like a lot of families facing a real crisis, we immediately stopped talking about it.*

Put Information into Context

Your narration needs to move the story along, which means it should not only impart facts, but also make it clear how they are relevant to the story you're telling. *The 390 people in the club now fought their way to an exit* is interesting, but I have no way of knowing if that's a lot or a little. If the club is Madison Square

Garden, it's a very small crowd. In contrast, *390 people—nearly twice as many as the club could legally hold—fought their way to an exit* tells you that laws were broken even before disaster occurred. The same is true for motivation. *The mayor called a late-night meeting* may not advance your story as well as *Hoping to avoid the press, the mayor called a late-night meeting.* Motivation must be fact checked, however. Never guess at what someone was thinking or feeling, unless your narration makes clear that it's speculation, as in *She might have been concerned not to hear from him; perhaps that's why she got into her car that night.*

If quantity is important to convey, offer it in terms that are comparative, rather than giving specific numbers. *From head to tail, the dinosaur would have been half as long as a football field.* Comparisons and context are also useful when discussing quantities from the past. It's common for filmmakers to imply that someone "only making $5 day" in 1905 was being exploited, without finding out what this amount meant at the time, what it might buy, and how it compared to other incomes at the time.

As you add this context, keep in mind that you're building toward story events. You need to remind the audience occasionally (not constantly) what's at stake, what information we know, where we're going. *The board will stop hearing testimony at 9:30. At that point, their vote will decide the future of this regional school system.* Offer gentle clues about the outcome as we move forward. *He had gambled everything, and he had lost. As Ransom's troops trudged wearily north . . . .*

Get Off the Dime

Like the story itself, narration needs to keep moving forward. It's surprising how often narration repeats the same information over and over, especially to remind viewers that they're seeing something for the first time, or that it's very dangerous, or that no one knows what's around the next corner. If you've told us once that a particular military unit is untrained and untested, don't tell us again; build on that information as you move the story forward.

Don't Drop Names

If people are worth mentioning, they're worth identifying. The first time someone's name comes up in narration, let us know who the person is, even if you think that we'd have to be living under a rock not to know. You don't have to go into a lot of detail, just enough to remind those who know and inform those who don't: *Noted composer Leonard Bernstein once said . . .* , or *He was filmed in performance by cinematographer Gordon Parks. . . .*

Along the same lines, try to anticipate words that your audience may be unfamiliar with, whether they're spoken by the narrator (and a more familiar word can't be substituted) or spoken by an interviewee or someone on camera. If the word's meaning is not clear in the context, you may need to set it up. For example, suppose the historic artifacts you're presenting on screen include a bill of sale for a frigate. You might set it up as *That day, the general placed an order for a new sailing ship, one outfitted for war.*

Put Lists in an Order That Builds (or Descends)

This is fairly straightforward. You want your paragraphs to pack a punch. Look at the following line of narration from the series *Liberty! The American Revolution*, describing the British invasion of New York in 1776: *30,000 troops. 10,000 sailors. 300 supply ships. 30 battleships with 1200 cannons. It is the largest seaborne attack ever attempted by England until the 20th century.* What's great about this is that the build is not by number but by power; in fact, the numbers decrease from 30,000 (troops) to 1 (attack). But the power goes from men to supply ships to battleships, and news of the force that's about to hit the newly-independent states is delivered with a sentence that jumps the chronology and lands us, very briefly, in the present. It's very effective drama.

Use an Active Voice

You want your narration to be as active as possible. For example, *A decision was made to allow Coca-Cola to advertise on school property.* Who made the decision, and how? A more active way to say this is *By a vote of 4 to 1, the school board decided to allow Coca-Cola to advertise on school property.* (Obviously, if we're watching a scene where we know it's the school board, and can actually see four hands up and one down, you won't say this. But if we're seeing a shot of the hallway with soda vending machines all lined up, you want narration that helps that shot along.)

Help to Differentiate among Similar Things

Narration can play an important role in getting a viewer through a succession of battles, or medical interventions, or political gatherings. Since you've been careful to film a series of events that build on each other, and not just three or four examples of the same thing, your narration may be needed to simply make that build a little more clear or fill in the details. *The operation on Bill's knee had only improved mobility. Now Dr. Fishman needed to add cartilage . . . .*

Do the Math for Them

If you write narration that says *Born in 1934, she was 18 when she met Mark*, there are viewers who will be so distracted trying to figure out the year she met Mark (1952) that they'll momentarily lose track of your story. Whether it's calculating profits or age or elapsed time, it's best to write it in a way that doesn't make the viewer do the work. This is not an issue of involving the audience in the story, it's a matter of not wanting to distract them from it.

Avoid Hype

If a story is truly astonishing or an event is truly chilling or a person is really sinister, that fact should become evident through the story or character or event and the way you present it. The cheapest and worst way to try to pump emotion into a piece is through adjectives and hyperbole. Frankly, audiences become skeptical when narrators begin to sound like over-caffeinated salespeople. If your story is really good, it will sell itself.

Know When to Stop Narrating

Prepare the moment, and then let it play. If you're building toward the battle of Waterloo or a lifesaving operation or a statewide volleyball tournament, get us there and then let it play for a bit. Audiences need a respite from the talking; they need time to feel those moments of humor or pathos or fear. Anticipate those moments and build them in, whether it means a moment of silence or a moment with music or just action and sync sound. This is also true when the information is very complex and needs to be processed; or when it's very funny, and the audience needs time to laugh.

15

Storytelling: A Checklist

Here's a list of questions to be asked at each stage of production, and especially as you near the end of the editing process:

- Given a choice between your film and the latest sitcom or indie drama, which would you choose? Are you telling a compelling and dramatic story and giving the viewer a reason to watch?
- Does your film *involve* the viewer in a story unfolding on screen, rather than talk at them?
- Are there interesting questions being asked and answered throughout, offering mystery, intrigue, suspense?
- Are you offering new information and an unusual perspective, or just rehashing tired, unchallenging material?
- Have you grounded viewers in your story so that they can anticipate where you're going and will be surprised when you take unexpected turns?
- Are you in the driver's seat of your film, steering toward emotional and intellectual highlights? Have you created moments of discovery for the audience, allowing them to reach their own conclusions before having them confirmed or denied?
- If there is backstory in your film, have you gotten a story under way that motivates the audience to want to go there?
- If your subject is complex or technical, have you gotten a story under way that motivates the audience to want to understand it?
- Have you "cast" the film carefully, with a manageable group of characters who fairly represent the complexity of an issue

and not just its extremes? Or, if your focus *is* the extremes, have you made that context clear?

- Do individual characters stand out and play differentiated roles in your overall story and film, or is their presence generic?
- Does the story that was set up at the film's beginning pay off at the end? Can you articulate that story in a sentence or two?
- Does the film seem like "just another documentary" or is it something that people might want to tell each other about the next day?

Part IV

CONVERSATIONS ABOUT STORY

Many documentary filmmakers, including those interviewed for this book, work in a range of job capacities and film styles, so identifying any one of them with any one type of storytelling is difficult. With that said, there are some organizing principles behind the following conversations:

Steven Ascher and Jeanne Jordan (Massachusetts) were asked about their two feature-length documentaries, *Troublesome Creek* and *So Much So Fast*, which they describe as "nonfiction novels."

Victoria Bruce and Karin Hayes (Maryland and New York) were asked about their first collaboration, *The Kidnapping of Ingrid Betancourt*, a feature-length documentary that aired on HBO's Cinemax.

Ric Burns (New York) was asked about his experiences as a filmmaker who specializes in long-form historical documentaries, often created using archival materials.

Jon Else (California) has created a diverse body of documentary work and is also a renowned cinematographer. Our conversation ranged from visual storytelling to the pitfalls and possibilities of digital video technology.

Nicholas Fraser (England) is the commissioning editor of *Storyville*, an international documentary strand of the British Broadcasting Corporation.

Susan Froemke (New York) and I spoke about her distinguished work in vérité filmmaking, and in particular the Academy Award–nominated *Lalee's Kin*.

Sam Pollard (New York) has served in a variety of roles as a filmmaker, but we spoke at greatest length about his experiences as an editor and coproducer of two documentaries with Spike Lee, both for HBO: *4 Little Girls* and *When the Levees Broke*.

Kenn Rabin (California) is a filmmaker and writer, although I spoke with him here primarily as an internationally recognized expert on the use of archival material in documentaries and documentary-influenced dramas, such as *Good Night, and Good Luck*.

Per Saari (California) works in dramatic feature development in Hollywood and, in his own time, makes documentaries. We spoke about *Why He Skied*, a personal and self-funded project about his late brother, extreme skier Hans Saari.

Onyekachi Wambu (England) is a Nigerian-born filmmaker and journalist. We discussed not only filmmaking but also the uses of documentary media for empowerment and awareness.

16

Steven Ascher and Jeanne Jordan

Steven Ascher and Jeanne Jordan have been making documentary and fiction films for more than 20 years. Jeannie recently served as series producer of PBS's *Postcards from Buster*. Her previous credits include coproducing and directing *Running with Jesse* for the PBS series *Frontline*, editing two films for the acclaimed series *Eyes on the Prize*, and editing dramatic films including *Blue Diner*, *Lemon Sky*, and *Concealed Enemies*.

Steve Ascher's work has appeared on networks around the world, and his films include the documentary *Life and Other Anxieties* and the drama, *Del and Alex*. He is the author of *The Filmmaker's Handbook: A Comprehensive Guide for the Digital Age* (with Ed Pincus), a best-selling text, and is completing a third edition for publication in 2007. Steve has taught filmmaking at MIT, and both he and Jeannie have taught at Harvard.

This husband-and-wife team have made several films together, including the two discussed here. *Troublesome Creek: A Midwestern* is a feature documentary about the Jordan family's struggle to save their Iowa farm. The film won the Grand Jury Prize and Audience Award at the Sundance Film Festival in 1996 and was nominated for an Academy Award. *So Much So Fast*, also a feature documentary, premiered at Sundance in 2006. It tells the story of Jamie and Stephen Heywood, brothers whose lives are changed when one is diagnosed with ALS (Lou Gehrig's disease). I spoke with the filmmakers separately for this interview in 2003, and with Steve again in 2006.

Troublesome Creek documents the Jordan family's struggle to save their Iowa farm. You began the film after a receiving a phone call from Jeannie's father, Russ.

STEVE: Russ called and said he thought this would be his last year of farming. If we were going to call ourselves filmmakers and not make a film about this, there was something wrong. To be able to do a story like this, to have that kind of access—I thought of it as both an opportunity to tell this story and also for Jeannie to be able to tell some of the wonderful stories she'd been telling around the dinner table for years about growing up in Iowa.

He felt that he'd have one more year of planting and harvest followed by an auction. [The Jordans' plan was to auction off their livestock, equipment, and personal belongings in order to pay off their debts and keep the land itself, 450 acres.] That gave us the possibility of a narrative spine. It would have been much harder if not impossible to just make a film about day-to-day life on the farm, and be able to get into the kinds of issues that we did. We filmed four times over the course of about a year and a half.

How did you plan for the visual storytelling? Did you write up outlines, a treatment?

STEVE: We had to write up various things in order to raise money, but they were never really part of our thinking. With stories like this, in part you're following events and the events dictate what you're filming. But you have in your mind certain themes that you're interested in. In this case, the year on the farm, which included all the tasks that had to be accomplished—planting, harvesting, preparing for the auction, the auction. Then there are themes about Russ and Mary Jane, their marriage and their raising of children; there were themes about Jeannie's childhood; and themes about the changing landscape all over the Midwest, all over rural America. You're kind of advancing all of these fronts together, and you shoot things that can work toward them.

At the start of the film, there's a sequence in which a cat jumps from the roof of a barn into the arms of Jeannie's brother, Jon. It serves as a metaphor: as Jeannie says in voice-over, "My family in a nutshell—incredible luck, incredible timing, and teetering on the brink of disaster."

STEVE: That's a real tribute to editing. We had been filming for over a week, on the first shoot, and nothing had happened. We filmed mostly just goings-on at the farm. A cow had died, and we were doing a stakeout, waiting for the rendering truck to pick it up. Just waiting, for hours. And then we heard people shouting, and there was this cat on the roof. At the time we were just incredibly depressed. If the big event is a cat on the roof, we're really in trouble.

JEANNIE: Plus, when the cat jumped, we were moving the camera. I saw the cat jump, and Steve got the end of the cat jumping. But we didn't get the cat jumping. So it was a disaster. We filmed the wrong thing and we didn't get the climax of it. But in *Troublesome Creek*, I cut every inch that we shot. So I just went at that. I thought, I'm going to see if I can find a way to make "missing the cat" work. I know we have "after missing the cat," and I know we have "before jumping," so let me just cut it and look at it. And I realized that missing it was part of the story and the metaphor, and that the metaphor was unbelievable. The fact that Jon would even walk up there and say, "Come jump into my arms, little kitty," was absolutely a thing about my family that's always driven me nuts. Totally unrealistic, and it worked.

Once I got it cut and realized it was a metaphor, I also realized that if this were the first thing you really saw in the body of the film, it would set you up to be ready for anything. I knew—because we'd been trying to raise money for the film for years at that point—that people had the most prosaic, small-minded reaction to what farming is or what people who farm are and that I had to fight that.

STEVE: The problem with doing a film like this is as soon as people hear the words *farm* or *farm documentary*, their eyes glaze over. "Oh, it's another farm film, and it's going to be sentimental," or "It's going to be, 'Oh, poor farmers.'" And when they actually see it, they're stunned to find out these people are funny, they're intelligent, and the film is doing all sorts of things that they just didn't expect. Our hope was that the film would resonate with universal themes and become something that's about the passing of time, and about a marriage, and about the history of America.

You shot only 27 hours of film footage, in 16mm, for a program that runs about 88 minutes. That's very conservative.

STEVE: That was mostly imposed by budgetary problems. Every time we'd get out there, we'd budget a certain amount to shoot, and invariably we would have shot that amount halfway through the time. And then we'd have these agonizing meetings up in the bedroom trying to decide how much more stock we could order, which we knew we couldn't afford to process. Most of the footage of the film we never saw for about a year. [It was stored in the freezer at their home in Massachusetts until they could process it.] The joke was that instead of having dailies, we had yearlies.

Would you shoot it in video today?

STEVE: Probably we would, but at the time we felt strongly that the landscape of Iowa and the texture of the farm would only come across in film. The beauty of the landscape, the feel of the animals, and the smells and the corn in the summer—all of those things are an important part of why farmers do what they do, because it's such a tough life. That had to come across, mixing the financial tension and strain with the rewards of being a farmer; it played into the structure of the story. So we made sure that the seasons were very much a part of the film. Ultimately, we blew the film up to 35 mm. There's no comparison between the beauty of the 35 mm image even to 16 mm projection.

But by the same token, there were a number of scenes that we missed or gave short shrift to because we were so limited in the amount of film we could shoot. In a typical evening, we might shoot a roll or a roll and a half of film. That's 10 minutes or 15 minutes of material, which is hundreds of dollars.

You filmed the Jordan family during an extraordinarily difficult time. Were you ever concerned that the filmmaking would add to their burden?

JEANNIE: I have a very political family. The farm situation, the farm question was something I was raised dealing with, a really viable big political issue in this country. So trying to capture what it was that we felt was so tragic and shortsighted about it, through what was happening to us, I knew they'd all be behind that. I also knew I wasn't going to betray them in any way. I wasn't going to show anything that they didn't want me to show or say anything that was a breach of their privacy.

The only time that I felt bad was when we asked my parents to go to Rolfe, where I grew up. [The filmmakers bring the Jordans to a farm they'd rented for several years before taking over the family property.] I knew that the house had fallen apart, and they didn't. It was very painful for them. So when we edited it in, I asked them if they didn't want that there. My mother wasn't talking by that time [because of her illness], but she agreed with what my dad said, which was, "If you don't see what eventually will happen, you don't understand what you're talking about. You can say farmers go out of business and farms go away. How do they go away? They fall apart. They tear them down." And he said, "You have to show something like that; this is as good as anything else."

STEVE: They never asked us to stop filming. We're very careful even with subjects that we've been filming for years, we still feel very hesitant about what we film and when we're being intrusive. In Jeannie's family the most you would get might be a look of "Why are you filming this?" or, as we approached the time of the auction, one of the reasons that Jeannie becomes more of a character on screen is that her sisters were saying, "You don't think you're going to be able to just film this without helping, do you?"

The idea that you can respect the privacy of your subjects and still present an honest story might surprise some filmmakers. Do your students ever ask about that?

JEANNIE: It's not so much that they ask about it as that I tell them. A lot of students do personal films; that's kind of what all of our first instincts are. Lots of times they'll have crossed the line. A young filmmaker I know did a film about her mother dying of cancer, and it was very raw. Her mother was a very beautiful woman who, when she knew she was being filmed, would get really done up, as much as she could. But sometimes her daughter would walk in the room filming, and her mother wouldn't be prepared for it, and she'd complain a bit. One of the things I said to the filmmaker after I looked at one cut is, "I want you to look at this through your mom's eyes. And I want you to look for moments where she looks good. As much as you can tell the story with those, I think that it will still work and you don't have to embarrass her. You don't have to make her feel like, "Oh, I look so horrible." Her mother probably wasn't going to see this film, but still, it's trying to instill that kind of respect. We all have a natural instinct to protect, but I think that a lot of students, when they're young, think that means you're not being honest; that you have to show something bad or raw to tell a good story.

The stories in Troublesome Creek—*both the overall story of the Jordan farm and the individual stories that Jeannie tells, such as "Daddy Date Night" (in which she recounts nervously preparing for one-on-one time with her father, even writing out talking points in her hand)—manage to be both very personal and universal.*

STEVE: When I think of the universals that mean the most to me in the film, they're about time and family connections and the passing of history, a history that means so much now but will be completely gone in a certain number of years. You're looking for true moments. Part of it involves giving the audience room to think and images that are suggestive of those themes. The drive from the house to town, the shot is out the back, facing backward, and you're seeing this beautiful plume of dust that was kicked up, backlit by the sun. And I remember shooting it, hanging out the car door, and thinking it was beautiful, but it's also clearly a visual metaphor for leaving the past behind. And it's while Jeannie's narrating this wonderful Daddy Date Night story.

As their daughter, are you revealing information to your parents, through this film, for the first time?

JEANNIE: Yes, absolutely. Mother knew that I was scornful of her Pollyannaish view of the world, as in the scene of me giving her shit because she thought that Charlotte at the bank was her best friend. But Daddy, we were all scared of him when we were little. We aren't anymore; he's mellowed incredibly. But he was moody, he was worried, and he was just a formidable guy. He was also 6-foot-4 and has those eyebrows. So in doing the film, the one thing I could not do is depict our childhood without some hint of that. So there were two places in the film: Daddy Date Night and the Bergman reference. ["Russ came to the idea of optimism late in life," Jeannie says in narration. "The Russ I knew growing up could give a Bergman film a run for its money in the Moody Darkness Department."] But if you say something good right afterwards, which is, "He's completely turned around and is the optimist of the family," he comes away from it thinking, "I'm the optimist." But he noticed the other. We were visiting Steve's mom and stepfather. We were sitting on the porch on Martha's Vineyard, and my dad said, "Bergman." I said, "He's this Swedish filmmaker, makes really, really, depressing films, but really good films." And he said, "When you were little, did you think I was like that?" And I said, "You were like that Daddy, I didn't think you were like that." Then we had a really interesting talk. One of the things I asked him was, "Did that hurt your feelings?" And he said, "No, because everybody seems to like me anyway, who saw the film."

Tell me about the westerns that we see the Jordans watching throughout Troublesome Creek.

JEANNIE: The first time we were there to shoot, it was like, they're going to watch TV every night. They're not going to talk about anything. This is a disaster. And then part of us started realizing, wait a minute, what they're watching, by and large, are westerns. We decided we could use that as a metaphor.

STEVE: Russ loved westerns, and the whole issue of his struggle with the bank is informed by clichéd storytelling notions of good guys and bad guys, cowboys and farmers, and making a stand against your enemy. *Lonesome Dove* was on the night before the cattle auction, and it felt like some incredible piece of serendipity or fate that this story about the end of the West would be on the night that Russ was about to shed the cowboy part of himself. When you're a farmer with animals, you're partly a plant grower and you're partly an animal wrangler. And this was going to be the end of his wrangling days.

Troublesome Creek *is narrated by Jeannie. Did you always know that she would narrate?*

STEVE: Jeannie thought that hopefully the film could stand on its own without narration. In the end, the narration is a very important part of moving the story along and giving you access to layers of knowledge and storytelling that go into the past, that you just can't film. Jeannie would sit down and write stories about, for example, Daddy Date Night. She'd write a few pages and then she'd give it to me and I'd pull things out of it and then she'd rephrase them and place them; it's a kind of an organic back and forth. Collaboration can be hard, but there's so much about how you interpret the material and what's really going on in a scene, and what does the audience need to know and when, that it's very hard to make these films alone.

I think of the film as both biographical and autobiographical. And it's always walking the line between "as seen through" Jeannie's eyes, she's narrating; my eyes, because I'm shooting; but also seeking to make that presence disappear at moments when we want the audience to just be immersed in Russ and Mary Jane's story without thinking about the perspective from which you're viewing them.

The film also conveys a strong point of view without becoming a rant.

JEANNIE: To be a political film, *Troublesome Creek* had to be charming. You had to like these people, to identify with them. If I had ranted, which was in me to do, I would have lost a part of the audience because the bias would have been too obvious. The bias is obvious, but it's tempered. I'm not positive I'm right. I had to show that I was angry that there are only three million farmers left, but I'm not saying I know how to fix it or whose fault it is. It's history; it's just happening.

STEVE: As partners, Jeannie and I had very different perspectives on what was going on. Jeannie had lived it and knew it intimately, and I was from New York and didn't know anything about farms. So we combined an insider's and an outsider's perspective. The film by turns takes you deeply inside the family and then steps outside and looks at the story in a more distanced way. I think that's a way that you can take a personal narrative and help the audience to see it in larger terms.

We felt that the film's biggest influence would be if it were a compelling narrative that people would want to watch. All of the other issues emerge from the story and are there to be talked about. We took it around the Midwest, and the fervor of the discussions that would come after the film—it raises the questions to a level that people feel passionate about. We saw that as its biggest kind of political contribution.

Is that why you avoided some "traditional" documentary elements, such as interviews?

STEVE: We didn't want to do interviews. We absolutely did not want any expert testimony about anything having to do with farming or economics that would make it seem like that this was a subject being studied as opposed to a subject that was being lived. At one point, [though] we felt we had to sit Russ Jordan down to try to get him to tell us his side of the story—

JEANNIE: —Steve and I had this whole list of questions to ask him—

STEVE: —And the result of that is the banker joke that he tells. And that's it. That was his response to, "How are you doing? What do you think is going on with the bank?"

JEANNIE: That's denial, but it's a good way to do it. At least it's funny.

So Much So Fast *begins with a prologue, a transition from* Troublesome Creek. *We learn that after you'd shot the film, Jeannie's mother, Mary Jane, was diagnosed with ALS. Five years after her death, in 1995, you began filming the Heywoods: one brother has ALS, and the other quit his job to start a foundation and find a cure.*

STEVE: When Mary Jane got ALS, there was nothing you could do about it, and it was hard to even find out anything about it. This was in the very early days of the Internet. By 2000, everything had changed. There was a real explosion of research, and the Internet made it possible to find out what was going on anywhere in the world. We had been looking around for a way to do something about ALS that wouldn't just be about somebody being sick and deteriorating, and in the Heywoods we saw the possibility of an extremely vital story with a lot of growth. And also, they're a very dynamic family, and very funny. That was very important to us, that we could get at the story with a lot of black humor.

When we first talked to the Heywoods about filming, we talked about how close we needed to be in order to do this story. Actually, Jeannie said first that Mary Jane would *never* have let us make a film about her illness, and so we totally understood if the Heywoods didn't want to do it. Which I thought at the time was perhaps one of the worst pitches ever made to a film subject! But Jeannie also talked about how we're really asking to become members of their family, in a certain way. And given the amount of time we spent together over those years—which included a lot of time of *not* filming—we did become very intimate. We went on vacation with them, for example. A small portion of the time was filming, but most of it was just hanging out and eating and doing all of the other things that you do.

How did you decide how much of the illness to show, and what to leave out?

STEVE: Stephen Heywood welcomed us filming anything. At one point, he started gagging, before he got his feeding tube. And I put the camera down and went to try to help him, and afterward he said, "Why didn't you keep shooting?" And my feeling was one, I can't shoot when somebody's in that kind of distress and I might be able to do something, but also, I just really didn't feel that that was something the audience needed to see. We're already asking the audience to see and think about things they normally might turn away from.

In becoming close to your subjects, do you risk losing your perspective, your objectivity? How can you be inside but also outside at the same time?

STEVE: I would say that *So Much So Fast* is much more about intimacy than it is objectivity. I don't particularly believe in objectivity; I believe that you can give a truthful account and an account that may be balanced in various ways, but I don't think objectivity really comes into it. That said, both Jeannie and I are capable of both being very close to the people we film and stepping back when we need to. We were both deeply involved with the Heywoods' lives, but at various times would say, "We're making a film here, we can't play a role." There's a scene in the film where Jamie is quoting Melinda, from couples counseling, where she said, "These people are making a film about us and they were wondering when I was going to crack." And I know that I never had that conversation, which is what I tell Jamie, and he thinks that Jeannie did, but she didn't. We wouldn't take sides in that way, because it would be inappropriate. But we decided that we had to leave that scene in, even though it deeply misrepresents our relationship. We felt that film subjects are often misquoted and have no control over what is said about them; we might as well subject ourselves to the same treatment. And we couldn't narrate our way out of it.

Jeannie once talked with Jamie about the prime directive from *Star Trek*: When you go back in time, you can't move a rock on a planet or you'll change its history forever. And Jamie said, "Well, you can move the rocks on my planet any time you want."

In contrast to Troublesome Creek, *you shot* So Much So Fast *on video. Was that a storytelling choice?*

STEVE: Yes. With *Troublesome Creek*, we had defined the story in such a way that we were only going to shoot for a certain period of time. Whereas with *So Much So Fast*, it was much more open-ended. There were many more story lines that we were following: Stephen Heywood's experience with ALS; the foundation growing from three people in a basement to a multimillion dollar research facility; the family itself; and aspects of ALS separate from any of those things. All of those different story lines called for a much higher shooting ratio.

How many hours did you end up shooting?

STEVE: About 200. But for a project that was shot over four years, that's still not extraordinarily high.

Did you find it took longer to edit than Troublesome Creek?

STEVE: It does take longer to edit, in that you've got a lot of stuff to wade through. And also, in this case, we were following different story lines and trying to do them all justice. At one point we had a really interesting cut that was about 2 hours and 15 minutes, but our feeling was that it was just too much to sustain the emotional arc. The executive producer at German television, one of our backers, said, "You really have three films here, that are individually interesting but no one person could follow them all." Which kind of supported our feeling that the film had to be 90 minutes or less, given the intensity of what you're watching.

What were the three films, and how did you choose between them?

STEVE: One of them was about the family, one was about the foundation and the business of trying to run this non-profit research organization, and part of it was the science. We gave a lot of priority to the family side of it. But we're hoping people will see this film in a lot of different ways. It's partly a topical film about an orphan disease and how people cope with it. But it's also about time and life, and we hope that audiences will find themselves in the film, and see the metaphors that are there for them.

As you approach material in the editing room, do you think about act structure?

JEANNIE: Act structure? No. I tend to be a natural storyteller; it's something I kind of grew up with. I start from the beginning of the footage, and I'm cutting whenever I see any kind of a story. The story might be Wendy, Stephen Heywood's wife, gets tired of watching [their son] Alex try to open his sippy cup and goes over and opens it for him, but there's a whole back and forth between them. I'm probably not a good person to talk to on some level just because I really don't want to think about the big picture until I have all the little pictures together.

Isn't that the same as editing sequences?

JEANNIE: It is, it's making sequences. And I'm stringing them together and then I'll get Steve to come in and we'll watch them together. So that whatever reactions I have already in my mind, he'll have his own. Because he had his own to begin with because he shot them. So we just kind of leapfrog over each other and try to sneak up on whatever is in the material that the other one doesn't see.

In contrast to Troublesome Creek, *Steve is the narrator of* So Much So Fast, *and in addition is occasionally heard and even seen on camera. How did that come about?*

STEVE: When filming the men, it worked out better if it was just me alone. If we were both there, Stephen [Heywood]'s focus would get split, and it just wasn't working. So I would shoot them and have these conversations—much more conversations than interviews. Initially I didn't even mic myself, but Jeannie encouraged me to do it. And then, because the conversations took on the importance that they did, she felt strongly that I should be the narrator, to continue that voice and be the audience's access to the story.

You're currently producing a third feature-length documentary, about an artist who's assumed responsibility for her mentally challenged sister. What's it like to create these kinds of films, which you describe as "nonfiction novels" because of their complexity and layering?

STEVE: I remember when we started *So Much So Fast*, the first time we went out with equipment—after not doing that kind of filming for a long time—we looked at each other: "Are we really going to do this again?" It's a tremendous commitment, and you have to develop this incredible kind of symbiosis with your subjects, where you're getting close to them. On some level you feel kind of parasitic, that you're living off their life in a certain way. In another way you feel invisible because you're filming all of this, but you don't know if they see you as a person or as a someone who's making the film. Those are questions along the way. But the reason to do it is you end up with a kind of film that you can't get any other way.

I think for both Jeannie and me, it's a matter of needing to really get on the inside of something, to be able to tell a story with that detail and deep knowledge. Having wrestled with those issues over that length of time makes for a much deeper film, and there's also the throughline of time, how the world changes over time. As much as we'd like to finish these films faster, they get a tremendous amount of power from showing life unfold.

Any last words of advice on storytelling?

STEVE: Think before you shoot, know what it is you're looking at, and have a sense of what you want a shot to convey. Shots don't just happen; they're an expression that is concocted between the camera person, the subject, and serendipity. And you should always be thinking, "What is it that I want to take out of this scene, what do I want audiences to see?" You're always putting yourself in a seat in the theater when you're shooting, or you should be, and thinking, "What am I revealing? When do I want you to know that this character is sitting over here or that this person is frowning?" And that's a calculation that you're doing both when you're shooting and you're editing. How to structure a scene to reveal things.

JEANNIE: Be respectful of the privacy of who you're covering, especially if you're making personal films. Even if you're doing a very intimate film you can do that. Unless there's some real evil that you're dealing with, I think that people need to be careful and respectful of who they're shooting.

17

Victoria Bruce and Karin Hayes

Although their fathers had been lifelong friends, Victoria Bruce and Karin Hayes did not meet until shortly before they began their first film, *The Kidnapping of Ingrid Betancourt*. At the time, Victoria was a science writer with a master's degree in geology, and the author of *No Apparent Danger* (HarperCollins, 2001), about a tragic expedition into a volcano in Colombia. Karin, a graduate of the University of California in Los Angeles, was working as an associate producer in Washington, D.C.

Following *The Kidnapping of Ingrid Betancourt*, the two filmed *Held Hostage*, a short film about three Americans who work for a private military contractor and are also being held by Colombian guerrillas. They are currently raising money for *Pip & Zastrow*, the story of two friends who joined together to keep peace in Annapolis, Maryland, after the assassination of the Rev. Dr. Martin Luther King, Jr., in 1968.

In 2002, Ingrid Betancourt was a senator in Colombia, campaigning for president and calling for reform of a corruption-plagued government, in a country that had endured 40 years of civil war. How did you first meet her?

VICTORIA: Ingrid had a deal with HarperCollins to do the English version of her autobiography, *Until Death Do Us Part*, which was first published in France. So she came here to go on book tour. A year before, I'd gone on book tour, and I had this wonderful publicist who knew that I'd fallen in love with Colombia when I wrote my book and that I wanted to do something positive, to show a positive side of Colombia. He was also the publicist for Ingrid's book tour, and he called me up and said, "Vicky, you have to meet this woman."

So I read the book and thought, "This is great." Because here's a way to put a face on Colombia, the face that I saw, which was bravery and beauty and compassion, which Ingrid encompasses all of. So I met with Ingrid for an hour, in January 2002. She was running around doing all these interviews. I didn't really have a feel of what I wanted to do with her, I thought maybe a magazine article. Somebody suggested maybe a film, a documentary. So I met with National Geographic Television and tried to interest them in the idea of following Ingrid on the campaign trail. National Geographic has some kinds of series where they have journalists out in the field, and I was thinking I would do something like that, with me as the journalist. They seemed interested, but a couple of weeks went by, so that wasn't happening.

It's already January 2002, the campaign is under way and the presidential elections are in May. So I imagine you had to move quickly. Is that when you called Karin?

VICTORIA: I had met Karin twice by then, and I knew she spoke Spanish. [Karin attended both the University of Guadalajara and the Universidad de Costa Rica before going to UCLA.] And I knew she knew how to make films, so I called her.

KARIN: I read Ingrid's book and just thought, "I have to do this, this is an amazing woman." At that time I was on contract still, I was an associate producer at Cronkite Ward and had a couple more months in my contract. But Vicky and I met in New York and we were trying to decide in what style we were going to do the documentary. Because initially she was thinking, journalist. And I was thinking about *The War Room*, that vérité style, like in the campaign headquarters.

At this point, she's a free woman, and you're planning to tell the story of the campaign?

KARIN: Yes, we were going to follow her on the campaign trail: Here's this woman running for president in Latin America, a woman who started her own political party, who's been very controversial in Congress and the Senate, she's led hunger strikes, she's pointed out all of the corrupt people in Congress, she's made a lot of enemies, and she's just taking Colombia by storm—or had the potential to. So we thought how fascinating it would be to follow her through these little towns and see people's reaction to her campaign.

Did you have any funding?

KARIN: No, [not] with all of this really happening in such a short time. The next thing I remember, I saw on CNN that she'd been kidnapped. [In February, Senator Betancourt was kidnapped by the Revolutionary Armed Forces of Colombia (FARC), a guerrilla group with whom the government had been negotiating.]

VICTORIA: We had talked to her right before that. Ingrid knew we were coming; it was sort of going to be more set up. "Well, if you want to go see the FARC, we'll see the FARC, if you want to do this—" because this was before the peace process broke down. There were a lot of journalists meeting with FARC in those days, and so we could have driven a bus through FARC territory. That's what we were planning on. And she said, "I'm going down to meet with the FARC on the fourteenth." And actually we have footage from that; we didn't shoot it—

That's the meeting in your film, with everyone around the table?

VICTORIA: That's the meeting at the table where she says, "No more kidnapping." And that was nine days before her kidnapping. So we knew she was going there, we were setting up, getting ready, and we were planning on going a couple of days later than we ended up going. But when she was kidnapped we just went into Plan B. Karin was still working, so I had to go down by myself.

From your press materials, it sounds like Karin gave you, Vicky, an all-night crash course in video production. You had Karin's PD150, your own video camera, and some rented sound gear. . . .

VICTORIA: She tried to make me bring a flak jacket. My pack's already too heavy—

KARIN: I was there with a mixer, explaining how to use a mixer in case she had to. And she said, "You've got to record this so I can remember how to do it." So we're filming my explanation of how to use the mixer and we're testing all the mics and all this.

VICTORIA: And white balance, I didn't know what that was . . . .

KARIN: I was trying to give her the crash course. Some basics, and then when she was down there we would talk. And I'd ask, "What'd you guys get?" and she'd tell me, and I'd [suggest], "What about this and this?" She's really good at interviews and knowing how to get the story, and I was more about the technical: Did you get shots of this, and b-roll, you know—

VICTORIA: And our cameraman [Cesar Pinzón] didn't speak any English. I speak a little bit of Spanish, and we got a great fixer [Mayra Rodriguez] who became our associate producer on the film, who was wonderful. But it was a little bit scary, for me.

KARIN: And she was shooting second camera.

VICTORIA: I shot a lot of second camera.

KARIN: And then the cinematographer used my camera. And then one of the best things was, she left her Panasonic one-chip camera down there when she left Colombia, after that first trip, so that if anything happened to Ingrid—

VICTORIA: We figured she'd be released, we really did. And that would be a happy ending, and they'd have a camera to shoot with. Because our cameraman didn't have his own camera—

KARIN: It was stolen when Ingrid was kidnapped; he'd given it to the sound guy, our sound guy [who was present but not held]. But with the camera we left down there, he captured the whole funeral scene—

VICTORIA: The father's funeral, and the kids calling Ingrid on the radio. We wouldn't have had the kids in there at all, because that was the only time they were back in Colombia. So it was great that we had left that camera there. And it was the brother, the cameraman's brother who shot it; the cameraman was out of town.

After she's been kidnapped, the family decides to continue the campaign without her, carrying a life-sized cardboard torso of Ingrid around with them. Given the changed circumstances, why do you think they continued to allow the film?

VICTORIA: They were surrounded by media because they were running a campaign. So it wasn't like we came into their lives during a crisis time and no one else was around.

KARIN: Many times, we blended into all the other media that was there. It was like a blur to [her husband] Juan Carlos, I think. And it was only in the very end, I remember the last day, we bought dinner for Juan Carlos and took it to his house, a kind of wrap-up. And he said to us, "Wow, I'm really going to miss not having you guys here. Because it's been company for me."

VICTORIA: Not that we'd really even talk to him very much. We'd ride in the car with him, he kind of always had us around. The hardest thing for me originally going down there was meeting Juan Carlos. When you first meet him you're like, "Oh please, he's going to be a drag, this can't be our main character." I mean on camera, he's not dynamic, he sort of mumbles. We only did one sit-down interview with him. That was it. The rest was just shooting. We didn't want to sit him down again. You didn't have to ask him, "How're you feeling today, Juan Carlos?" Which is the question he was getting all the time.

KARIN: He's a little closed off. Hard to get to know.

VICTORIA: But when you cut the film together, then the human being comes out. Trust that the character will come out in your shooting, if you spend enough time with them.

KARIN: But also, I was kind of hypersensitive about not wanting it to become sappy, to show every scene that [Ingrid's mother] Yolanda's crying in. I mean, she was strong, but at some point in most of our footage there was a point where she usually broke down. But I didn't want to be . . . what's the word? Exploitative. I didn't want to put in crying just to pull people's heart strings. I really wanted to be honest with it, not force it.

VICTORIA: The kids hang up the phone [after leaving a voice message they hope will reach their mother, via radio], and then it immediately goes to this happy music, and it's campaigning again. We made a real conscious decision to pull you out of that: It's sad, and then, onward.

In terms of vérité filming, were there ever times when you intervened? I'm thinking, for example, of the powerful image in which Juan Carlos appears to be holding his wife's cardboard hand.

VICTORIA: We have so much of that, we had so many shots. Our cinematographer was very good. Sometimes he would cut off audio in the middle of somebody saying something wonderful, it drove me crazy, but when he had a good shot he would be on it. That's the way Juan Carlos carried her, and sometimes he'd just look at her and sometimes he'd touch her. The one thing we did ask him to do is ride his motorcycle. It's not pivotal, it's sort of a transition, the end of the act, coming down before the election.

You were there in March, and again in May, for the election?

KARIN: Sixteen days for the first shoot, and then ten days for the second. And in between that time, we thought, okay, March/April, we're going to cut a trailer together, and we're going to get funding, we're going to get grants.

VICTORIA: So we could go back in May and have the money. That didn't happen.

So you really didn't become part of the family while you were there— you blended in with the media instead, and weren't there for that long.

VICTORIA: We've become closer to them after, especially Karin. But we were there for four weeks, total.

In all, you filmed about 100 hours of material. Tell me about the process of editing it.

VICTORIA: That's another thing; we didn't realize that we'd have to learn how to edit until we came home with the second batch, and we were like, "Now what do we do? We still have no money." My ex-boyfriend gave me $15,000, and we spent that on the first shoot.

KARIN: And then the second shoot, we just said, "Okay, we're each taking this much out of our savings, and the rest we're putting on credit cards."

VICTORIA: We ended up being able to pay it all back, but after our second film. With Ingrid we would have broken even, because we've had international sales.

KARIN: We thought we'd hire an editor, but we had no money. We started doing the transcribing ourselves as soon as we got home. We had said we wanted to have the film done before she'd been kidnapped for a year.

VICTORIA: The goal was to apply to Sundance and Slamdance.

So you taught yourselves Final Cut, and worked on borrowed computers in Karin's parents' dining room?

KARIN: We bought Final Cut and we bought six Final Cut Pro books, and then we sat down and just started cutting. And we had already started trying to collect all the interviews from radio that Ingrid had done in English [during her book tour].

VICTORIA: The reason we did that is because, okay, here we have all this footage but who cares about Ingrid? We have some campaign footage, but you're not going to like her much, you don't even know her. So Karin started contacting all of the media outlets where she'd done interviews, to get the tapes from there, and that's where we ended up cutting her whole audio narration from.

KARIN: We had five different interviews to cut from. *Fresh Air* [NPR] was probably the longest, it was an hour. The others were maybe half hours.

And you also use some stock footage—home movies, campaign footage, etc.—that you got from a range of sources.

VICTORIA: Some of the campaign footage was shot by Cesar. And then we got a lot from Colombian television. Cesar was really connected, he had seven brothers working in TV, and so he was able to negotiate and get us the Colombian stock footage for very little. I think we ended up paying for 14 seconds (20-second minimum) of CNN that cost us $1,800. But most of the footage and audio, Karin and Cesar negotiated, we got for very little.

So this is late in 2002, and you spent about three months editing, still without any financial support.

KARIN: Four months, maybe. To January, because we were up to the last wire.

VICTORIA: We used to put sticky notes on our computer, that said, *How's Ingrid's life?* Because we'd get so miserable, start complaining to each other. Neither of us had boyfriends, we had no social life, we used to sit by each other, at 3:00 in the morning, editing.

KARIN: And another thing we did is, I think it was Vicky who came up with this idea, the Shoeless Children's Fund. And whoever complains next has to start contributing—

VICTORIA: —a dollar,

KARIN: And whoever complains the least gets to choose the charity.

VICTORIA: The Shoeless Children's Fund. We still say that every once in a while when one of us starts complaining too much.

Did you hope your film might make a difference?

KARIN: We were really hoping that it would have some kind of effect. And mobilize people in a way. We just got two calls, Amnesty International wants to screen it in Chile and Bolivia. So it's starting to get out there. But in terms of mobilizing in the U.S., I mean certainly the people who have seen it, the overwhelming response is "What can we do?"

VICTORIA: But they can't do anything,

KARIN: That's the hardest thing.

VICTORIA: Write your congressman or something.

In the fall of 2002, I was at an industry gathering where Vicky did what audience members are never supposed to do—it was a panel of commissioning editors, and when they opened the floor for questions, you pitched your film. The audience was a bit riled, but an editor at HBO asked to see you.

VICTORIA: "What's the question?" Well, I did PR for NASA, so I have a PR background. I was really nervous because I knew I was going to do it. I told Karin I was going to do it.

KARIN: From the very beginning, when I was imagining where did I want my film to be, and what style did it need to be, I was thinking HBO.

VICTORIA: And then I wouldn't give her [HBO] the tape, that was the best. Because it was going to be playing at Slamdance, so I told her to come see it. That's what they tell you, that you never should give a screener. You should never let them sit alone with a TV on a bad day. Get them in a room with other people, get audience reaction, a full house, and then you get your distributors to watch your film.

The film screened in competition at Slamdance on January 23, 2003 — a few weeks shy of the first anniversary of Betancourt's kidnapping. The title was Missing Peace. *When and why was it changed?*

VICTORIA: After Slamdance, HBO acquired the film for two years. They wanted to do some re-editing, and we worked for another two months with their editor, Geof Bartz. The most important thing they changed was that they wanted you to know that Ingrid was kidnapped up front. We had a slow build of getting to know this woman. And Sheila Nevins [said] that you will care so much more about her time with her kids in the home video if you know she's going to be gone soon. It's brilliant.

It's a really nice first act. Once you've made it clear that she's been kidnapped, you build a sense of who she is and what she's doing, and she herself, in voice-over, narrates. At the end of the first act, the story returns to the kidnapping, and she's no longer in the picture — except as a cardboard cut-out.

VICTORIA: I think that's just sort of a "gimme" storytelling — that's what happened to everyone around her, that's what happened to her family. To keep bringing her back wouldn't have had that effect. And I think that we also realized that this isn't a story about a woman, it's the story about a man. Really. And it became the story of Juan Carlos, how he changes from a guy who never votes to a guy who's a huge political animal at the end.

KARIN: We still see her and how she's in it, but it's about him and the family and the campaign and what a family of a kidnapped person goes through, even though she was in an extraordinary situation, being a presidential candidate. Here's Ingrid, and she's a face for all of the hundreds of other people who are kidnapped and the 50 to 60 people who are being held as political hostages now.

Betancourt was still in captivity when your film was released, and remains in captivity as of now, June 2006. Were there steps you had to take to ensure that the film didn't make her situation worse?

VICTORIA: We let her family watch it [before it was done]. Typically I would recommend that you not let your characters watch your film, but we didn't know what things were scary politically. They definitely didn't want to make the current president look bad, whoever was going to win, because that's their only hope to get Ingrid out. Some people said, "Are you making her so high profile that the FARC's going to think she's even more valuable, and keep her kidnapped longer?" But the family themselves, and especially Juan Carlos, a former advertising man, were always of the opinion, "Keep it in the media, keep it alive, keep the story alive." And it has turned out that the family is very supportive of the film. But at the time I think they were very worried, it's a very personal film about their family.

Did you intentionally use dramatic three-act structure for the film? The first act ends, as mentioned, with the kidnapping. The second act drives to election day. The third act continues through to the outcome—she doesn't win, but she does get enough votes to save the party she's founded. And then we see the videos released by the kidnappers, to prove that Betancourt is still alive.

KARIN: Vicky's really good with storytelling. She wrote her book, she was a journalist. And for me, I knew about the three-act structure, and I knew that it had to have an arc, our story. And that's what I was focusing on.

VICTORIA: We got a lot of advice from a lot of friends, we would have people watch rough cuts along the way.

KARIN: There was one point when we had some friends of ours who had gone to film school, and they came and sat with us at one point for like six hours, until 3:00 in the morning, going through our film, bit by bit, the rough cut, advising us on how we're editing. And I remember they sat down with me and said,

"Karin, you have no second act. There's no character arc, nothing. It sucks. You have to do something."

And then after HBO acquired it, there was the additional editing, in New York.

VICTORIA: We'd go up there and see what Geof was doing, and he would send us things.

In some of the reviews I've read, people have taken the film to task for not offering more time to the other political candidates, or to FARC. How did you decide to just give a platform to Ingrid, and not, for example, let her assertions about corruption be challenged?

VICTORIA: We did interview all of the other candidates, except [Alvaro] Uribe; we interviewed him after the election because we couldn't get an interview previous. And the reason that we didn't put them in—I mean, we didn't have her specifically attacking any of the candidates. There was something in one of her audios that said, "I saw how all of the Congress was bought by so-and-so's money." And if you listen to the audio very carefully that "all" was taken out and we found a "some" somewhere in her audio and stuck it in there, for legal reasons.

A lot of times, some very strongly-opinionated Colombians or even Americans will say, "You didn't tell the FARC side" or "You didn't tell the paramilitary side." And you say, "Colombia is such a complicated country. There's just no way to do a political story and a personal story." But then we did *Held Hostage*, and so now we tell people, "Buy our next film." Because we cover the drug dealers, the paramilitaries, the guerrillas; these are all the factions. To me, it's not hard, because I feel like I'm more of a storyteller. You can pick one side. This is a narrative and that's Ingrid's opinion.

KARIN: I think that in doing documentaries there's that freedom, because you can choose how you want to tell your story. People challenge us and say, "Ingrid did this, and Ingrid did that, and she wasn't all this good." Well, that's fine, because everyone's going to have their own opinion on that. We wanted to make a film where people would see the story, maybe it would inspire them to find out more about her, find out more about Colombia. The next step is for the audience. It's not up to us to say, "You must believe this, you must believe that." You need to think about it and make your own decisions. We're telling one story.

VICTORIA: If you are an activist, as many documentary filmmakers are, a way to really touch people is by finding a human story. Rather than an issue piece. I watched *China Blue* [produced and directed by Micha X. Peled], which is about the Chinese garment industry. And they actually got inside one of the sweatshops and lived with a 13-year-old girl who works there, followed her from her home town. It was extraordinary.

You're onto a third film collaboration. What's the secret to a successful partnership?

KARIN: I think we both bring different things to the table, which is a good thing. Someone was asking me once, how do we figure things out, like if we both disagree on how something should go. And I would say that if either one of us has a stronger argument for why it should be this way, then the other one says okay, fine—

VICTORIA: Or is more passionate about it—

KARIN: —More passionate about it, we'll say fine, we'll try it that way—

VICTORIA: We always tried it the other person's way.

18

Ric Burns

Ric Burns won two Emmys for *The Civil War*, which he produced with his brother, Ken. Through his own company, Steeplechase Films, he has created an extensive body of award-winning work, primarily for American public television. His films include *Eugene O'Neill*, *Ansel Adams*, *Coney Island*, *The Donner Party*, the six-hour series *The Way West*, and the seven-episode series *New York*, completed before the September 11, 2001, terrorist attacks. He followed up with an eighth episode, *The Center of the World*, about the World Trade Center, which he was completing at the time of this interview in 2003.

Of the ideas that cross your desk, how do you decide which to make into films?

For me, in the bundle of words "historical documentary filmmaker," there's no question that the word "film" is the most important. And that's because of how powerful and dreamlike film can be. Certainly the experience of film that I value most is an experience of being taken to some very deep place by the flow of light and shadow and sound and words and music, which are the elements of film. It's always about contrasts. Visually, thematically, emotionally. Think about the Donner Party. Read a one-paragraph account of the Donner Party, and if it's accurate, you'll feel that interplay of brightness and darkness. In one of the biggest years of the American dream, 87 people go West thinking they're going to find Paradise and end up in a terrible nightmare. Say the words "New York" and try not to have in your mind, very swiftly, the New York skyline. Its most powerful moment is at twilight, where it's both tremendously, luminously shiny and also powerfully black and dark.

In choosing a story, the pilot light goes on when you sense that this is material that will allow you to exploit that dream power of film. Use that basic feeling to ask yourself, well, what's the story here? What's the structure of a film that will penetrate and elaborate the story? And in the case of New York, I think the most gratifying thing about working on that project—which sprawled to 14.5 hours and now we're working on another two-hour film about the World Trade Center—is that, at the very center of it, a very simple, provisional explanation revealed itself as to, why did New York become such a shining and dark place? And that was that at the very beginning it was founded as a relentlessly commercial colony, unlike the religious colonies that were its rivals at the time.

From there, how do you focus a historical topic that's broad and complex?

Every step along the way you ask, "What's absolutely crucial to telling the story? What advances the story?" You've got to start with the Dutch [settlers], you understand that. Then there are the English; you don't spend that much time with the English—they did some things that were different, but many things that were the same. So you apply the basic narrative yardstick, which is: try not to tell any story more than once. So there's only one riot. There's only one fire. There's only one burst of skyscrapers. There's only one war. In other words, always find that moment where the nature of the particular story you're telling is caught at its highest arc. Tell the story of the draft riots of 1863, the most catalytic and, to this day, the worst instance of civil unrest in American history.

You try to be as severe as possible as you go through the chronology of your subject matter. Ask, "What are the central themes that structure the material? Which are the moments that elaborate those themes most powerfully?" And you use those central themes as a kind of divining rod to show you—amongst the literally infinite amount of material, in the case of something like New York—where the gold lies. Where's the stuff that's most powerful? Where is the stuff that most embodies the themes, elaborates them, and drives them forward?

How do you define theme, and how do you handle themes in your work?

Theme is the most basic lifeblood of a film: *This* is what this thing is about. The story is the vehicle and the theme is the tone and emotion; theme tells you the tenor of your story.

Theme makes you see and feel the correspondences between different elements of your story. How do Harlem in the 1920s, the explosion of mass media, Al Smith, the stock market rise, and the skyscraper wars all correspond with each other? Theme is, in a sense, vibrating through all of them. At its worst, the theme becomes a kind of cookie cutter which causes everything to look the same. At its best, it makes you understand the metaphoric relationships between things which are, on the surface, more or less dissimilar, more or less alike. Al Smith's pursuit of the presidency, F. Scott Fitzgerald's pursuit of Zelda and the great American novel, a modest investor's pursuit of wealth, and somebody else's pursuit of the highest building in the world, all stand in a corresponding metaphoric relationship to each other, which doesn't mean that they all mean the same thing. You understand them as resonating within the same ambiance, and that can't help but make each of them more powerful.

Not all historical documentaries explore themes; some present a story or situation without that added complexity.

What I know from my own work is that if you do it quickly, you can't possibly get the themes. It's one thing to understand the theme and write it out on the back of a matchbook. But then to actually cause the theme to flow through the film, that's really difficult. First, you find the right theme. That can take a while. You articulate it correctly, in relationship to the actual material, the research, the stories, which can take another while. Then you have to stitch it together in such a fashion that the theme actually stands up and walks like some Frankenstein monster. That's where so much of the work of filmmaking, in the writing and editing, takes place. And you keep comparing what you've done to what you intuitively know it could be and should be.

When and how does the storytelling take shape?

You create your first description of what the film is. Sometimes it's in the form of a letter to a colleague, sometimes it's in the form of a two-page proposal to get seed money. But every iteration in some sense is a version of the film, and you try to give that iteration as powerful and intense an articulation as you can. And then, when you move to the next articulation—longer, more detailed, more structured, more intense, hopefully more involving—you don't abandon the previous iteration. You use it as the point of departure. And as you do that, it begins to vary. Not four episodes but five; not one hour each but two. In my case, it's never shifted in a way that has retroactively obliterated the original intuition; it elaborates it. It's very much like rolling a snowball down a variegated hill. The snow is sort of wet here and dry there and dirty here and pristine there, and as you move, the snowball acquires its own eccentric shape and velocity. But it's always growing organically in relationship to the material and the hillside that it's moving down.

When there's a potential to research indefinitely, how do you know when to stop?

I think any successful creative project exists within an oscillation between obsessiveness and decisiveness, and you can't abandon either. The obsessiveness that makes you keep on looking for more material, another photograph, shoot another interview, delve deeper, is in a sense always there. A metaphor might be Odysseus strapped to the mast, listening to the sirens singing, and what they're singing is, "There's more stuff here. There could be more material. There must be more." But you create a structure in which you're not only Odysseus strapped to the mast with his ears unwaxed, you're also a disciplined crew moving forward, making decisions. "We're going to use this and go with it." Anytime anything works, you never let go of it. And that's the decisiveness. You say, "Right. It really works." Always rare. That's not to say that at some point you don't discover in the process that the things you like best are no longer going to fit. But you hold onto them, and by holding onto them, they take up space and begin to delimit what you can do.

Do you write a draft of the script before you shoot?

It's really happening in tandem. For example, right now we're working on a biography of the World Trade Center, an eighth episode to *New York*. We have a very clear outline of what the film is, and a kind of a treatment that's about 50 pages long, a corralling of the material likely to be in the story. But it's not a script. It's a chronologically-arranged treatment of what feels like the principal historical materials, an iteration that has enough structure in it to tell you where the themes of the film are going to emerge, where they develop to their highest point, and where they transform.

Armed with that, you can do interviews; you know how to craft questions. And you can always go out and shoot live cinematography, whether it's cinéma vérité shooting or live shooting of landscapes. The ideal thing is to do at least some of the production, in addition to interviews, while you're doing the script, because you're going to find that there's material you didn't expect.

For example, everyone knows of Philippe Petit, the man who walked on the tightrope between the Twin Towers. What I didn't know until doing an interview with him was that he's going to be a huge part of the film, not just a little five-minute moment halfway through. Here was a man who in 1968 conceived, sitting in a dentist's office in Paris when he was 18, the fantastic ambition that he wanted to be a high-wire artist and walk between the two towers of the World Trade Center, which had not even been started. When he did it, in August of 1974, the buildings were reviled for their brutality and their kind of inhuman scale in lower Manhattan. And suddenly here was this slender, unlikely Frenchman, dancing on the edge of nothing, as crowds of New Yorkers looked up in astonishment. That juxtaposition of fragility and power—and sort of vertiginous aerial theatricality—is the essence of a crucial aspect of the World Trade Center. So you discover that this person you thought was a little footnote expands to become part of the psychological center of the film.

Six months ago, if someone had said, "Will you interview Philippe Petit?" I would have said, "Probably." But luck is a residue of design. The design comes from that intuitive conviction that the story is powerful, and from the themes that you articulate on the basis of that conviction. That design then allows you to go out in the world and chance, so to speak, upon all sorts of elements: interviewees, places that you might shoot, quotes from a book, episodes of the history that you knew nothing about. And that's why that interplay between obsessiveness and decisiveness is so crucial.

Tell me about your process of editing.

The analogy, I think, is writing, by which I don't mean to say that it's verbal. You're trying to create a sequence that is as powerful and intense and engaging a sequence as you can. And in a way, that's what writing is. You start out with a sentence, and then you elaborate it into a paragraph, a few pages, a treatment, a script. And all the while you're collecting material for the film. When you sit down to edit, in a sense, you're writing—not with words and ideas alone, but with words and ideas, images, interview moments, spoken material, archival newsreel footage, sound, music. You're still trying to sequence them, still trying to elaborate that sequence, which, like a five-word summary of your film on paper, sings a little bit and has some shape to it and engages somehow.

Do you use a dramatic act structure?

I think that that's a very sophisticated way of thinking about it, which probably one does whether one knows one is doing it or not. If you get to the point where you're actually driving forward the process of creating a story—and it's getting better—that's what you do. We have a very simple, very homely formula, which came up in the editing room of *The Civil War* 15 years ago, which is, just give and take away. It moves by the old structure of contrast. Now, if those contrasts were simply alternating back and forth, the film would be completely repetitive, like a red light going on and off and on and off. So that dynamic of giving and taking away has to itself have an arc of change in it. A value is posited, you care about something, some problem is put in its path, and it develops and transforms over time.

And your protagonists aren't necessarily human. In the series New York, *the city itself is the protagonist.*

Right. You have to be true to your subject. A mistake that's often made is to confuse the component parts of a subject for the subject itself. Say, for instance, you were doing a film about the West, the conquering of the American West in the second half of the 19th century. Immediately, the building of the transcontinental railway, the Battle of Little Bighorn, George Armstrong Custer,

Sitting Bull, or the events leading up to Wounded Knee—all those stories, events, people, moments, clearly compete to be part of your story. But what can happen is you can be seduced into thinking that your film is really about that person or that moment or that thing. It may very well be fine to spend all your time talking about George Armstrong Custer. But if you've determined that you're doing a film about The Way West between 1845 and 1893, you can't take the cheap and easy solution of just being beguiled and distracted by the most dynamic, dramatic, component part. And I think that what happens in historical documentary films very frequently, to their detriment, is that the people who make them get diverted and don't stick to their guns, which is "I started with this subject. There's only one hero to this story."

That's the most challenging thing, I find, in doing these films: The part is always seductive and the whole is very elusive. Yet it's the whole which is your subject. It's the thing that creates coherence and narrative trajectory, relates incidental components to deeper themes. It's the whole that gives you dramatic movement. Not a kind of dramatic movement that keeps you penned within the circumstances of a local story, but dramatic movement that sends you arcing out across a vast amount of space and time. And if you discover that there's even as many as two heroes, you've got two stories. You've got two films.

How do you ensure that a film is balanced in its storytelling?

One big difference between a certain kind of written history and historical documentary films is that the former can afford to be discursive and self-qualifying and nuanced, without jeopardizing, necessarily, their power. The latter, films, cannot afford to do that. In my view, the way complexity gets into film is not by trying, at the same time, to say something is five different things, but by over time showing the many different facets of something.

I gnash my teeth at academic historians who seem to have dipped into 10 minutes of a film and say, "You claim that New York is all about commerce and greed. Doesn't that seem a powerfully capitalistic position to be taking?" Well, right, there are those moments where that was the facet of New York that we were holding up. Because film is, in certain ways, a reductively simple medium. It wants you to be transfixed at every moment by one simple thing. So how do you get complexity? Not simultaneously, but consecutively. You get the banker now, and then later you get the labor leader. You get the poet here, and later you get the master builder. When you're with the poet, don't say, "And at the same time, there was a master builder and there was a politician." To try to do more than one thing at once compromises the intensity, which is the promise of film's engagement with the audience.

I think viewers, filmgoers, TV watchers, understand that film works best by engaging you very powerfully in a sequence of "nows." Now we're here, and now we're here, and now we're here. New York turns out to have the logic of capitalism, but also the logic of alternatives to capitalism. It's a place about building fantastic public works, but it's also a place about stopping the building of fantastic public works. It's about powerful men who rule for 50 years, and about 144 disenfranchised women who in their fiery deaths catalyzed tremendous social change. It's all those things. And I think that what filmmakers are always vulnerable to is that any moment extracted from the flow of a film seems to be reductive. If it weren't reductive, it wouldn't work as film.

Do you think about what you want the audience to take away from a film?

The illusion that film performs, when it's powerful, is it gets people to confuse the experience of the film with the experience of the past—to get audiences to almost unconsciously confuse the aesthetic experience they're having as the film unfolds with their imagination of what it must have been like to be there in the past. In a way, I think that for historical documentary filmmakers, that's the way you animate the past. By creating, paradoxically, a present, which is the film that you're watching now, which is so aesthetically and psychologically and emotionally and intellectually engaging, ideally, that people say, "Right, that's the past. How amazing Coney Island was at the turn of the 20th century." But, of course, it's not the past. And that's the great poignancy of historical films. You're using the elements which history has handed down to us, or which we have created in the present, to stand in for those things.

The thing I've always found most difficult to describe about filmmaking, which I think is the most important thing, is that you must get people to believe in the existence of something other than what they're seeing on the screen. They have to believe that beyond that frame they're looking at—up above it, off to the left where they can't see, before the moment they're looking at, after the moment they're experiencing—there's something more. If you do that, which is, I find, very difficult to do, then what you see is that people are transfixed. They're not just looking at a shining screen. They believe that these are real people, real events, real moments, caught in a whole dynamic which is infinitely mysterious and dense and they're not sure where it's going, but they sure as hell care about the outcome.

Which means you've engaged the viewers; they're active, not passive.

Right. It's easy to tell people what a story is; it's very difficult to tell a story. When films simply tell you what the story is, they're basically two-dimensional maps rather than four-dimensional universes. Storytelling is "once upon a time." It's a ship that comes around a corner, and you can see it and you're somehow thrilled by it, caught in the "now" and a whole bunch of potential futures which haven't yet occurred. You're saying, "What's going to happen here?" When films tell stories, when they engage you in the process of a story, then they work.

In terms of the ethics of using archival material, are there guidelines as to what you will or won't do in your work?

I think there's kind of a contract which any film or filmmaker establishes with the viewer. And that is you, the viewer, trust me. I will always use the thing that's closest to the truth that I possibly can. Now, that may turn out to be not very close at all sometimes. The purity of the intention of the filmmaker is crucial. And the intention is double—the truth, but the intensity of its presentation as well. If you're on the Donner Party trail, which took place 150, 160 years ago, there were no cameras there. Therefore, if a shot of a wagon train—which is, in fact, a still shot from a film made by the Church of the Latter Day Saints in the 1940s—works and is not a lie, it's because a moment's reflection will tell people there were no shots of the Donner Party. So why do we believe it? Because we're being taken there by an assembly of story elements: verbal elements, facts, artifacts, quotes, interviews, shots that are plausibly, clearly, demonstrably, from the route.

I think that there's a way in which you can be absolutely faithful to the archival elements and ruin a story. There are historical documentary filmmakers who apparently believe that having the original photograph is all you need to bring somebody into the truth and to make the film powerful. That's nonsense. It may well be that the shadow of a hand of a live actor, at a certain moment, will bring you closer to the truth of Abraham Lincoln than all the Brady photographs in the world. Conversely, maybe it won't. Maybe the reenactment will be terribly done. So it really has to do with the ingenuity of the filmmaker. Sometimes, you might actually choose to use an element that's less historically authentic, because it works better and is therefore a better thing to do. The essential purity of the intention of the filmmaker—to tell you the truth but to bring you intensely into the dynamic of the story—is being honored.

What about the underlying research?

Not only do you do book and archival research, but you always work closely with academic advisors. Tampering with the facts is absolutely inconceivable. It doesn't mean that you don't make a million mistakes, but you fact check and you change it. When filmmakers begin to play fast and loose with a fact, they begin to rupture the essential contract that they make with the audience. Even though the audience can't quite tell where or how or why, they may not have that knowledge, they swiftly and intuitively understand that somebody's bullshitting them. You need to feel the integrity of a film. It's solid. It's well wrought. It's made of materials that seem apt. It's well balanced. We bring an enormous amount of expertise, we viewers of films, when we sit down and let the lights go low. And in that sense, viewers are the best critics of films.

How do you begin to think about visualizing a subject for which there is no photographic record?

[Photographer] Alfred Stieglitz formulated the idea that a photograph was not an objective representation of an outer external reality but was an equivalent of an inner state, an emotional state. And I think that film, being a sequence of images, is in a sense simply a more elaborate version of that. Sometimes a plethora of available archival visual imagery can make you think that that's what the movie is, and not pay as much attention to the fact that it's always about finding an equivalent. When you're obliged to invent the imagery, it in a sense focuses you on what your job should be anyway.

The great example of this is Custer and Crazy Horse. The most photographed American of the 19th century, except for Abraham Lincoln, is George Armstrong Custer. And there's no photograph of Crazy Horse. I'm not convinced that it was easier to bring the emotional reality of George Armstrong Custer to life just because there were all those photographs. With Crazy Horse, you were obliged to go to landscape shots and modest recreations to find the psychological resonance. There was no easy way out.

Will you talk about the rhythms of editing, how you know when to fade to black for a moment, or when to let a sequence play?

The units of construction of films are scenes that have beginnings and middles and ends and their own rhythms and climaxes. In a story like *The Donner Party*, when you've had one climax, you need to fade out and have that moment of emotional pause and closure. Film is essentially musical, like any temporal art form. It's all about incremental progressive effect of all the events that make up the flow. Do you need a beat, will the flow become too relentless if there's not that pause? Do I need to receive the information I was receiving in that last scene at a slightly statelier pace, or do I need to speed it up? What you're trying to enhance, it seems to me, is the axis of clarity and the axis of emotion. Because the two are totally related. The clearer the event, the more powerful the emotional impact of it.

What I love about the final phases of making a film is when you can just feel everything is exactly right. Not that there couldn't have been something else which was also right, but that given what you've chosen to do, it's right. The language, for example—that there's no gap between articulation and understanding. That's what makes these scripts so mind-bogglingly difficult. It's not the concepts or research that are the challenge, it's finding the articulation within the flow of this particular film. What are the words that are clear, in the simplest, best way for this moment in this film? I think of that line of Geoff's [writer Geoffrey C. Ward] from

The Civil War: "The spring rains had washed open the fresh graves from the year before." You're done. You could come across the same historical fact or moment and articulate it differently, and maybe that different way would be just as good in its own context. But you're done.

19

Jon Else

Jon Else directs the documentary program at the University of California, Berkeley Graduate School of Journalism. His films, which have earned him four Emmys, several Academy Award nominations, and a MacArthur Fellowship, include *The Day after Trinity; Yosemite: The Fate of Heaven; Sing Faster: The Stagehands' Ring Cycle*; and the PBS series *Cadillac Desert* and *Eyes on the Prize*, which is where we first met. He has served as cinematographer on hundreds of films, including *Tupac: Resurrection*. He is currently producing and directing *Wonders Are Many*, a documentary feature about nuclear weapons. We spoke in 2003 and again in 2006.

Is the common thread in documentary a need for story?

The common thread that we've overwhelmingly embraced for the last 50 years is story. We haven't figured out a way to do documentaries very successfully without stories. The adoption of the story devices of *dramatic* film—that's a relatively new thing.

Story, in the sense that I think we all bring to it from Western literature, from the theater, from a good novel and narrative films, has served us extremely well. It's kept a lot of viewers from changing channels to watch a soap opera or *Desperate Housewives*. But in a way, that's our deal with the devil, our Faustian bargain. I've spent a lot of my career trying to make real people in the real world behave like Lady Macbeth or King Lear or a character on *Homicide*. Trying to sort of force them to not be quite so messy and nonchronological in how they go about their struggles with life, and trying to make it fit a Shakespearean mold.

When I did the film *The Day after Trinity*, about J. Robert Oppenheimer and the building of the first atomic bomb, we had people on the production staff read *Hamlet*, and there was a lot of discussion around the big table as we were shooting and editing about the similarities between Oppenheimer and Hamlet. What we ended up doing, I think, was kind of bend whatever Oppenheimer's real-life character was so that it more closely approximated a tortured young Danish prince trying to figure out what to do. The same was true with Henry Ford [*A Job at Ford's*] in *The Great Depression* series. There was a great, I think, unconscious effort on my part to make Henry Ford's reversal of fortune at the hands of his workers reflect King Lear's reversal of fortune at the hands of his daughters. I'm not sure I would do it that way again.

But isn't that a valid biographic device, as long as your work is also accurate? Print biographers do it.

Both films are structurally very successful, I think. But whether they're successful history or not—time will tell. Robert Oppenheimer and Henry Ford are an awful lot more complex and their lives are messier, in terms of their forward motion, than either Hamlet or King Lear. And another problem in both of those films is that I attempted to make myself invisible, jumped through a lot of hoops to make the filmmaker vanish entirely.

Even then, shouldn't viewers realize that someone is telling the story?

But I believe very firmly that audiences take documentaries to be somehow truer than nearly everything else they see on screen. And that at the end of a film, when the lights come on or the commercial comes on, there are certain events that the audience believes actually happened in a certain order. The audience doesn't say, "Well, that's Jon Else's version of how the events in Henry Ford's life unfolded." People are going to take it to be something unnervingly close to the actual way in which actual events happened.

I try to get it right; there's nothing in either of these films that hasn't been fact checked to within an inch of its life. And that's why I feel comfortable putting out my version. There are other spins and versions that also can be fact checked. What I don't have patience with are stories that get put out there in which the filmmaker is too lazy to fact check it or the story is too good to be fact checked. To kind of let it go and then say, "I'm not a journalist, so it doesn't matter." I don't buy that.

Part of the problem seems to be that there's no common definition of "documentary." Even filmmakers are divided: Are they artists, journalists, something else?

In a way it's not up to us. We don't have the luxury of defining ourselves as documentary makers or not. Our films say, very loudly, "I am a documentary." The whole seduction of the audience succeeds because audiences place great value on something they believe in their souls to be true. You can say, "No, I'm not a journalist, no, I'm not a historian, I'm just a storyteller"—but what you put on the screen is going to be taken by the vast majority of the audience to be factual.

You can't have your cake and eat it too. You can't tell a story that is too good to be true, and not let the audience in on the deception. But what I try to do with my students is point out that in making these films you don't have to stretch things like that. Having a passionate personal voice doesn't mean that you can't be journalistically ethical. You can be a journalist and an artist at the same time. It's all about letting people know what kind of truth you're telling.

You've talked about the role of documentaries in advancing public awareness of issues and events. Can you explain?

I'll limit myself to discussion of documentary as something that's important in civic dialogue, in the national conversation. One role of documentary is to provide the American public with a basis for conversation, a basic and accurate understanding of what the issues are and what the basic facts are. Documentary in fact does have a secret life among policy makers. President Clinton was famous for watching lots of documentaries in the course of briefing himself for a particular issue. There was a screening of the Yosemite film in a Senate caucus room for seven senators, even before it was released on PBS, unbeknownst to me. *Cadillac Desert* had a screening on Capitol Hill in a Senate caucus room with about 100 people in attendance from the White House, OMB, the Congress, the Senate, the Department of the Interior. The first copy of *The Day after Trinity* was purchased by the C.I.A.

If you went to the sixth grade in California in the 1990s, you had to watch *Cadillac Desert*. Now, there's no question that public television is also hugely important, simply because of its large but diminishing reach. *Cadillac Desert* was seen by about 9 million people on the night it was broadcast. The book only sold 50,000 copies. By the time the sun sets on my life, the series will probably have been seen by 30 to 50 million people around the world. Fine with me.

As a director and director of photography, how much do you plan your storytelling in advance?

In approaching a film, I always try to find at least two stories that unfold simultaneously. One of them almost always is a very simple, straight-ahead, forward motion through time. For instance, in *Sing Faster*, the forward motion is just the simple story that is told in Wagner's *Ring Cycle*, in the operas. It's this crazy soap opera about the gods fighting, a giant Aristotelian drama with characters and rising conflict and resolution and all that. And then parallel to that is the much less linear story of the stagehands preparing this production for opening night.

In *Cadillac Desert*, the same was true. In setting out to tell what, on the surface, were not enormously riveting tales of how canals and irrigation were developed in the West and how dams were built, I first looked for a narrative. Just a simple, forward-moving narrative that went through time and involved people in conflict. And it turns out that there was a lot of that, [it] took place in Congress and had an enormous effect on how we live in America today.

The second thing was to find some sort of a visual chronology, something visual on a grand scale. And it turned out that was fairly straightforward. The American West was at one time very, very dry. What we did was that we slowly, in the course of each hour, showed the water being re-engineered. Helicopter photography was extremely important in *Cadillac Desert*, in getting up above these landscapes to see how much they had been changed. You really can't tell how much the plumbing system in the West has been turned on its head until you get up above and look down and see that the rivers and canals are running in the wrong direction. It's dry where it should be wet and it's wet where it should be dry. We also did a lot with the visual concept of "unnatural" farming—at night, in the middle of the desert, etc.

Yosemite: The Fate of Heaven tells two stories as well; the story of the park today and the pressure it's under from tourism, and the park as it was encountered by Lafayette Bunnell, on an Indian raid in 1854. Yosemite's an interesting case because all of the footage on screen is in the present; it's a historical film which takes place entirely in the present. All of the narration is from an 1854 diary that I discovered about halfway through the preproduction period.

Did you excerpt and use passages in the order in which they were written?

The unfolding of events in the diary, the story of what Lafayette Bunnell and the Mariposa Battalion actually did—arriving at the valley, chasing Chief Tanaya and his tribe, and finally burning Chief Tanaya's village—those in fact are in the correct order, a nasty parable of conquest. On the other hand, Bunnell's ruminations about Yosemite and his transcendental experience, those paragraphs are shuffled around pretty substantially. I teach in a school of journalism now and I take a much tougher, hard-ass view of all this than I did.

Isn't there a logic that these are his thoughts, which were likely ongoing?

Yes, I think that's true. But we'll never know, will we? When the lights go on, we are responsible for what the audience believes to be true. And that includes not only what happened and what things looked like, but the order in which they happened, which is crucial to cause and effect.

Do you ever storyboard your work? For example, the scene of the workers at Yosemite National Park, in Yosemite.

Never. What I do is I plan very carefully and work extremely hard to figure out, what is the concept behind this particular sequence that we're shooting? Why are we watching these people blowing up a boulder on a particular trail in Yosemite? What is this shot or sequence telling us within the developing narrative of this film, and what is this shot or sequence telling us about the world? Are we there with the trail crew and the dynamite because it's dangerous? Are we there because all the dynamite in the world is not going to make a bit of difference in this giant range of mountains, where people are really insignificant? Are we there because these people are underpaid and they're trying to unionize? You've really got to figure out what the concept of the sequence is and what it is not, otherwise you just fire hose everything.

How would answering those questions change how you shoot the scene?

If the sequence is about man against nature and the futility of trying to tinker with these billions of tons of granite, it may be important to show that the boulder is huge compared to the people. And you can choose to do that by how you place human beings in relation to the boulder, and in fact we did that with that particular boulder. The thing I remember about that particular scene is that it was to some extent about danger, that people were using dynamite to clear a trail so that hikers could enjoy their Sunday afternoon going up to the lake to catch some trout. I remember having a lot of communication with John Haptas, the sound guy, to make sure he was getting this grating and to me very scary sound of a pocketknife cutting through a stick of dynamite, because of the danger involved.

If that scene was also to some extent about the camaraderie between the members of the trail crew, all of whom had lived in these mountains together, in camp, for many months by that time, you try to do a lot of shots in which the physical relationship between people shows. You show people touching each other, looking at each other. They weren't trying to unionize, but if in fact we had been doing a sequence about the labor conditions for trail workers in Yosemite, we probably would have made it a point to shoot over the course of a long day, to show how long the day was, show them eating three meals on the trail, walking home really bone-tired in the dark. Basically, the more you're aware of what you want these images to convey, the richer the images are going to be.

The danger is that we always have to be prepared that the scene may be conveying something different from what we expected it to convey. It may be that you shoot a sequence and somewhere along the line you unearth some material in front of your camera or some research or a new angle that means that this stuff suddenly has a new meaning. That can be good or bad.

It can be bad when the producers insist on bending it into the old meaning. I do a lot of camera work for other people, and I see an awful lot of sequences that I've shot end up on screen being pumped up to mean something which has really nothing to do with what they were at the time.

Why do you think this happens?

There's a lot of misunderstanding that tape is cheap and that it's a good idea with miniDV to shoot everything in sight and figure out later what it's about. That's one problem. The other problem is going out with an inflexible preconception, shooting a scene which doesn't match the preconception, and then coming back into the editing room and trying to force it with narration, tricky cutting, steroid music, or by shooting bogus footage to add to it. We've gotten to the point where producers need to have things be dramatic and unambiguous often gets the better of them. I take a very firm view about documentary ethics in general, and I think that there's an alarming erosion. The great thing about low-cost video production is that it democratizes documentary. But one of the downsides is that there's no oversight. And there's a danger that people's enthusiasm or rage or advocacy or ratings lust is going to get the better of them.

Do you write outlines and treatments before you shoot?

I do. Well—I do two kinds of films. I do films about things that have already happened, which are historical films. And films about things that are actually happening as we film. And you have to treat them differently.

The reason historical films are so popular with funders is that they know what they're going to get; they know what happened, no surprises. And the same is true for planning the film. It's your job as a maker of historical films to spend whatever it takes, six months or a year, to figure out a way to write an engaging treatment that draws on every bit of research, to turn over every stone, find out who are the interesting characters, find out who are the good witnesses. I write very, very detailed treatments for historical films. Most of my historical films take place in the present, by the way, there's a huge present component to them.

On films about events which unfold as you film, it's nearly impossible to write a treatment; that's one of the reasons they're so hard to fund. What you can and must do is to write a document, a quasi-treatment that clearly lays out who the film is about and what the conceptual underpinning of the film is. If it's a film about a baseball team, are you there because you care about the mathematics of baseball, or do you care about the profit the owner makes? Do you care about the relationship between the players and fans? Are you there because there's a Japanese player on the team? Are you there because these players relate to the legacy of the Negro Leagues? Why are you there? Then, whatever you write needs to lay out what might likely or possibly unfold as an order of events. It has to lay out pretty clearly who the characters are likely to be, what their relationship to one another is likely to be, and what's likely to change over the course of the time that you're going to be filming. No matter how you do it, there's a little bit of folly in it. And the problem is simply the money, who's going to give you the money to go out and find out what's happening in the world? Who would fund *Salesman* [Albert Maysles, David Maysles, Charlotte Zwerin] today, except maybe Sheila Nevins [HBO]? I think vérité films get funded almost solely on the reputation of the filmmaker or on the basis of a good sample tape.

Do you shoot to the treatment?

I treat it sort of like the airplane evacuation instructions. When all hell's breaking loose and you're out on location and you're sick with malaria and half your crew has mutinied, you can glance at this treatment and figure out this fail-safe way of making the film. You hope that you'll find something vastly better, but the original treatment is a way of ensuring that you can get the film started on the screen, and most important, that you can figure out some sort of ending.

Do you work with an act structure?

I try to have the rearrangement of time, the flashbacks and flash forwards, carefully worked out within that ever-advancing present tense in the film. That almost always gets changed in the editing, but at least going into it I have something that I know, if all else fails, I can use this model and it'll be at least a passable film that won't embarrass us all. The film I'm doing now has no acts; it may be embarrassing.

At what point do you know what you want your audience to get out of the film?

It's probably a mistake to begin a film without some notion of what the audience should feel and believe and understand at the end. Those are three different things. If you've chosen a complex and deep and robust subject, there are going to be things that emerge in the process of making the film that are going to change your notion, your idea of where you want the audience to be. You know, you spend 80 percent of your effort on the first 10 percent and the last 10 percent of the film. The middle part's easy, sort of like the space shuttle.

What about casting?

For better or for worse, casting is everything. Sad sacks who mumble are just not too interesting on film. I used to describe it in much more charitable terms—we used to say, "Look for the good storyteller." In practical terms, most documentaries now require having two or three lead characters, and then sort of a second tier of the supporting players. You can look at dozens of documentaries, good ones, and that's the model that they use. It gets bent a little too often, particularly in historical films, in the direction of powerful leaders. The thing that's tough is to find the little people, but they're always there if you look hard enough. In *Cadillac Desert*, we tried to find people who worked on the dams, people who remembered the West as it was before the rivers were redirected.

In finding people to help tell a story, I'm always very direct about calling people who may have a different point of view on the story than me and encouraging them to be part of the film. Respecting what they have to say, putting it in the film. On the afternoon that we sealed up the deal on *Cadillac Desert* [based on the book by Marc Reisner], the first phone call I made was to Floyd Domeni, who is the dam builder from hell in Marc's book. He turned out to be a wonderful man who was more than happy to talk very forthrightly about what he did and why he did it. I make an attempt to either have the film be fair to everyone on all reasonable sides of an issue—and being fair doesn't necessarily mean giving everyone the same number of seconds on the screen—or to make it very clear that I'm doing a rant, if that's what I'm up to, and not try to trick the audience into thinking that I have no stake in this.

But fairness is in the eye of the beholder. On *Cadillac Desert*, I thought that our story unfolded with enormous fairness, but it got a lot of people angry on both sides. Some environmentalists felt that we were too easy on the forces of development. There were a lot of big agricultural groups who thought we were way too tough on big agriculture. There were people in Los Angeles who thought we had disgraced the memory of William Mulholland. I disagree with them all. [But] it's okay if people don't like our films; it's not okay if we get it wrong, and it's factually inaccurate.

Your current film seems to break some of the narrative strategies you usually employ.

This new film, *Wonders Are Many*, is the most complicated narrative that I've ever done. It weaves together (1) the story of the making of *Doctor Atomic* [an opera composed by John Adams and directed by Peter Sellars] over a two-year period, with (2) an archival history of the arms race with (3) the life story of Robert Oppenheimer, with (4) the story of the final 48 hours before the Trinity test. But the unfolding of each separate story is nonlinear: We begin with the end of the opera and end with the beginning of the opera. The film is 92 minutes long and Hiroshima gets destroyed [the bombing that marked the culmination of Manhattan Project research] about 20 minutes in.

It's the first film I've worked on where decisions about what comes next rest on a very simple visceral sense of what works cinematically. I've got a great editor, Deborah Hoffman, who can look at a scene and say, "This next scene, even though it happened six months before, is visually and emotionally what makes sense. So let's go from that shot of wreckage at the Nevada test site to the chorus singing about plutonium, not because it makes textbook sense but because it moves the film forward in a musical, emotional, and visual sense without hurting the logic." This intuitive way of working is not for every subject. The thing that makes it possible is that the stories are incredibly rich and broad; I mean, it's an opera and an atomic bomb, so we're seldom at a loss for something jaw-dropping to put up on screen. And it takes a really brilliant and grown-up editor—Deborah has saved me on many films over the years. It's also a lot of work. It's stories braided together, and only one, the historical story of the Manhattan Project, is narrated. When we're on stage with the people making the opera, the narrator goes away. The irony is that it's a very data-dense film; you learn a lot about nuclear weapons.

In your program at U.C. Berkeley, you try to identify the types of stories that lend themselves to lower-budget filmmaking—films in the $100,000 range, as opposed to the $500,000 or more that's typical for an hour carried nationally on PBS or HBO.

In the system we're trying to develop at U.C., it's a mistake to first find a story and then figure out how to make it inexpensively. You have to first figure out how much money you realistically have available, and then figure out what story fits with that. It's the polar opposite of what we've been doing all our lives.

There are some straight-ahead litmus tests that you can apply. It's almost impossible to do inexpensive films which include commercial archive material. You have to find stories that'll withstand moments of inelegant storytelling, that will not be destroyed by the loss of a particular character or location or action. You want to look for stories that can be done without travel. You want to look for stories that have a built-in narrative timeline, narrative arc.

Films don't go over budget because you paid a sound guy too much and put the crew in a hotel for an extra day. They go over budget because people waste two months of editorial time figuring out what the story is. If you're talking about doing inexpensive work, that's the single most important thing, finding a story that comes with a ready-made through-line. It's much more cost-efficient to figure out the story beforehand. The downside of that is that you're never going to be able to make *Salesman* or *Soldier Girls* [Nick Broomfield, Joan Churchill] or *Control Room* [Jehane Noujaim, Hani Salama, Rosadel Varela] if you do that. And the fact is that it's very, very tough to do any kind of cinéma vérité film—which involves really discovering the story—inexpensively.

A few other things. You want to do stories where you don't have to burn up a month getting any administrative access. You know, if you want to do a story about the history of Disneyland, that's a textbook example of something that's not going to be inexpensive no matter how you do it. If you want to do a story on the inside of a political campaign for a month with a Panasonic 100B, you probably can do that inexpensively. It's got a built-in story arc, two leading characters, somebody's going to win, some-body's going to lose. You've got rising action, rising tension, and an ending.

We've commissioned three documentaries to date. Lourdes Portillo did *McQueen*, a short film about Steve McQueen that pre-miered at the Whitney Museum. Peter Nicks did *The Wolf*, an hour-long film about his struggle with cocaine and crack that ended up being broadcast on *ABC Nightline* over two nights. And then Al Maysles set out to do one chapter in a long-term project of his, getting onto cross-country trains and following the stories of people who were riding. And it didn't quite work: Some voyages of exploration find something and some don't, and his didn't. So he's rearranged what he's doing and is involved with a short film about a dance troupe in New York. It may be that in this "cookbook" model, the open-ended exploration of cinéma vérité is problematic. If Albert can't do it, maybe nobody can.

What are some of the other challenges of making a quality film for less money?

I suspect that the most important element and in some ways the most difficult is how you break up time. How do you take the order in which real people have done real things in the real world, and how do you stretch and shrink different events to last more or less screen time? And how do you reorder them in a way that gives the greatest drama, without leading the audience to believe falsehoods, that certain things happened when they didn't? The editorial process, which can stretch to months or even years on documentary projects, that reordering of time, that's what burns up money.

It's all about, first of all, finding the point at which you enter the story. And the mysterious art is then figuring out at what points do you flash back to reveal portions of the backstory, and at what point to do flashbacks within flashbacks? In real history, Harvey Milk and the man who eventually killed him, Dan White, were both elected in the same election on the same day. But Deborah Hoffman and Rob Epstein, in structuring *The Times of Harvey Milk*, carried the audience through the first third of the film, getting Harvey Milk elected to his seat on the San Francisco board of supervisors with hardly a mention of Dan White. It's only after Harvey Milk has been elected that we then flash back to the same election and meet Dan White, and go through Dan White's ascent to power. And those two men will eventually meet and White assassinates Milk.

Are there common structural problems that you encounter in your work with students?

The most common difficulty is finding where to enter the story. Almost all first-time filmmakers start their film at what later turns out not to have been the best place in the chronology. The second most common difficulty is a refusal to give the audience enough basic information, because students are very reluctant to use narration or text of any sort. They've grown up exposed to nothing but *bad* narration and often have trouble imagining narration that's brilliant and artful, or even useful. But words in a film can be wonderful or horrible, just like camerawork or sound or music or editing. The third most common problem is the ending, bringing the film to a soft landing, or a crash landing, or any landing. And that's the one we have the least success in solving.

When people think of documentary today, they're likely to think of the big-screen blockbusters like Super Size Me, *and perhaps some of what's on public television. But for working documentary filmmakers, the bread-and-butter is likely to come from the often very low-budget documentary programming that dominates commercial television. Some of it's excellent, but there is also no shortage of material that's unimaginative, if not journalistically unsound. How do you prepare students for this world?*

You have to be a realist. It's perfectly possible to do beautiful work when you're on someone else's payroll (look at Robert Flaherty). But at some point, you're going to be asked to turn out shit, and you're going to be asked to turn it out in a way that's unprofessional and doesn't do justice to your skills. When that happens, hard as it is, you have to find the line that you won't cross, especially the ethical line. We've had some experiences with recent grad students seeing stuff in the field that was just plainly, clearly unethical and struggling with that; seeing a producer posing as policemen in a drug bust, for instance.

But I'm convinced that students can fight to do good work in those settings. If a producer asks you to fake things, cook up phony stock footage, falsify your reporting, fudge the drama a little more than you're comfortable with in order to drive the ratings, you somehow have to find it in yourself to say no in a constructive, orderly way, through the chain of command. Sometimes you're not going to get asked back, but that's okay. The more folks at all levels of documentary can blow the whistle very loudly when they see stuff that's just plain dishonest, the better. You will work again. Documentary filmmaking is about showing an audience what the actual world is, and that involves skilled ethical filmmaking. It's especially hard to speak up when you are young, but do it clearly and carefully, and have confidence that you're going to be able to work in a place that does have higher standards.

20

Nicholas Fraser

Since 1997, Nick Fraser has been series editor of *Storyville*, which each year presents up to 50 documentaries from all over the world on BBC Two and BBC Four. Roughly a third of the films are bought as completed films, while the rest are "prebought" or commissioned jointly with other broadcasters. (For example, *Storyville* coproduced *So Much So Fast*. The film's credits read: "A production of West City Films in association with WGBH, ZDF/ARTE, BBC, with support from TV2/Danmark." In the United States, the film will air on PBS's *Frontline*; in the United Kingdom, it will air on BBC's *Storyville*.)

Prior to joining the BBC, Nick was a commissioning editor at Channel Four and operated his own production company, Panoptic Productions. A former print journalist, he continues to be a contributing editor at *Harper's* magazine and is the author of books including *Evita*, *The Voice of Modern Hatred*, and the forthcoming *The Importance of Being Eton*. We spoke by phone in 2006.

There is quite a range of film subjects and styles on Storyville— Trembling before G-d, The War Room, Why We Fight, My Terrorist, Me & My 51 Brothers & Sisters, Murderball. *You've said that the requirement for the series is that films "should all be strongly narrative." Do you explain to filmmakers what you mean by that?*

I don't. There's a backlog of *Storyville* they can go to, to figure out what we've shown. But I think it's bad for me to say, "Well, this is what I want." It's rather irritating, because it means I spend a lot of time saying what I *don't* want. We don't want films that are flat and look like current affairs. We don't want illustrated scripts.

We want films where the narrative is important, and what you discover comes from what you see.

I like the dictum of D. H. Lawrence, when he said that you should always trust the tale, not the teller. I think that when documentary films have a very strong ideological point of view, they're not very satisfactory. I have no objections, necessarily, to strong ideological points of view, but it seems to me when a film is put to the service of a point of view—and it can be ideological, or it can be a point of view that comes over the script that's pre-written—you feel pushed into conclusions, and you feel the filmmaker decided what they wanted to say before they set out to make the film. So I would say I'm interested, firstly, in people who have a desire to tell a story because they wish to find out about something themselves. That just accords with my temperament: I tend to write articles or books because I want to find out about things, because I really don't know what I think about them. I may feel ambivalent; nothing wrong with feeling ambivalent.

You've compared today's documentaries with the New Journalism of the 1960s and 1970s, the nonfiction narrative prose of writers such as Norman Mailer, Truman Capote, and Tom Wolfe.

That's right. Documentaries are probably the most interesting form of nonfiction at the moment. It seems to me that with the exception of *Vanity Fair* and *The New Yorker* in North America, there's been some sort of decline—and *Harper's*, obviously I love *Harper's*, I'm a contributing editor—there's been some decline in the value given to long pieces of reportage. About thirty years ago there were far more pieces. They've been replaced by blogs. Blogs constitute instant controversy and opinion. And although I used to be in the business of instant controversy and opinion, I now find it sort of tiresome, because there are too many opinions. I think one should try to shed opinions in life, rather than acquiring them.

What appeals to me about documentaries made at the moment is that they do, consciously or not, seem to hark back to this moment in the late 1960s when everything seemed possible in the long-form story. That you could send a good writer out, whether it was Joan Didion or Norman Mailer or whomever, you could send them out to cover a story and they would come back with something remarkable. Well, you can do the same now with digital video cameras. It's a niche market, documentaries, but probably a broader niche market than journalism was in the 1960s. More people can be lured into seeing good documentaries than could be lured into reading *Esquire* in 1967. I want to get this right: It is a sort of democratic medium, but alas, at the moment these films are not reaching wide enough audiences. They should be, but they're not. But more and more good films are being made each year. And obviously the funding of these films has changed, a lot of private money goes into them, they're made with an eye on cinemas, they're not destined solely for television. And if they do go to television, they don't go to the usual outlets like PBS or the networks as they might have done 20 years ago. They go to cable channels, satellite channels, and they will go over the Internet on demand. That will be the way these films will be distributed in a very short time, I imagine.

Wendy, Alex and Stephen Heywood, from *So Much So Fast*. Photo courtesy of the filmmakers.

Steve Ascher and Jeannie Jordan (So Much So Fast) describe their films as nonfiction novels, because they're shaping a narrative that's layered and textured.

That's exactly what they are doing, and it's exactly what Norman Mailer prescribed. *Hoop Dreams* is a good nonfiction novel; *Guerrilla: The Taking of Patty Hearst* is just excellent. Numerous films that come out each year are great nonfiction novels. And they exist, if you like, at the boundary between the long piece in a magazine that you love to read on a plane, and the nonfiction novel. And that's a very good place for documentaries to be, in my view.

How important do you think journalism training is for documentary filmmakers?

In terms of actually getting stories right and knowing who to trust and all that, it seems to me that's largely—I hate to say instinctive, but if you're well educated and ambitious you can figure that out. You can read a book about ethics, or you can go out with an executive producer who'll tell you what you can and can't do. If you invent everything, people are going to figure it out quickly.

A film like *Hoop Dreams*, its journalistic standards are impeccable. And yet it's not just a piece of journalism, it's something bigger, it's got bigger ambitions. Journalism makes use of characters for journalistic purposes. People exist in a story because they've been shoved into the story to back up the point of the journalist, or as source material for the story. In documentaries, it seems to be the other way around. You go with the characters and then the story builds itself around them.

The other similarity between New Journalism and the kinds of documentaries seen on Storyville *seems to be one of authorship. But not all documentaries are authored to the same extent; much of the documentary programming that dominates commercial television, for example, can feel sort of mass produced.*

Right. However, I think that authorship can be defined in a lot of ways. I think Robert Greenwald's films *(Outfoxed, Wal-Mart)* are authored; they're very journalistic. It's said to be a question of recognizable voice, but whose voice, and is it in the film? You can't be dogmatic about it. Sometimes it's very explicit. Sometimes the author has to be on camera, like Michael Moore. Other times, the films are very authored, such as the Ascher/Jordan films, but you rarely see them. You have the commentary [e.g., Steve narrated *So Much So Fast*], but even if someone else read the commentary they'd still seem like very personal, authored films.

In a way, it's very confusing, this discussion about authorship. A reason for this confusion comes from film theory, which is obsessed with *auteurs* and fiction. That's probably a very bad mold for a documentary, which is a hybrid of film and journalism. And just as you can be an author in a number of different ways, writing a nonfiction piece, so you can in a documentary.

Do you see differences in storytelling across nationalities?

Yes, absolutely. Documentaries are more ambitious in America at the moment, because they *can't* go on television always. I mean if you're guaranteed a place on a mainstream channel in Germany or Britain or France, and it's a place in the middle of the schedule, well, what you're going to be asked to do is something for quite a big audience. So you tend to make something that's quite explicit, quite comprehensible—a bit like what you were talking about earlier, a bit like Discovery output or PBS output—some of PBS output, not all of it. But if you're an American, you don't know where it ends up, so you tend to make a different calculation, like, "What am I saying, and will people want to watch the film?" And that brings you to start every film from scratch, in a way. To say, "What is the point of what I'm doing?"

If you look at the totality of output from the United States, it's extraordinarily rich. And—I'll probably be shot for saying this—one of the reasons it's so rich is that it's actually reasonably hard to get commissioned to make a documentary in America. So that, coupled with the fact that they *can* get interest and they can get private money, means that people have to struggle and they have to be very ambitious. Or they have to be very rich. And that means that you get a certain winnowing out of people who are just doing hack work. I mean, there's a huge amount of hack work on American TV, there's enough hack work to keep one going until infinity, but it's not on the whole in the field of documentaries.

I also think that the American tradition that we were talking about, of 1960s New Journalism and direct cinema, is very rich. And in addition to that, I think Americans are disposed toward empiricism. You really do have this preparedness among very intelligent American filmmakers to spend forever on a subject until it's absolutely right, and that's why their films are very good. Very enduring. And why I love them so much.

I think that there are many good documentaries made in Europe. The subsidy system works both ways. Sometimes it's very good for films to get funded easily, and you don't have to suffer to make them. And other times it means there's a certain orthodoxy, you have a machine set up for commissioning documentaries and all documentaries conform to what the machine is used to getting. So the machine tells you, we believe in innovation, but actually they're churning out the same form of innovation every year.

I think there are good French documentaries, there are good German ones—I thought *Darwin's Nightmare* was very good. There's less pressure to make documentaries in Europe, because to be absolutely blunt about it, the European media are less crass than the American ones. I discovered a website [complaining about] my complacence and elitist views when I said I thought the BBC did a good job being impartial. But the fact is that it does. There is a crisis in news and reporting in Europe, but it's not as acute as the crisis in America. I think the crisis in America is why these very talented young people are being impelled to make documentaries, as a sort of compensation for the failure of what they call mainstream media.

And at the same time, it seems, the market for documentaries crosses national borders, so filmmakers need to work to create stories that will appeal to different cultures, lifestyles, viewpoints.

But I think it isn't so much down to national cultures, it's down to the receptiveness of documentary producers in each country as to whether they want to do this, whether they get it—the notion that you're not just making these films for a group of lefties in a smoke-filled cinema at a festival. That these films have to cross frontiers, and they have to deal with what is limited, what is special, what is often minute, what is local, but at the same time they have to go around the world. They really have to do that.

What I like about documentaries is they're very pluralistic. I'm not asking for a whole lot of documentaries to be made from the neo-con political position. But it seems to me that somehow, sometimes documentaries suffer from the fact that most of the people that make documentaries agree politically with each other. And I think the strength of filmmaking, like journalism, is that people should be unpredictable in their views, or they shouldn't have perceived views. They should actually rather *look* at things than have views about them. I mean, do we care that Cartier-Bresson was a lefty? No, we don't at all. Or Robert Capra. Well, ultimately

I know what the filmmaker's views are, but that doesn't always translate into their documentaries, and they're much more subtle and richer because they're about narrative.

Al Maysles is great on this subject, he expresses it far more beautifully than I ever can, because he has an interest in human nature that's very rich. All his films, their lasting appeal comes from the fact that he loves his characters. I think it would be fine if he hated some of them as well as loving some of them, but he only loves them. And I think that's more important than ideology. Ideology, political positions—they go out of date in a week. No one can remember, what did Michael Moore really want to say about George Bush [in *Fahrenheit 9/11*]? All people can remember is the little goat book. All they can remember about Wolfowitz is licking his comb. The rest of the ideological stuff, you probably go back to it now and say you agree with only half of it.

Among the films you've commissioned are A Cry *from the Grave (1999) and a sequel,* Srebrenica: Never Again? *(2005), both written, produced, and directed by Leslie Whitehead. The films concern the 1995 Bosnian massacre at Srebrenica. I've read that you originated the project, sending articles about the massacre to the filmmaker and helping to shape the film through the questions you asked.*

I spent a lot of time with Leslie, because I was interested in the massacre at Srebrenica, and I thought the story was going to be very difficult to do. It was very politically sensitive, a huge subject.

What sorts of questions do you ask when you're working with filmmakers?

Quite basic journalistic questions: who, why, what, when, and where, really. I think that the most useful thing I can do is to ask people simple basic questions about what they're doing. "Why would you want to make a film about this subject? What's the point of the narrative? Why did you choose this situation and the subject? How does the situation and the subject you chose translate itself into this narrative?" If you chose to examine the film from this point of view, you have to tell me why. A lot of filmmakers, including Leslie, are very savvy at figuring this out. I mean, Jehane Noujaim—both *Startup.com* and *Control Room* are very well thought out. She tells me that she has no idea what she'll end up with when she starts filming, but this is hard to believe.

When you get a pitch from her, it usually lasts about five minutes, but she knows exactly what she wants to do. The characters seem created in a very solid way, very early in the process.

This might surprise many new filmmakers, who still seem to have the misconception that documentaries are spontaneous and unplanned, not "discovered" until late in the editing process.

You should know much earlier what you're doing. You should know why and how you're telling the story. I mean, there are many, many films about Chinese factories. But if you're going to a Chinese factory, why are you filming the Chinese factory, what are you trying to tell people? There was one film we showed, *Made in China* [distributed as *A Decent Factory*], which is about a Nokia supplier in China. And what they filmed was a visit to a factory by a Nokia ethical consultant and a Nokia executive.

[*According to material on Storyville's website, French filmmaker Thomas Balmes was approached by YLE in Finland to take an "anthropological" look at the Finnish corporation, Nokia. He says he spent 18 months "filming boring Nokia meetings all over the world" before he met Hanna Kaskinen, Nokia's environmental expert. "She was just starting to push the Nokia management to take a new position with ethical issues," Balmes told the BBC Four interviewer. "I found it very interesting because it touched on the issue—can you be a capitalist and be ethical at the same time?" He also notes that he was in the right place at the right time: "Hanna was about to do Nokia's first ever ethical assessment." And so the film took shape and gained international coproduction support. The story—the film's train—is deceptively simple: Balmes follows Nokia executive Kaskinen and English consultant Louise Jamison to China, to visit the factory of Nokia's major charger supplier.*]

As soon as he said, "That's what I want to film," I could see the film. I could see why you would go around a Chinese factory in the company of these people looking into whether the Chinese factory conforms to European safety and health requirements, and whether that would be a comedy or not. And in fact the film was very funny, though a lot of people didn't get the humor. Somehow filmmakers manage to tell you, through an image or a description of the situation, that that's why they want to approach the story. And that tells me what the story's going to tell the audience.

Because you see a point of view?

Not so much a filmmaking point of view, but you see what they want to look at. You get a phone call from Cartier-Bresson, and let's say he is in the middle of Russia and he says, "I'm doing a sequence in a worker canteen, and there are people dancing there." You'd say, "That's great," and then he'd come back with 20 frames, and one of them will be that immortal picture of two peasants dancing in the middle of the canteen. And you'd know enough [when he called] to know, well, that's going to work very well.

This is the difference from print journalism: You'll be told by reporters what the story is about; documentary filmmakers are telling you what they *see*. My background is writing, but I write differently now because I've learned a lot from documentary filmmaking. My writing's become much more visual, and pieces are constructed more like documentaries, with scenes in them. I think it makes them easier to read.

What do you see when you walk into Big Edie and Little Edie's house in Southampton [in Maysles Films' *Grey Gardens*]? You see these crazy people at the top of a staircase in their funny clothes. But what you really see is this extraordinary performance put on by the daughter and the mother, not only for themselves but for the camera. And if you get a phone call from Al Maysles saying, "They were singing today, it was a wonderful day," you know it's fine. What you're getting is the situation and the way the filmmaker is filming it, not the paraphrase of what it's all about.

In considering projects for support, you've said that while filmmakers can come to you just with ideas, it helps, especially when it comes to filmmakers whose work you don't know, if they've shot at least a few minutes of material.

You should always have tapes, because if you don't send tapes, if it's all bits of paper, it's very hard to know what you want to film. Again, the analogy is, if you're commissioning a Magnum photographer to go somewhere, you want a piece of paper saying this is where I want to shoot, but you'd also like some work from the Magnum photographer that tells you *how* they're going to look at what they want to film.

What do you look for in a reel?

Often the problem with reels is that they're edited to look like TV shows. So you think, well, that's the subject, and it could be turned into a TV show, but you don't know how good the film is going to be. In other words, they shouldn't be too slick—or, they *should* be slick, but [you want] to edit them so that they look like the final film. Tapes can be much rawer, but something attractive on them tells you what the impact of the final film would be.

Among the topics covered in submissions you receive, do you get a lot of misery?

Much too much misery. You just can't supply a diet of unrelieved misery. "Miserabilism" is the handmaid of "reportorialism"— you've got to find other ways. And when you do cover things like the Iraq war, you've got to find interesting ways into the subject. For us to do a film about the horrors of Baghdad—a film we showed, called *The Liberace of Baghdad*, is very funny. And very telling. [Filmmaker Sean McAllister spent eight months filming Iraq's most famous pianist, Samir Peter, playing for journalists and others in a hotel bar.] But it's also seductive because you can watch it for a whole hour and ten minutes without being *too* depressed. Absolutely unadulterated dollops of misery are no good, and audiences stay away from them.

How do you see documentary changing, in terms of both filmmakers and audiences?

I think that you can reach sizable audiences through the documentary form, because if the story is very attractive, people are prepared to sit down and watch it. I'm encouraged by that. It seems people don't have problems watching them, they don't find them difficult. You don't necessarily want to read a book about something; you should be forgiven for not wanting to read a book about the Iraq war because it's so depressing. But you're prepared to go to your local movie house and watch a film about it. Or better still, you'll watch a miraculously good film like *My Architect*, which does so many things: It tells you about architecture, about growing up, about being abandoned by your father. And I think these films have easily found a niche audience. It's not a big enough audience—for commercial purposes in America it's just about big enough, but it should be larger. The only thing that stops the sector being precarious, making documentaries, is that the cost is falling. That's not necessarily a wonderful thing for documentary makers. They can make cheaper films, but they may not get rewarded for doing them. I worry about people devoting their lives to documentaries, they don't make a lot of money at it. But I think you can survive if you're clever; there's money from lots of different sources around.

21

Susan Froemke

One of the nation's leading direct cinema (also known as vérité) filmmakers, Susan Froemke is currently completing a long-term project about addiction for HBO. Her company, Susan Froemke Productions, creates corporate and independent work.

When we spoke in 2003, Susan was chief administrator and principal filmmaker at Maysles Films in New York, a company she joined in the 1970s. Her first production with Albert Maysles and his late brother, David, was *Grey Gardens*, a now-classic portrait of Edie Beale and her mother, Edith Bouvier Beale, reclusive relatives of Jacqueline Kennedy Onassis. While at Maysles, Susan made more than 20 nonfiction films, including the Academy Award–nominated *Lalee's Kin: The Legacy of Cotton* (HBO), a look at poverty and education in the Mississippi Delta, and the Grammy Award–winning *Recording* The Producers: *A Musical Romp with Mel Brooks* (PBS), about the making of the Broadway hit's cast album. We spoke about these projects in 2003, with an update in 2006.

I've heard direct cinema described as "the drama of life—without scripts, sets, interviews, or narration." Many people think this means you just go outside and start filming.

Right. But that's not at all what happens. It's one thing if we're recording an event, and the client wants us to be somewhere at a certain time and we show up with our cameras. And as you start recording that event, you see, "Wow, this could be a really interesting film; there's more than just this Rolling Stones concert that I'm filming [*Gimme Shelter*], or there's more than just these meetings with the Gettys [*Concert of Wills: Making the Getty Center*]." Pretty soon, you have to start thinking as a filmmaker and ask yourself, What story are you telling? What direction is your subject taking you in, and is that something that's going to make a good film?

What about films that begin as a general topic or idea, such as Lalee's Kin?

The genesis of *Lalee's Kin* was HBO calling me up saying, "We'd like you to take a look at poverty at the end of the millennium." So how do you start to find a story? We researched and researched. We had to become educated about the current issues of poverty. We wanted an answer to the question, "Why is there so much poverty in this rich country?" This was 1997; the welfare reform bill had just been passed. Initially, it seemed that the obvious story line was to follow three welfare mothers and see how the changes in the welfare laws were affecting their lives. But as I researched the topic more—and it wasn't just me, I had two smart assistants on staff here—I realized that I wanted to look more at the systemic causes of poverty.

Through talking to a lot of academics and policy makers, including Senator Paul Wellstone, we identified the systemic causes of poverty as illiteracy, illegitimacy, and racism. Larry Brown, who had written the book *Hungry in America*, told us, "If you're doing a film about poverty, you've got to be in the Mississippi Delta." He said, "There's this one school superintendent that you've got to meet, Reggie Barnes." And when I called Reggie Barnes, I got that intuitive feeling over the phone that this is my subject. Reggie said, "If you can educate the child of illiterate parents, you can stop the cycle of poverty." And that struck home. It's a simple statement but it's a powerful statement; let's investigate this. I went down to the Delta and met Reggie, who had a Herculean task ahead of him, getting an impoverished school system off academic probation. This was a real narrative, the first I'd found after searching in four different states for almost six months.

So you have the genesis of a story, what then?

At Maysles, we say that casting is everything. We choose to call it "researching," because people think that casting means actors, like a Hollywood film. But we do have to find our subjects, they don't just fall in your lap. Once we found Reggie, we needed to find a family whose lives were going to intersect with the school superintendent's story, so you could see how difficult it is to try to stop this cycle of poverty that's been passed down for generations. Since this is the Mississippi Delta, we couldn't find any production personnel who could help us cast, so I asked Jim O'Neill, who was affiliated with the Delta Blues Museum in Clarksdale, to drive me around the cotton fields.

When we drove through Lalee's neighborhood, I saw her family pulling down a house, an old wooden structure next to an old trailer she was living in. We stopped and watched, and Lalee soon invited me inside. We sat down at the kitchen table, and she just talked. And I thought, "This is the dream subject." Because I could say one or two words, and she would start to pontificate. Also the fact that she was giving me access to her house, the first time I met her, is exactly what you need when you're doing vérité. It's all about access and getting the trust of your subject. I think Lalee started trusting us very early on in the shoot. And she'd never seen a documentary in her life, so it's not like I could say to her, "Just let us film your life, and if you don't like something that we're filming, you can always tell me."

We also loved Lalee's children; they just charmed us. That was another reason why Lalee was cast. Main and Redman were the first two kids that we met. Redman was so curious and adorable, and Main, although somewhat withdrawn, really opened up around us. And it was after the second time we filmed that we met Granny [another child]. Right away I thought that Granny was a fascinating character and had a lot of potential as a main or secondary story line.

You filmed Lalee's Kin *over a period of time, traveling from New York City to Mississippi periodically to shoot. What would motivate a trip?*

We went down to film Lalee soon after I met her because she was getting a new trailer [from the government]. And it's really a metaphor for poverty. Lalee's so excited that this new house is going to arrive, she's full of hope and expectations, and when she finally gets it she realizes it's this rat-infested dump. It was a year before she could get a stove, a refrigerator that worked, and electricity. I mean these are gargantuan efforts for a family to overcome. And you see her crushed, which is what we experienced filming this very poor population. They couldn't have hope for long. But they had this resilient spirit; they would say at the end, "Well, I thank the Lord for whatever I've gotten."

The story kept changing every time we went down there. It was really hard to track. We would go down for events, like the arrival of the new trailer or the beginning of a school year. We went down on Granny's birthday, which also happened to coincide with the school announcing that it was going off probation. We would always check in with Lalee and Reggie, especially with Lalee, and get a lot of textural things. And oddly enough, a lot of things would happen on birthdays or Mother's Day, I guess because a lot of people would come into the household. On Mother's Day, she found out that Eddie Reed, her son, was in jail.

We would often go down thinking we were going to film one thing and something totally different would happen; a whole new chapter would unfold. And I just would not worry about it. Your subjects, in many ways, are directing the film. You follow the directions their lives take; it's always much more interesting. Even the minutia of daily life fascinates me, like when Lalee is teaching Granny how to cook. It tells so much, that there's no meat in the house, and what Lalee ends up cooking with is bologna.

As a direct cinema filmmaker, a style that's observational or "fly on the wall," how do you approach issues of storytelling?

We're trying to make scenes, because we're trying to make nonfiction films. I never think that we're making a documentary. I think that we're making a film, just like a feature film director makes a film. I've got to get cutaways, I've got to get an end point of the scene, and I've got to get into the scene some way. Usually you're going to miss the beginning of the scene, unless it's total serendipity and something unfolded while you were filming. Often you're sitting waiting and something happens and you just miss that first line. You've got to get it some way. For instance, the scene at the end of the film where Lalee breaks down. We went into the trailer and Lalee was incredibly upset. She's talking to her daughter. And so Al [Maysles] and I just started filming because we could see that something had happened, something very emotional was going on. As I started to understand—a neighbor had come to tell her that Eddie Reed had been taken back to jail—I knew that I didn't have a beginning to the scene. I had to get a beginning, but I didn't want to just ask Lalee, "What's going on?" I don't like to do that, to cut to an interview to explain what's going on in this beautiful emotional scene, and we're not going to be using narration, so I have to figure out how to nudge Lalee to give me an opening line.

That's, to me, a real skill that you develop after you've shot a lot of vérité and you know what you need to bring back to the editing room for the editor to be able to craft a scene together to tell a story. Lalee didn't know what Eddie Reed had been taken to jail for. So what I did is, I asked Jeanette, Lalee's daughter, "Why don't you call the police, to find out?" As soon as I said that, Lalee said to Jeannette, "Why don't you call the police?" That allowed Jeanette to talk with them and then tell Lalee [as we were filming] what had happened. So that we did have a beginning to the story.

So you're working on several levels—as the technician recording sound, the producer worrying about Lalee, and the storyteller watching for a scene's beginning, middle, and end.

Completely. I feel like that's something I learned very much from being able to watch David Maysles work. When David and Al were shooting *Grey Gardens*, there was no one in the house but the two of them. But I worked on the editing, and so I saw how David talked to the subjects, and I'd seen it on other projects, too, where David would get certain information out of a subject. And so I know you have to do that. You're like a psychiatrist, you say things like, "How did that make you feel?" When Lalee was telling about the death of her son George, that was a situation where she was so emotional, it was very hard not to intervene and comfort her. But being sympathetic and hardly saying anything keeps the scene going to where you feel like you have an ending. And to me the ending was where she said, "You want to love your children but don't love them too hard," which is a really amazing line.

What other storytelling issues do you face?

I'm always trying to figure out how to tell the backstory. Often over the course of shooting I'll just throw out a question: "What about your mother?" or "What about Redman?" Especially if there's someone else around and some comment about the past goes into a discussion about the present. You throw out a thought and let the subjects bounce that around and see where it goes. That's how the "school or jail" scene started, with me just chitchatting. Lalee talks about how she started caring for Redman, and then she says, to Redman, "You know, you're gonna have to go to school or you've got to go to jail." And Redman says, "I want to go jail." And so the scene offers a way to explore one of the film's themes; that these little boys are being programmed to jail.

I don't think it pays off to try to manipulate in vérité; it doesn't ring true. We would never ask anyone to do anything other than, for instance, I noticed that Lalee didn't have any water. She was always pouring water out of a Clorox bottle to wash her dishes and things like that. She'd go to the jail and get it out of a hose that was attached to the building. And so one trip when we were down there, not much was going on, I said, "Well, are you going to go get water today?" Because I knew I wanted to get that scene of them hauling water. But that's something Lalee's family does all the time anyway.

How much footage did you end up shooting?

I think the ratio was 70:1 [70 hours for each hour of the final edited film]. But that's 16mm. I think *Grey Gardens* was about the same. *Grey Gardens* was shot over six intensive weeks and I think it was about 36 to 40 shoot days. *Lalee's Kin* was about 42 shoot days.

It's funny, because when we were at Sundance with *Lalee's Kin* [Al Maysles won the 2001 Excellence in Cinematography Award for the film], there were other filmmakers who would tell me they had 400 hours or 300 hours or something. You should be making choices. That's what filmmaking is all about, making choices in the field. What a handicap going into the editing room with that much material. Because to me you really have to explore your footage.

Tell me about editing Lalee's Kin.

We started editing about a year and a half into the shooting. Our approach to editing is that you screen everything and then you make selects. These films are not easy to structure. We screen all the footage, and then we talk about what we think is strong. The content dictates the form, the way we approach it. What you originally think might be the story, you realize you might have a much stronger story but it's going to be harder to craft. And so there's a lot of experimentation and restructuring and recutting.

Do you use an act structure?

We often call it Act One, Act Two, Act Three. We'll say, when we're screening, "This is Act One information"—it's setting up the situation. We don't yet know where it's going to appear in Act One, but we put it in that section. And then Act Two and Act Three.

Act Two is always the hardest in vérité, it's the hardest part of the film not to sag. You've got to get a few of your feisty scenes into Act Two. Reggie with the pep rally, where you see Reggie's passion, really held up the middle of the film and kept the story going, which is so important. In vérité you don't often have a lot of scenes that tell the story, you have to be very careful how you place them.

Were you still shooting when you started editing?

Ideally, it's better to start editing once you have shot. We usually try to cut the end of the film, the climax, so we know what we're building to. We want to have some kind of a dramatic arc, whether it's a story line arc or an emotional arc of some sort. Some realization that the character has, or some understanding about life, something like that. But with *Lalee's Kin* we hadn't finished shooting, so we just started cutting scenes. Let's say that there are 10 moments, or maybe 20, that we think really could make great scenes, so we cut those together. And then we do a very rough assembly, like four hours long. And you see how the scenes play against each other.

At this point, a scene could go in many different directions. Sometimes you have two or three points in a scene; often you try to assign a value to the scene. For example, "This scene is going to tell Lalee's backstory, her family upbringing." Or, "This scene is going to explain what Reggie's dilemma is." Or, "This scene, you're going to understand Granny's despair." One scene may stand for something for a two-month period, and then you completely reedit it to stand for something else.

That's why we give our editors director's credit, because they work very closely with us in structuring the film and giving the film a beginning, middle, and end. We do the selects and then the scenes, and once we cut the scenes, we start to put them in an assembly. Right away you start to see which story lines are working and which ones are weak. And you keep editing down, you keep sculpting, down and down. The hardest part for us has always been the opening. Trying to set the scene and introduce a lot of characters.

In general, direct cinema expects viewers to work a bit to follow a story, to figure out the players and themes.

Charlotte Zwerin—a phenomenal filmmaker to have learned from—said to me early on, "I don't see what's wrong with making people work a few minutes in the beginning of a film." And I think we all feel that way. I think it's different when you're cutting just for television. In a theater, no one's going to get up and leave; they've committed two hours or 90 minutes, part of their day, to going through this experience and they're ready to sink into a story. Television's a lot different; you'd better grab them right away. It's a different way that you start to edit.

How do you keep track of the material as you're editing?

I think most filmmakers use three-by-five cards. You write the topic of the scene and one or two points of what the scene's going to accomplish, and you have a bulletin board and keep rearranging these cards. About 10 years ago, [editor] Deborah Dickson and I started taking notes and putting them into the computer. It's much easier to look at your structure on paper and quickly see, for example, I've got a lot of Lalee, good Reggie, now I've got to weave in the kids. You can see what you're missing.

What kind of editing schedule do you follow?

We edited *Lalee's Kin* in a little less than two years. *Grey Gardens* took two and a half years; it took a whole year just to figure out what you had in the footage and what story line you were going to go for. Nothing happens in that house in *Grey Gardens*. So how do you structure a film about it? It took a long time to figure out that there was a balance of power between Little and Big Edie.

Vérité is a time-consuming process.

I think you get a much richer, more layered, more complex film in the end. You have to see where your subject is taking you. You've got a kernel of an idea and an intuitive feeling that this is going to lead you somewhere really interesting, but you have to have nerves of steel while you're making it. A lot of stuff doesn't happen the way you thought it was going to happen or in a timely manner. This is where the faith and the experience of making these films comes in, where you just know that life is going to reward you in some way. Sometimes you can get really lucky with a subject, like *Gimme Shelter*. The Maysles got an assignment to film a Rolling Stones concert at Madison Square Garden, one concert. And then they asked the Stones if they could, on their— the Maysles'—own money, follow them on tour, and then the Altamont concert happened.

    In *Lalee's Kin*, when the school district got off probation, Reggie's story, you could have stopped the film there. But Lalee's story . . . We thought one of the most revealing moments was when Lalee said, "I don't know much about love." It's really an amazing thing to hear a woman say; she's never really experienced romantic love. But you realize that she does love her children very much. She doesn't show it so much, but deep down she loves these children, and she especially loves her son. You see her devastation when her son is going to go to the penitentiary, probably for life. And that's when Lalee breaks down. But then she raises up again and it's her "keep on keeping on." When Al and I walked out of the trailer after we'd filmed that, we looked at each other and said, "We have an ending." And Deborah Dickson felt the same way.

Let's move on to Recording The Producers, *which you filmed as Broadway stars Nathan Lane, Matthew Broderick, and, of course, Mel Brooks made the cast album for* The Producers. *How was that film to make?*

That was all about gaining the trust of these celebrities. They have to do this very difficult recording of a cast album in one day, because of the union rules, and here's this film crew that I think everybody thought, "This is going to really prevent us from getting it done." Mel Brooks was very skeptical at first. He even said to me, "I hate cinéma vérité."

    But Nathan Lane was a big fan of D. A. Pennebaker's film, *The Company*, and so Nathan right away was very willing to wear a mic, and then Matthew Broderick came right on board. And what surprised us—and that's what's great about doing this because you never know what you're going to get, it's always a sense of discovery that's so exciting—is that they were very close, and big fans of each other, and they were very funny together. Nathan kind of interviewed Matthew, and Matthew played the role of Marlon Brando, and it's just this wonderful kind of vérité moment that you would never have anticipated. Talk about holding up the middle! It gives you a whole new insight into who these men are and how clever and bright and fast on their feet they are, in terms of humor.

Mel didn't want to be miked, but he was sitting next to [director/choreographer] Susan Stroman and she was miked, and so I could hear him. And as he could see that we weren't interfering, he said, "Look at this film crew, they have so much patience." We started at seven in the morning. I would say by two in the afternoon, he started to relax with us being there. There was a lot of chitchat going on, it was an off moment, they weren't recording, so I just threw out, "Mel, I'm curious, was there really a Max Bialystock?" And Mel just lit up and told us this great story. I mean he's a showman, obviously, and it was a wonderful story, and we all laughed, and then he came up to me afterwards and said, "You know, I think this is going to be okay." And I said, "But you know Mel, we are going to need an interview." And he said, "Oh, I don't know."

It wasn't until seven at night that he agreed to be interviewed, and then he basically did a stand-up monologue. As soon as I got that I said, "I've got a film, and I've got a great film." And afterwards, he was willing to sit and talk to us, and it was very heartfelt, and we got another layer that way. And then it was just a joy in the editing room; we edited that film quickly. It was wonderful material.

What kind of gear and crew did you need?

When you only have one day to shoot, there's a lot of pressure on you as the director to make sure you're getting everything. We could have used four cameras, but we only had the budget for three—two in the recording studio and one in the control room. I used the most experienced vérité cameramen, I think, in existence: Bob Richman, who grew out of Maysles; Don Lenzer, who's done years of work with us; and Tom Hurwitz. You had to go in with people who are also filmmakers in their own right, because you couldn't be everywhere at once and there was almost no way to have a communication system because it would interfere with the recording process.

How has your work been affected by the emergence of digital video?

It's been hard for me to get used to the rhythm of shooting in video. I grew up in 16 mm. I like the fact that you have to change film [magazines] every 10.5 minutes because it makes you really think about what you're shooting and what you're getting and what you need to get. A half an hour [a video cassette length] goes fast—when you're shooting it's all very intense—and then I think, why did I keep shooting?

In terms of editing, it has made a tremendous difference. With *Lalee's Kin* [which was shot on film and edited on video], we did selects and digitized selects. I don't really understand how we ever edited without the Avid, to some degree, even though I miss being able just to get on a Steenbeck and look at footage—not selects, dailies. But all the different versions you do in the [nonlinear] editing room, I mean, you can work it out so much quicker.

Still, you've got to have time to think about what's really the best story to tell with your footage. Any team in the editing room is going to tell a different story. You could have cut *Lalee* in a variety of ways. You could have cut *Grey Gardens* differently as well. You've got to think about what you're doing, and you need time to process the material. To me, that's never going to change. Telling a story is telling a story, and it's not always easy—especially in vérité—to see what structure is going to be best; there's a lot of working with material that's required. I've been in editing rooms where the editor gets a call from a cable station, "We're hoping you're available, we've got one month to make this hour-long film." And we're always just stunned. The truth is that *Lalee's Kin*, whether you're shooting in video or film, was going to be big budget. You needed the time in the editing room. You needed to pay a good editor. You needed to be going on many trips into the Delta to shoot. Those are expensive. And you can't run a film company on these tiny video budgets, either.

Update: Your first film at Maysles, Grey Gardens, has been adapted for the stage and is now a hit musical on Broadway. What do you think accounts for its success?

I think it's a situation of finding characters that many people can relate to. Little Edie's yearning to leave Grey Gardens and her inability to leave Grey Gardens is something a lot of people connect with. And it's a very powerful story between a mother and a daughter. I think that's why it's adapted so well—it's a great story.

22

Sam Pollard

Sam Pollard has been working as a feature film and television editor and documentary producer/director for nearly 30 years. He and I worked together on two documentary series for PBS, *I'll Make Me a World* and *Eyes on the Prize*. His other documentary credits include *Goin' Back to T-Town* and the series *The Rise and Fall of Jim Crow* and *American Roots Music*.

Sam has edited several dramatic features directed by Spike Lee, including *Mo' Better Blues, Jungle Fever, Girl 6, Clockers*, and *Bamboozled*. For HBO, he and Lee produced and Sam edited the documentary *4 Little Girls*, an Academy Award–nominated film about the 1963 church bombing in Birmingham, Alabama, that claimed the lives of 11-year-old Denise McNair and 14-year-olds Addie Mae Collins, Carole Robertson, and Cynthia Wesley. More recently, they coproduced and Sam was supervising editor on *When the Levees Broke: A Requiem in Four Acts*, a documentary about New Orleans during and after Hurricane Katrina.

Sam is a professor at New York University's Tisch School of the Arts, where he teaches first-year and advanced film and video editing. We spoke in 2003 and again in 2006, while Sam was editing *Levees*.

As an editor, what's your role in structuring the film's narrative?

You get three types of documentary producers. The first type will say, "I went out, and I'm doing a film about these four girls who were killed in Birmingham, Alabama. Here's my script, here's my structure, we'll screen the dailies together, and I want you to follow that template."

313

Second type of producer says, "I went out, I shot this footage about four little girls who were killed in Birmingham in 1963. I filmed their parents, their nieces, their cousins, I talked to ministers in the community of Birmingham, I also talked to Andrew Young and other people involved in the civil rights movement, because Dr. King went there in 1963. I think the story is going to be not only about the girls, it's also going to be about the historical event of Dr. King trying to break down the walls of segregation in Birmingham. That's my story. I haven't written anything down, but that's the idea." That's the second approach.

Third approach, the producer comes in, says, "I shot all this footage about the four girls killed in Birmingham, I'll be back in eight weeks, you let me see what there is—create something." I've done all types of documentaries, all three types.

In the case of *4 Little Girls*, Spike was like the third producer. He basically said, "I've got to do this story about these four girls; it's been in me about 15 years, I need to do this story." And he went down and he shot. He never really figured out what the arc of the story was, but he'd been carrying this story around with him so long—and his aesthetic is so artistic. He just knew he didn't want to make an ordinary-type documentary. Just not his style.

He came up with a list of people he wanted to interview, and after he shot for a month the family members and people involved in the movement, we went into the editing room. For about three weeks, from 7 to 11 in the morning, we would screen dailies and talk. I came up with the idea of trying to do the parallel story. On one track we have the girls' lives unfolding; on the other we see the movement as it moves into Birmingham, and then they collide with the bombing of the church. And that's how we basically approached it.

One of the strengths of the film is the stories and storytellers, particularly Denise McNair's father, Chris.

They were good stories. But you know, it was interesting. I was on that shoot when he did Chris. This was like a feature shoot. Spike had a truck, he had tracks, he had dollies, he had all these lights. I said, "Jeez, what's all this equipment?" And Spike had done a lot of research, but when we got to the interview that day, he didn't have any questions on paper. I was sitting behind him, and I had my own sheet of questions. And I swear, I thought he was so haphazard in how he was asking questions, his style is, to me, so indirect, I thought, "He's not going to get anything good out of this guy." But Chris really connected with Spike; he was able to convey emotion and was such a good storyteller. Mrs. Robertson [Alpha Robertson, mother of Carole] was also a good storyteller. They'd been living with their children's deaths for so many years, and they had stored so much, probably, things they wanted to say. And they all trusted Spike.

From your own experience, how do you think filmmakers establish that kind of trust? I'm thinking, for example, of Big Black (Frank Smith), a former Attica inmate you interviewed for Eyes on the Prize.

You know, it's a funny thing. Sometimes when I interview people, there's a kind of connection where I feel like I'm with family. I feel just very open myself. I don't feel couched; I don't have anything to hide. And I think people feel that and connect. Sometimes, I don't feel that comfortable with the person I'm interviewing, and it comes through. I interviewed Nell Painter for this Jim Crow show. I didn't feel I had done my homework in terms of what questions to ask, and I never connected with her. Everything was very stiff.

What if you're interviewing someone whose views you strongly oppose?

You still try to be as human as possible. For *The Rise and Fall of Jim Crow*, I interviewed this white gentleman in Florida who, when he was 16 years old in Georgia, saw four black people killed. At first I said [to the other series producers, Richard Wormser and Bill Jersey, both of whom are white], "You want *me* to do the interview?" Because this guy was 70 years old, he's still a redneck; you can see it, he still carries that baggage. But somehow, when I sat down and interviewed him and really touched on some areas that were so painful for him to remember, and really understanding his ambiguous relationships with black people—this guy opened up to me.

The only person that we knew I wasn't going to interview was in northern Georgia, this gentleman named Gordon Parks [no relation to the filmmaker]. He tells a story in Bill Jersey's show, in show three, about how when he was 15, his grandfather took him to a lynching of a black man. And even now he's unrepentant. I mean, he's surrounded by young white guys who are Klansmen, he's still a Klansman, so they knew that one I wouldn't do.

How do you feel about projects where the footage is handed off to an editing team and the initial connection is lost? Someone like the old man in Florida could be treated very badly.

Mutilated. I've been fortunate enough to not yet have someone else take the footage that I've shot. I feel it's my responsibility to be the one to help shape their story, and tell that story in the editing room. If somebody in *Jim Crow* says, "Well, I never said it like that," then I'm the one they're going to have to deal with. It's a delicate thing. You have to make editorial adjustments, sometimes, to try to get the story across clearly, concisely—because it's always about trying to be concise. The problem is that most times when people do their interviews, they don't quite understand that they're going to be edited. I've had it happen so many times. Someone will look at the interview and say, "What happened to what I said? I talked to you for two hours and you used two minutes?"

How much of a story do you work out before you film?

With *T'Town*, I did a treatment, and then when I got back, before I gave the footage to [the editor], I worked out a complete structure, a 20-page template. With *Jim Crow*, basically, I had a 40-page script from Richard Wormser. When we went into the editing room, I followed the script, and when we looked at it, it was terrible. Slow. Meandered. And then we went back and restructured, and then we looked at it again; it looked a little better. It's a process. He went and reshot; we put a whole new element in that was never in the script.

But the thing is, it's always better to have a foundation, a template. So you know you have something there in front of you. Most documentary filmmakers, even the students, go out and shoot and they don't have a clue what the story is. I mean, I'll do it. I've been trying to shoot something about my father, and even though I know I'm not doing it the right way, I'm still just going out and shooting. But I don't have any money, no deadlines, I don't feel constricted. When someone's paying me, before I start editing I will always write down the structure.

Do you look for a story arc?

I usually do. A transformation of a state of being. Sometimes I don't have to have a character take me through. And sometimes I can feel there's a sense of artifice. Part of me with Ali [a story about fighter Muhammad Ali, in *Eyes on the Prize*] always felt that—even though Ali's a great character, even though it's his real story—it feels a little jerry-rigged. It doesn't feel like it quite unfolds, it feels like you see the hands of the filmmakers moving the pieces. And that always throws me.

4 Little Girls *begins in a cemetery, with Joan Baez's "Ballad of Birmingham" on the soundtrack relating the tragedy that's about to unfold. How do you feel about the need for a "hook" at the start of a film?*

I have two feelings about it. Sometimes you've got to give them a hook right up front, like the bombing. Years ago, I did a film about Langston Hughes. We basically kill Langston off at the beginning. "He's a wonderful poet, but then he died." Then we backtrack and tell you the story. I always kind of liked that, that old movie thing. But I thought it was a mistake in retrospect; it underwhelmed the whole film, dramatically. Sometimes if you give them the hook up front, then when you build up to it again, you say, "Oh, I already know that." Sometimes the hook can be detrimental. In *4 Little Girls*, it wasn't. The reason we started with Joan Baez was because the song was so great. And Spike had had Ellen Kuras [director of photography] shoot the cemetery footage in that very weird style. He didn't know it was going to be at the beginning, but he shot it.

How do you approach issues of balance in your work?

Even when we were doing *Eyes,* I always questioned that, having to get the opposing point of view to give you the balanced perspective. I think the word shouldn't be "balance." I think that if you interview people that have contradiction, that to me gives it a more textured perspective. In *4 Little Girls*, people said we took a cheap shot at [former Alabama governor] George Wallace. Well, I don't think so. He was not in the greatest health, as we know. But it wasn't like he had just been thrown the questions and didn't know what to say. He knew. Before he even consented to do the interview, Spike had to send him all the questions. And when

I look at the outtakes—I put the whole outtake of the interview on the DVD—I really didn't cut that much out. So I didn't think we did him a disservice. It's a funny thing about people. Part of the reason George Wallace did the interview, I think, is because Spike Lee wanted to interview him.

What are the biggest storytelling issues your students face?

The biggest pitfall is understanding what their film's about right from the beginning. Before they sit down to write a page of the narration or script, what's the theme? And then on the theme, what's the story that they're going to convey to get across the theme?

For me, the theme of *Jim Crow* is how a people of color who were given their freedom in 1863, with the Emancipation Proclamation, had to struggle mightily against tremendous odds to be able to find that window of opportunity, and the things they had to do on all levels to move themselves forward. Richard and Bill may have a different approach, but that to me was what it was always about. So the next step was to find the stories that were going to help convey that. What I liked about *Jim Crow* is that there's an ambiguity in these real-life characters. Look at Booker T. Washington. On the one hand, he's this great man who starts this wonderful school [in 1881] to help black people. On the other hand, he basically says to black people, "Don't try to go but so far; take it to a certain level but don't rock the boat." None of this is simple. I always believe that nothing is black and white, that it's textured, shades of gray. To me, if that comes through, we did our job.

How do you evaluate story ideas?

What makes an idea great for a documentary is if you're introducing me to a world I've never heard about, and there's some story within that world that's going to be new and attention-grabbing. A student of mine who's Muslim came to me; she was down in Trinidad one summer and shot all this footage, so she wanted me to take a look at it. When you say Trinidad, my assumption, the first thing I think of is, Carnival. People in costumes dancing, having a good time; everybody's trying to do a film about Trinidad and Carnival. So I figure this is what she's going to show me.

She puts the footage up on the TV, and it's about a Muslim sect in Trinidad that's been in conflict with the government about being able to have freedom of choice in their own mosque, their own communities. Their government feels that they're like a terrorist group and they've been clamping down on them. There's been violent struggle, shootouts. So all of a sudden I'm saying, "Wow, this is interesting. I never knew there was a Muslim sect in Trinidad. I didn't know there was all this tension that's been going on for about 12 years." It's very interesting material for a documentary. Her problem is, she just went out and shot. Her father's Muslim, he knew about this group, introduced her to some people. Now she has no clue how to put the film together. What I said to her is, it's like doing the homework in a backwards way. You have to sit down and write down on paper, "What am I trying to say? What's the arc of this film?"

As a filmmaker, do you work to ensure that your storytelling is inclusive, that it covers voices and experiences that might not be readily available in archival material or secondary research?

I met filmmaker St. Clair Bourne in 1980, when I did his film about the blues in Chicago, *Big City Blues*. He basically became my mentor, in making me understand, as an African American, that the voice of "the other" is an important voice that has to be conveyed because you rarely hear or see it. Since that time, I've always believed strongly that, be it films about African Americans or Native Americans or Asians, women, it's important to be involved in those films. And if you're involved in a film that doesn't have that, you try to find that in the material.

Bennett Singer came to me a few years ago, wanted to do a documentary that I'm now executive producer of, *Brother Outsider: The Life of Bayard Rustin*. That to me was important. Not only because Rustin was so active in civil rights, but because he was a gay man who wasn't afraid to say that, no matter what the consequences. That probably drew me more to it than the fact that he was the main cog for the [1963] March on Washington.

With any documentary, music is an important part of the storytelling. At what point do you start to think about it?

All the time. I love music. You have to be a little careful because sometimes music can overwhelm the storytelling and undercut the drama of just letting the images play. Years ago, when we were doing the *Eyes* show, you were opposed to a piece of music,

"Keep on Pushing," that we put in at the end of the Ali story. You thought it was going to detract from just listening to Ali and the narration. And I argued with you, "No, no, Sheila, you're wrong." But in retrospect, you were right. I watched that show recently—the music was too specific, too on the nose. You've always got to be careful about how you use music. I like it to be a little more indirect now, as I get older.

Tell me about your most recent collaboration with Spike Lee, When the Levees Broke, *which premiered on HBO in August 2006, a year after Hurricane Katrina. How did this film come about?*

We were driving downtown [in September 2005], and Spike says, "You know, Sam, I've got a great title: *When the Levees Broke.* I want to do a documentary about New Orleans." So that night, I did some research on the Internet and wrote some notes. And the next day, I said, "We could do a doc that looks at the complications and the evolution of the hurricane and the personal stories of the people who were there." So Spike called Sheila Nevins at HBO and set up meeting.

When was your first shoot in New Orleans?

Thanksgiving. We went down with this mammoth crew of 25 people. Normally when you shoot a doc, it's you as the producer, camera, an assistant (if you're shooting film), sound, and maybe a PA [production assistant]. But when we flew out of Newark the day after Thanksgiving, it was Spike, me, a line producer, three cameramen, four assistants, and six graduate students from NYU. Then, when we got to New Orleans, we got a location manager with his four location people, five vans, five drivers, a camera loader—I mean, it was like an army. And Spike gave us our assignments: This crew goes to this parish, this crew goes here.

Spike returned to New Orleans several times, and also filmed evacuees in New York. I've read that there were about 130 interviews in all, some 200 hours of footage. I'm curious about your role, not only as supervising editor but also as coproducer.

Basically, my charge is to figure out how to make this thing a film. As with *4 Little Girls,* I'm given a task of combing through all this material and trying to figure out a structure to make it come to life.

Spike will come in and critique it and want changes, but I'm trying to build it, trying to tell a story and figure out how to make it exciting. And I've got about 18, 20 weeks to make it happen.

When did you start to edit?

I brought three assistants on in February 2006 to start logging and digitizing the interviews, and they were all transcribed, and the assistants went through the transcript books and wrote down the time code numbers. Then I figured out what I call subject bins, such as *The Days before the Hurricane; The Day Katrina Hit; They Thought They Had Dodged the Bullet.* If anybody talked about one of those particular subjects, the assistants put that bite into that bin. And then when I started, on March 6, I started going through each bin, putting together all the interview bites and whittling them down, shaping them. I don't go but so far, because I know that as soon as I start to put footage in, which is the next stage, it'll change.

Do you draft a script on paper before you cut?

I don't usually do a paper cut, I'm more instinctual now. But I will write out a structure—where I want to start, how I want to get to the end. I sketch out scenes and what the order should be. Then I start adding footage and stills, assembling edited sequences. What happens in this process of building is that I'll see things from my paper structure that aren't working, so I start to move things around. And I'll go back through the transcripts sometimes, like when I need a way to transition to certain footage. And then when I show Spike a cut, he'll ask, "How come you didn't put this in, how come you didn't add this sequence?" So I'll go back and look at the material and rebuild.

Do you find that your subject pulls—those bins—stay intact as sequences?

Not always. For example, initially I had a *Superdome* subject bin. But I've opened up: One sequence is about when people first got to the Superdome, another is about people dealing with it after they were there for four days, and another is about people evacuating the Superdome. So it's broken up into different sections.

With 130 storytellers, isn't there a risk that the film will be a long montage, and not a coherent story that carries viewers through an experience?

That's the challenge. Everybody's got different pieces of the story, and someone who might be good at the beginning is not so good when it comes to talking about the evacuation. Someone who doesn't say much in the beginning is great when it comes to talking about the flooding. So I'm trying to find the rhythms of these people, to create a journey, an arc. I've noticed in a lot of sequences where we've tried to intercut people telling the same story, I've gone back and I've taken out some voices, to allow one person tell the story. If you find the right characters, the right interviews, they can give you a visceral sense of immediacy, of being there, so you feel emotionally connected to it. When this man tells you about finding his mother's body under the refrigerator, because she hadn't gotten out. . . . Or this woman whose daughter went to stay with her father in the Ninth Ward, and she couldn't find her and was having dreams that she was falling, falling, falling, and then a few months later they found her daughter's body. . . . That's powerful. You try to get out of the way, not to condense too much, edit it too much.

You also have a unique challenge in that the four-hour film will be shown in various configurations—as a four-hour special, in 2 two-hour blocks, and as individual hours. How do you make each of those presentations feel complete?

I have a beginning, middle, and end for each hour, and we're also doing it by acts—my first hour is Act One, the second hour is Act Two, and so on. The first hour begins pre-Katrina and ends on people who were in the Superdome, who do anything— songs, games—to keep their spirits up. Act Two looks at the city in tremendous chaos, and the evacuation of people, and ends with all of these dead bodies. Act Three picks up with where the people landed, and what happened when they arrived there, and builds to the question of staying or coming back. And also deals with the psychic and emotional toll of the hurricane. The fourth act gets into what happened when people did come back, and rebuilding.

If each of the hours is an act, what is the overarching story?

A people under siege. One and Two are chronologically driven; Three and Four [edited by Geeta Gandbhir and Nancy Novack, who started in April] are more thematically driven.

How do you think your experience editing dramatic features impacts your work in documentary, and vice versa?

What we're involved in, always, is trying to tell a story. Before I became a producer in documentaries [in 1988, on *Eyes on the Prize*], I had edited a lot of docs, but I wasn't always thinking about how to tell a story and have it escalate dramatically and emotionally. That's something I learned from the irascible Henry Hampton [executive producer of *Eyes*, a series that used a three-act structure to tell historical stories.]. And then right after, Spike called me about cutting *Mo' Better Blues*, and I've worked with him since on a series of narrative fiction features. What I've learned from both is to always make the story dramatic. Get the characters up a tree, how're we going to get 'em down? I apply three-act structure to everything. I don't always adhere to it as closely as we did on *Eyes*, but it's always in the back of my mind.

Last question. Given their cost, which is money that might be spent elsewhere, why do documentaries matter?

Being documentary filmmakers, I think part of our responsibility is to be able to make people aware of history: social history, racial history, economic history. Nine times out of ten, people can only deal with that history when it's in the past, 30 years, 40 years. Sometimes you've got to jolt people a little. Because if you don't deal with what's happening now, you're just going to repeat the same problems, which we can see now in New Orleans. I think, because of Spike, that this film will have tremendous impact. It will reawaken people's outrage and frustration at what happened last year in New Orleans. It's present history, that needs to be considered, needs to be evaluated.

23

Kenn Rabin

An archivist, filmmaker, and writer, Kenn Rabin is one of the nation's leading authorities on audiovisual research and the use of stock footage and sound. His credits include the series *Vietnam: A Television History*, which involved more than 90 archives from a dozen countries; *Eyes on the Prize*, for which he received an Emmy nomination; *500 Nations*, by Kevin Costner; and Barry Levinson's *Yesterday's Tomorrows*, on which he served as writer and associate producer. More recently, he served as the archival scene researcher for the dramatic features *Good Night, and Good Luck* and *The Good German*. We spoke in 2003 and 2006.

As someone who's a storyteller and an archival film expert, what do you see as the strengths of using archival material to tell documentary stories?

I think that we've become more and more a visual society, and our storytelling relies so much on wanting to see what people are talking about. If we see it, we believe it's true, which is a tricky trap to get into, especially in this digital world. But we're raised on visual images, so we tend to think that that's the only way that stories can be told, and it's funny how you start crying out for those moving images if you don't have them.

What people don't realize is that moving images contain embedded in them certain types of information that is different than information in printed material. It's not a strength or a weakness, it's just different. To give you an example, I know of an archivist who's got a local news collection, and she's adamant about not throwing away stories on local fires, that kind of thing, because it shows what a fire truck looked like in 1950, how the firemen dressed. And she's got a point, that there's all this social information that's encoded in those visual images.

If you're telling a story with archival material, at what point should you start finding that material?

There's an interesting chicken or egg thing that the producer faces when dealing with the kind of crosstalk that you get between archival footage and the interview process. Very often the interview subjects will suggest where to look for archival material or what to look for. Examples: "I was there with my friend and he had a movie camera", or, "I remember NBC News was there." And what you find in the archival footage will sometimes suggest, "Oh, here's a lot of coverage of a particular event, let's expand on that." Or you'll see someone in archival footage and say, "I wonder if we can find that guy, is he still around, can we interview him?" That's the kind of crosstalk you get when you really do your homework. You've got some of your team going after the archival and part of your team doing preinterviews and shooting interviews. That kind of ideal way of doing it often implies the need for a higher budget and particularly more lead time in preproduction and more time in the edit room. There's no time to do that when you're doing one of these short-form, assembly-line things that has to be done in six or eight weeks for a miniscule budget.

With schedules and budgets that tight nowadays, are producers taking shortcuts with archival research?

Generally speaking, most filmmakers I am contacted by don't understand that the way you make a stock footage documentary is that you go to the original creators of the archival footage (the networks, newsreel houses, collectors, filmmakers) and hunt around for it, see what they shot, look through cards, look through computer printouts, screen material, order it up, and bring it all into the edit room. Their understanding of the process of making a compilation documentary is that your research consists of finding all the other documentaries that have been made on the subject, getting copies of them on tape, screening them, identifying the shots that you want, and then lifting them, or at best trying to get the producers of those films to tell you where they got the shots. Or contacting someone like me to try to find those shots, somehow, by just looking at them and intuiting where they originally came from—usually about a week before the show has to be delivered.

There also seems to be a change in how archival material is used, especially in lower-budget films.

Because of the quickness and cheapness with which documentaries are now being produced, people use what's called "wallpaper," which is generic images that stand in for narrative points that are being made. So when you say, "the city of Saigon," you can show an image that may be the city of Saigon, but it may not be the time period you're talking about, or it may be a city that looks like Saigon that you kind of get away with. It's really just an image that you're putting up on the screen to occupy the viewer's eyes for the three or four or five seconds during which the narrator is finishing their sentence. Sometimes people wallpaper with the correct image, and sometimes they wallpaper with the wrong image. It's not very good storytelling however you do it, because it's not organic. It's "pegs and holes" filmmaking; in other words, it's trying to fit a peg into a hole, rather than letting the process unfold organically in the editing room.

What about either slowing down or speeding up archival material?

This is something that's routinely done today. Changing the speed of archival footage, particularly slowing it down, will subtly or not so subtly change the emotional flavor of a piece of archival footage. It will make something seem more heroic, more sorrowful, more gruesome, depending obviously on what the content is. And that's something that people don't think much about when they think about whether they're using archival footage honestly. They don't think it's a cheat.

Is your bottom line that you just don't manipulate archival material, period?

Well, that used to be my bottom line. I would say something a little different now, a little more complicated than that. My bottom line now is, there are a lot of different kinds of nonfiction projects you can do. If you are doing the standard historical documentary and you are setting up that type of storytelling vocabulary, and that's the expectation you want your audience to have of you, then yes, you follow these journalistic rules and you use your footage with complete integrity. If you're doing another type of documentary, then you create it in a way where you are setting those rules up for your audience, and your audience understands that you're going to be playing a little different game.

I'm excited by the idea that filmmakers are finding new and different ways of using archival that set new rules that break the old rules. I like the fact that some people are using archival to make very personal documentaries; other people are using it to make what once upon a time was called video art. The only rule is that you've got to tell your audience what your rules are. I really like Jay Rosenblatt's work; you watch one of his films and you know he's trying to do something that's emotional and visceral and is not some representation of historical accuracy. It's something else; it's an art piece.

We often see early film footage—Charlie Chaplin, the Keystone Cops—played very quickly. Why is that?

Turn-of-the-century footage was, at the dawn of the technology, mostly shot at about 14 frames per second, approximately. If you screen *The Birth of a Nation* [D. W. Griffith, 1915] correctly, you're screening it at about 14 or 15 frames per second. And then as you go through about 1916 to 1918, it starts to standardize on 18 frames per second, which really is what the standard was for silent film through the 1920s, and then you get to sound film, which is 24 frames per second. Of course things varied; before there were electric motors, the cameramen were hand cranking the cameras. Even as they filmed one shot, their hand motions might change slightly. So it's an inexact science, but if you present early motion picture that was filmed 1917–18 through 1928–29 at 18 frames per second, then the motion will look normal to you, and it will look like what it looked like to the people who watched it at that time.

I worked with the original copyright frames of Griffith's film *Intolerance*, when I did some work for the American Film Institute. These were the frames of the film that were submitted for copyrighting in 1916. One frame of each shot of the film was stapled to a card and submitted to the Library of Congress, and we could see how the shots were tinted and toned. [The film-makers] had people hand painting each frame of the film; for the Babylon sequence they would have someone paint the king's throne with gilt. These things were stunningly beautiful. They're not the scratchy, dark, black-and-white, running-too-fast things we usually see; they're tremendous works of art.

Have the visual archives for the 20th century been kind of picked over, or are there still surprises to be found?

The archives have been picked over fairly well for the subjects that everyone has done, that's true. But having said that, there's still the rest of each shot, and there's still, how do you use the shots and how do you put them together and how do you put together all the different elements that you have, and why do you pick the subject that you pick? I mean you have to go back a step and say, "Why do you want to make another documentary about the Kennedys? Do you have something new to say? Does the world need another documentary about that?" People should ask themselves, "Why am I picking the subject I'm picking?" But the other thing is, they've not only been picked over, they've been conglomerated and overly computer-cataloged, because they've been retrieved so often. The same keywords pull up the same footage again and again. Creativity is being taken out of the search process.

An example of that: When we were doing *Vietnam: A Television History*, we got down to the last episode, about the fall of Saigon. I was at Sherman Grinberg, which held the ABC News footage at the time, and I was looking for all the footage I could find on the evacuation of the American embassy. I pulled everything I could find in the computer, and then I started pulling in some other words like *Saigon, embassy*. And then I started putting in phrases like *embassy roof*, that would not necessarily have been put in if, like today, you're no longer at the archive but telling some sales rep at the archive what you're looking for.

You can't go to the archive?

It depends on the archive, but less and less can you go to the archives. As collections get bought up by these conglomerates, they have their people who are paid little and who turn over every six months, who sit at computer terminals and do these searches for you. So you tell them what you want, and they punch in the most obvious keywords. And then they pull that stuff, they put it on a VHS cassette, and they send it to you. And that's your film research.

Are you allowed to suggest unusual keywords?

You can if you can think of them, although you don't know how their computer systems work. One of the things about film research is that you pull some reels, you look at some stuff, and then you think of other things you want to pull. You also put in date ranges and personalities and things like that. And so I was looking for everything on the fall of Saigon and closing down the American embassy, and because I put in some unusual keywords, I came up with this one fairly large reel of film. I put up the picture on the flatbed and started watching it, and it looked like chaos at the embassy. People trying to climb over the fence to get into the embassy, people trying to grab onto the bottom of the helicopter as it's trying to take off from the roof, and all this. And I'm watching it and all of a sudden from chaos everything stops, and everybody becomes calm and walks away and sits down at tables, and then there are random shots. And I'm thinking, what's going on here? To make a long story short, I discover that what I'm looking at is footage not of the embassy in Saigon but of Thailand, where Michael Cimino is shooting *The Deer Hunter* and recreating the fall of Saigon. And he had yelled, "Cut," so all these actors had stopped recreating the fall of Saigon and had gone back to a cup of coffee from the craft services table. It was the eeriest thing.

The previous episode of the *Vietnam* series was ending with the fall of Saigon, and we were going to pick up there at the beginning of the last episode and go on to talk about the legacies of the war. And we thought, this is amazing, we'll start the last episode with this thing, which is a recreation of this event that we'd seen the real footage of at the end of the previous episode. And I never would have found it if I'd had to phone in, you know, "Give me what you've got on the fall of Saigon."

Is it possible to make an archival film on a low budget?

It's possible, but it has to be something for which the archival materials are relatively inexpensive and accessible, and are not owned by heavily commercial third-party sources or bound by increasingly strange legal encumbrances. There are now all kinds of rules and laws regarding likenesses of famous people, which get you into all kinds of financial trouble. I worked on a film recently that wanted to use a clip from something that normally would be in the public domain by many years. But because an actor appearing in it had their likeness trademarked, the use of that clip was going to be prohibitively expensive or not even available.

I would like to see the government step in and be heroic—issue exemptions to the copyright laws that allow nonfiction filmmakers working on primarily educational projects to be less encumbered by various restrictions—but I don't see it happening. Congress is moving in the opposite direction, favoring corporations maintaining control over their copyrights for longer and longer periods, which is not the original intention of the law.

What should storytellers know, and how should they compensate for, the various biases that are inevitable in archival or third-party material?

Producers should know about the material they're using—where it comes from, what the history of that company is—at least enough to know what the bias might have been. The more you know your subject, the more you're going to know how things might have been manipulated.

As an obvious example, if your subject is the Stalinist era in the Soviet Union, you're going to know that the materials produced out of that environment were manipulated in certain ways and showed certain sides of issues and not other sides. As a producer, you can include that as an actual subject. You can do a section on the use of propaganda in the Stalinist era; you can show photographs that have been doctored, before and after. You can show film footage that was released in the Soviet Union and then show footage of the same event as it was released in another part of the world.

It's really your responsibility to educate yourself about these kinds of things knowing, for example, the history of the newsreels. A lot of documentary filmmakers rely on newsreel footage if they're dealing with the early or mid part of the 20th century. Newsreels ran from about 1910 through the late 1960s in various countries. They were manipulated in lots of different ways, and of course narrations of the newsreels were heavily propagandized and newsreels were often restaged. One of the great newsreel moments in my research was when I was at the National Archives looking at some *March of Time* newsreels, produced by Time/Life.

I found outtakes from the story on Kristallnacht, the night when the Nazis raided all the Jewish shops. Actors dressed as SS storm troopers were sitting around a studio smoking cigarettes while prop people brought in glass plate windows with Hebrew writing on them, that were obviously meant to be windows of Jewish shops. And they were setting up to shoot a scene that was supposed to be Kristallnacht.

Above and beyond that, anyone using audiovisual materials should understand in general that these materials have a point of view. Things are edited. What is in the frame and what isn't in the frame, what shots are and aren't being used. Whenever you inherit audiovisual materials, you are inheriting something that's been edited in a variety of ways. That's a basic fact that anyone working in media needs to understand.

Another issue we noticed during the making of Eyes on the Prize *was that the quality of archival news coverage changed fairly dramatically between the 1960s and 1980s, and beyond.*

There are two different types of changes here, the changes in nightly news and the changes in network news documentaries. The 1960s were also the glory days of such long-form documentary series as *CBS Reports* and *NBC White Papers*. These were researched and shot over months and then presented as periodic specials, these incredibly in-depth stories where reporters followed people around for long periods of time. They're a great source of archival footage, and that kind of source doesn't exist anymore. In the 1980s and '90s, you have basically leading up to a sound bite. It's almost like the newsreels, which are often frustrating to use because you've got these short shots that you can barely edit into a sequence—one minute on each story.

I think that one of the things that begins to happen as you get good committed documentarians in the 1990s and beyond is that they start covering their own stories.

And this work, in turn, becomes an alternative to archival news material for the next generation of filmmakers.

Yes, and that footage will be wonderful, intimate footage that is not like anything the networks would have shot. People have been making their own films all along, but I think that now, more people are making their own films about contemporary subjects.

Good Night, and Good Luck is a dramatic feature, but the film includes a lot of stock footage and sound, and in addition David Strathairn, as Edward R. Murrow, recreates Murrow's actual broadcasts for CBS. How much archival material is in the film?

We bought about 21 to 22 minutes just from CBS. When you add in what we got from NBC and other sources, it would have to total more like 25 or 27 minutes. There's a lot of archival going on at the same time as a lot of nonarchival. There are scenes, for example, when Murrow is waiting to speak to William Paley and he's in Paley's outer office with his secretary. There's a little monitor near where she sits, and she's watching a 1953 soap opera. When Don Hollenback commits suicide, he's watching an episode of *The Beulah Show* from 1953, 1954. There's a lot of archival that the average viewer will barely notice; there are some prime-time shows playing on monitors in the control room, and there are even little things that are archival, like the CBS cloud logo. That was actually a major feat of clearance, all that CBS branding.

It's interesting the way documentary and dramatic forms blend in the film.

One of the most exciting things for me was that George Clooney created this film as a labor of love. It was, essentially, a documentary story from 50 years ago. It was pretty much all talk, in black and white, made for $7.5 million. And he thought, as did everybody involved, "All right, this will play for a week or two in 400 houses, and it'll do well at the film festivals, hopefully." And it played for months, and we were all happy and thought that maybe this would contradict the studios' notion that if you're going to do a film in black and white, they've got to cut your budget by two-thirds—it'll go straight to DVD and the sales will be abysmal, so they've got to underfinance the film.

And instead it was nominated for an Academy Award. Tell me about the other Section Eight film you've been working on, The Good German, which also involves a lot of archival imagery.

The Good German is an adaptation of a novel by Joseph Kanon. It's not a docudrama, it's not a documentary, but it is a historical piece. It's about an American journalist, played by George Clooney, who goes back to Berlin at the end of WWII, right when the Potsdam

Conference is happening. He gets involved in an intrigue having to do with a very young American soldier who's over there, played by Toby McGuire, and his own former secretary, played by Cate Blanchett. It takes place in divided Berlin, when Berlin's in four sectors: American, Soviet, French, and British.

The original plan for the film was that every shot would be digitally placed over archival footage. So that literally, the film would be "shot" in 1945 Berlin; the actors would be green-screened over archival. There was a scene in a butcher shop, for example, and I had to find every camera angle we needed in a butcher shop in 1945 Berlin. If there was a scene outdoors, a destroyed park or a zoo, I had to find those camera angles. There was interplay between the writing, directing, and archival research—what I could find that was in Paul Attanasio's script, and whatever else I found in my research that might work or that piqued Paul's interest, or [director] Steven Soderbergh's.

Basically it was going to be done so that it looked like a 1940s Warner Brothers film, like *Casablanca* or Hitchcock's *Notorious*, where a lot of full exterior scenes were done with process projection. But because of budget constraints, because of the decision to work in black and white, we had to not do that. We ended up just doing it for some exteriors and for what traditionally you use process projection for—images out of car windows and tram windows and things like that—and in certain selected scenes and cutaways. The rest of it was created, but because I'd spent almost three years finding them millions of feet of archival footage, they used it as reference. They literally built destroyed Berlin on a back lot at Universal, based on the archival footage. And costumed all the extras, who were playing the Berliners, based on the archival footage and on stills that I got from the Imperial War Museum. A colleague of mine in the art department, Joanna Bush, created an amazing database of all the footage I'd collected. It was organized based on the geography of Berlin. So that on Steven's computer, he could click on a map of Berlin and it would find all the archival footage that I had gotten on a particular plaza or a particular street or a particular location, and pull up all that archival footage and all the stills. Steven could know where he was situated in Berlin, and the art department could recreate a particular *strasse*. We'd know the ruins and we'd know how much that area was bombed out and all that.

I got footage from various places; Germany, Moscow, London, Paris. The most useful turned out to be at the National Archives and the Library of Congress here in the U.S., because that material was vast; it had been shot by Signal Corps camera units headed up by George Stevens and William Wyler. A lot of it we got into a digital form, and then it was linked to this database.

Can you give me an international perspective on your archival work?

Hmm, how to answer that . . . I'm increasingly working internationally, but much more recently. Although I began my career doing this work on a much more international level.

Because of the Vietnam *series?*

Because of *Vietnam*, yes. At *Vietnam* we accessed something like 90 archives. I forget how many different countries, but it was a lot. Asian countries and middle European countries; we got footage from Poland and from Austria, we got footage from a lot of different places. And then after that I did some projects at WGBH [the PBS station in Boston] that involved Central and South America. In fact, we did a show on Cuba at WGBH and got some stuff out of the ICAIC [Instituto Cubano del Arte e Industria Cinematográficos] collection at Cuba. In the intervening years that's become harder and harder to do, and now there's a major push by FOCAL [the Federation of Commercial Audiovisual Libraries International]— and particularly by Lord Putnam—to rescue the ICAIC material. It's disintegrating rapidly and there's very limited access to it.

Is there communication, internationally, between archives?

There's an attempt by archives to coordinate, on an international level, more than I've ever known them to before, through organizations like FIAT, and FIAF, AMIA, and FOCAL [see the Sources and Notes section in Part V for details]. There is a sense that archives are becoming multinational corporations. So if you get on the website of Gaumont Pathé, it's now multilingual and they're prepared to handle you if you're making a request from the U.S. or France or the U.K., and that's true of a lot of, archives. It's not true of some archives from smaller countries, but certainly archives in the major countries in Europe are getting more business from other countries. It's a good thing in terms of access; it's a bad thing in terms of the fact that more and more of these archives are behaving the way large multinational corporations are behaving. They're setting their prices high and making accessibility for the little guy a lot more difficult.

They're consolidating, too, aren't they, with the bigger archives buying up the smaller ones, even across international borders?

They're gobbling up archives like nobody's business. The BBC, as an example, now represents NHK in the U.S., they represent the Australian Broadcasting Corporation, they represent CBS, they represent Nugus Martin, which is an archive that includes a lot of presumably public domain material as well as other material from the earliest years of the 20th century through World War II. And various other collections.

On one level, these large archives can be seen as stewards, can't they? Conserving and cataloging materials. And then perhaps on another, they're exploiting it commercially, which is where many documentary filmmakers get stuck.

On one level they're stewards, they're one-stop shopping, they're digitizing the material, putting a lot of information on their website so you can search and find things easier. On some other levels, there are problems. The lowest priority is the stuff that you need for your documentary. What's getting up on the website are the sound-bitey things, the little visual things, the quick and easy clips for your corporate presentation or TV commercial. It's not anything with any context, where someone can build a sequence in a documentary.

What will it take to keep documentary filmmakers and their work in the equation?

I think that money's going to talk. At this point, and increasingly, archives are charging more and more money. And they're organizing their pricing structure on this model that, a few short years ago, only the archives that provided beauty shots used to charge. By the shot, 10-second minimum: "Okay, that's going to cost you $2500 for a minimum 10-second shot of sunrise over the Statue of Liberty." Because their clients were TV commercials. Now, more and more archives want to do it that way, which is absolutely impossible for documentary filmmakers. Some archives will say, "Yes, if you're a documentary, if you're non-profit, we won't do it by the shot, and there'll be a 30-second minimum." But I can feel that changing. And so part of the conversation is "Well, these clients that you need to create accessibility for, build this part of your website for—and it's going to be a lot of work, because some of what they need isn't even digitized or indexed—these clients are not going to be able to pay $150 a second for licensing."

But of course, you need to have the license if you're going to get your documentary shown on television, or in theaters, or distributed for any kind of home or educational use.

More and more, the way filmmakers are handling it is to say, "Okay, I'm going to say, 'I'm going for film festivals and that's it.' When the time comes, if I get distribution, I'll buy whatever [rights] I need for that distribution. I'd like to go theatrical, I'd like to buy out a theatrical package, but there's no way I'm going to be able to afford $95 to $150 a second right out of the gate."

To be fair for a minute, the expenses that archives face, in terms of restoration and cataloging and vaulting and all that, continue to rise. They do. And you have to remember that as time goes on, what these people have to store increases. The amount of material that's being shot increases. And all of their expenses increase. And so they face huge expenses, including personnel, everything. So I can always argue that side of it. It's no cliché: Some of my best friends run these archives.

But somehow, they have to meet in the middle. I would like to think there's a way that the more expensive clients can help subsidize the documentary filmmakers. If these archives are so geared up for corporate clients, they must have a lot of them. Can that help subsidize the documentary filmmakers? And in fact, some archives will tell you that that's exactly what happens, and that otherwise they would be charging more than they even are.

I think that documentary filmmakers, especially those who create films that are used in educational settings, should be more up front about where their archival material is from. So that if or when they make substitutions, audiences would have the tools they need to decide for themselves if the substitution is valid or misrepresents the historical record.

There are pros and cons. In a way, you're giving away your proprietary information, and I think that discourages primary research by the next filmmaker who comes along. The problem, as I mentioned, is that particularly in the last 10 or 15 years—and particularly since the era of cable documentaries—we've gotten to a point where filmmakers are not given enough budget and time to actually look through archival footage themselves, thereby stumbling on things that haven't been used a million times before. Instead what they do is this kind of second-generation audiovisual research, where they call someone like me and they say, "Now where did those shots from *Eyes on the Prize* come from? We want to use them again." Thereby perpetuating the use of the same stuff, and possibly perpetuating errors. Not so much in *Eyes*, because we were very careful, but in other films where people might have used some generic shot of a B-52 to represent some other plane on some other date flying over some other city. It's not good filmmaking and it's not good documentary scholarship. That sloppiness is made a lot easier when you start putting every source of every shot out into the public like that.

And I can make an argument *for*, which is the footnoting argument. Footnotes mean that you've done your homework, you've been accurate, you're showing that you used the accurate sources. And I suppose if someone makes a film the sloppy way, then they can't footnote it as easily, except to say, "Such and such shots taken from *Eyes on the Prize*." It won't say, "Taken from ABC News, such and such date, such and such can number."

But also, for viewers who want to develop better media literacy and understand the filmmaking choices that are made, to make the archival sources more evident might help.

I think that's a good argument. But the people who want to have that conversation will go to the website; other people, maybe the majority, won't know to even have that conversation, they'll just watch the film. How do you make people aware that they need to have the conversation to begin with? And then, what would be included in the footnotes? Is it good enough to say, "ABC News, such and such date," or do you want the can number and everything in there?

Good questions. For now, any other thoughts for filmmakers who want to use archival images and sound in their work?

I think the whole issue of fair use, and what's happening now, is really important. I'd definitely send folks to the Center for Social Media "best practices" statement [*Documentary Filmmakers' Statement of Best Practices in Fair Use*, available for download at www.centerforsocialmedia.org/fairuse].

24

Per Saari

Los Angeles-based filmmaker Per Saari is head of development for Nicole Kidman's production company, Blossom Films, and previously worked at Robert Redford's Wildwood Enterprises. On his own, he makes documentaries. His most recent film is *The Magic Knot*, a 30-minute film about the Khumbu Climbing School, which was established to teach technical and safety skills to Sherpa climbers. I spoke with him primarily about an earlier film, *Why He Skied*, a 45-minute documentary he began shooting in 2002, a year after his older brother, Hans, died in a skiing accident near Chamonix, France. This interview was conducted in 2006.

People handle grief in so many ways. Some write poetry or essays; some compose or perform music. Why documentary?

When you go through such a personally momentous thing, you have to come up with a way to organize it in your head, just so you can rationalize it and deal with it. And for me there's nothing more analytical and ruthlessly self-critical than a documentary film, and especially a documentary film that is all about yourself. So for me it was actually a pretty logical approach to handling something as personal and intimate as grief.

How did you think of the film when you first started out?

Initially it began as a way to tell his story. My sister said she was afraid that people would forget who my brother was, and I started thinking about that and wanted to make a film about him. But I wanted to do it in a way that was helpful to me, and helpful

341

to the people who knew him. I approached it from the personal angle of "How is this affecting me?" and then from the angle of "What's an approach that might make people interested in finding out about it?"

The film has an interesting structure. It begins with text on screen, describing the tragedy that occurred in Chamonix, where your brother fell. It cuts to you in Chamonix, about to climb the same mountain, to retrace his last steps. But then it cuts back to six weeks earlier, when you first set out in a car with two friends to retrace Hans's larger journey, from the West Coast home he lived in as an infant to the East Coast where he went to college, and then on to Europe.

I read in a documentary filmmaking book that you can never go wrong with a road trip. No matter what, the physical journey always keeps people interested. And so I took that idea and put it together with a fairly convenient map of my brother's life, which literally went from west to east across the United States and then to Europe. We followed a chronological road trip from A to Z. But I stole the idea from somebody's book.

Along the way, you meet with people who knew Hans and ask questions not only about who he was and what he did, but also about why he did it—and whether or not he'd considered the potential cost to others.

Before I started, I asked all the people that I knew—not necessarily the people who are in the film, but people who knew my brother—questions that they had. And I pooled the questions and came up with a master list of things that I wanted to ask people. Actually, I wanted to get more into the stories of the people we were visiting, to find out what they were doing and their adventures. But that stuff wasn't needed in the end, it was fat, and it just sort of fell away.

Leaving the questions that you ask, and also the questions the film asks.

There are two mysteries. One is, why did he ski? Why did he go that day, why did he make the decisions that he did, why did he do in general what he did? But there's also a more formal mystery: You're trying to piece the film together as you're watching it, and there are different story lines going on so the audience is forced to question what they're seeing and where they're going, and where their preconceptions are taking them. So that's a more sort of structural mystery. It was a way to keep people engaged in a story, just on a formal level. To try to keep this a mystery was really important, because I'm dealing with a subject that's so personal.

The film unfolds with two forward-moving stories. One is the road trip from west to east. The other is your presence at Chamonix, which is intercut with the road trip. You're there to follow your brother's last journey up a mountainside, but there's a question of whether or not you'll succeed.

That was designed initially as sort of a gimmick, because of course you're going to climb the mountain. But in the end, we were tricked; we almost didn't climb the mountain because of weather and all the things that we saw unfold in the film. So it actually was true drama unfolding.

How much did the film change as you were editing it?

I would say the film didn't change as much when we were cutting as it did when we were shooting. I didn't have the structure in my head, other than the road trip. But in the six weeks that we were shooting the film, I started imagining how I wanted to put it together: If I wanted to tell it linearly from the beginning of the road trip to the end and cut in my brother's story along the way, or if I wanted to start with the mountain climbing and go backward, as we ended up doing. That was all stuff that I had plenty of time to think about along the journey itself.

How long did it take to edit?

The editing went on forever, mainly because there was so much emotional baggage and it was really hard to get my head into the project every night. The editing took two years, if you can believe it, as opposed to the Sherpa film, which took six weeks. I think when you're dealing with something so personal, and you're really formulating and modifying a thesis statement over and over and over—and it's a really difficult thesis statement to conclude—you just keep at it.

It was also hard because the crew hadn't done this before. My best friends were the two people who went with me, and technically it was a little tricky to get stuff to fit together. There was more footage than we needed and technically it was not where it should have been. So it took a lot to cull the footage and then to piece it together, more than if you'd had a very clear plan and an [experienced] crew.

How much did you shoot?

We shot 65 tapes, which is approximately 45 hours. Which isn't too bad, but I'll tell you, there are tapes that we just didn't even use, and there are interviews that didn't even get looked at because there's so much material. Unfortunately, we went into the project with a vacuum cleaner approach, which is never ideal. On the Sherpa film [produced later], we shot a fifth as much material and ended up using a lot of it. So I learned a lot.

What did you shoot with?

We were using a Sony PD150 digital camera. We also had a small video camera that we took with us as a way to document the documentation, because we knew it would be a pretty self-referential film. Someone actually gave me a little advice before I left: They said even if it's a $200 camera, just take something with you that someone can always just turn on—you don't have to get it all geared up, you don't have to have sound that's great. And that little camera saved us; a lot of the really terrific stuff that we have in the film came from that camera, some of the best stuff. And I never would have guessed that that would be the case.

Can you give an example?

One thing are my reactions, that we wouldn't have had otherwise. There's a moment in the film when these wacky cousins of mine are talking about their own adventurous lifestyle, their parrot farm. But what they're saying is very interesting and, to me, the core of the film. They say, if you really look beneath the surface at what's going on in your brother's life, you'll come away with a whole new meaning—and not just a meaning about Hans's life, but a meaning about your life. And we were lucky to have footage of me reacting to what they're saying.

Also, there were spontaneous little moments along the way that we were able to catch, the texture of the trip. And I think when you're doing a road trip, a lot of it is spontaneous and you don't have time to open the trunk and get out the camera. So the small camera was actually very helpful. In fact, the mountain climb was shot almost all with the little camera. People get so worked up about shooting on high-quality film and video that they forget that the story isn't really dependent on how grainy the image is. As long as the subject is there, that's really important. And that was something that I took away from the whole process.

I'm curious about how you cast the film, the people you chose to interview.

There were two factors for me in deciding who we wanted to include in the film. Because we were making a road trip, we were at the mercy of the map. So one was, who is geographically convenient, and who was going to be at the right place at the right time? The second factor was what people had to say. I wanted to make sure that we found people who were going to be honest and who had interesting things to say about my brother, even if they were critical. And I think we did a pretty good job of balancing those things and finding people who had honest and not always easy things to say, not only about my brother but also my parents' approach to life. That was probably the most important thing for me, was making sure that we had brutally honest people to interview.

The one person clearly missing, who appears in photographs, is Hans's girlfriend.

I spoke with her before the film to ask if she wanted to do it. And for her it was so close; it was over a year after the accident but for her it was just absolutely too difficult to go into. And in fact my parents said the same thing, but were able to compose themselves more than she would have been able to. So she was a big supporter of the film and obviously her family was, but she just decided that she didn't want to be in it.

And her grandmother speaks so eloquently for her, and for your brother.

And again there's someone who is honest and eloquent and beautiful.... That was probably the most difficult part to shoot, of anything, because of the personal intensity of it.

The film uses text on screen to identify places and certain other information, such as "expedition." Otherwise, the only narration is a voice-over recorded by you. When did you write and record it?

The voice-over was written way after, that was the last thing that I did. And I really struggled with it, because what it said not only bridges the pieces of the film together but is the thesis statement. The voice-over goes from what I postulate at the beginning to what I conclude at the end. It was really difficult to make it concise and to come up with a conclusion that made sense; I reworked and rerecorded it probably a hundred times.

Recording voice-over is very difficult; it's a difficult thing to pull off without seeming either like you're a newscaster or like you're just talking in an interview. There's a unique tone that you have to achieve, and it was a real struggle to accomplish that. I'm still not convinced that I did a good job.

There are a few places in the film where it looks as if you're alone, talking to a camera that you've set up.

Right. That was in France. After some really intense days, I just set up the camera and interviewed myself. Molly Stratton, who was the sound person on the film and is one of my dear friends, wrote a list of questions that she wanted me to answer. And so I had this little card with me that I referred to every once in a while, and I'd turn the camera on and basically interview myself. Which is an interesting process.

Did you show rough cuts to people to get reactions?

I did. I showed lots of versions of the film to different people, and it became much more personal as the cuts went on, because from the beginning people were noticing that I was shying away from showing myself on film. I was afraid that putting yourself in a movie was too self-involved. My friends and the people who looked at the film talked me out of that, and encouraged me to include more of myself and to focus less on the silliness of the story, pieces of the film that involved my friends and the texture of the road trip that in the end weren't nearly as important as my arc as a character. And so I ended up including a lot more of myself, as much as I could. But it's also very difficult to be honest on camera, to be yourself, to open up. And I'm not a very sort of gushing person as it is. So if I had one more thing to include it'd be more of myself opening up.

How did you determine the final length?

The final length was determined just by the cut. It felt like it was done; it always hovered around 45, 47 minutes.

Did you raise money for the film?

The film was entirely self-funded. I didn't have a lot of time to pursue funding before the shooting window was upon us, so I had to break the piggy bank. The large percentage of my budget that was dedicated to purchasing equipment—including sound gear, I firmly believe that sound will make or break a project—I considered to be an investment toward future projects. As a result, my next film, *The Magic Knot*, cost almost nothing to shoot.

What was it like to screen the film with your sister and your parents?

It was really scary, actually. Because they didn't want to see the film before I was done with it and before we could see it in a public space. So our first screening was in Jackson Hole with about 1500 people. It was a very large screening and I was worried that the film wouldn't play well, or that people would be restless, or that my parents would be disappointed. And probably the most important thing that came out of that first screening was that people were re-engaging about my brother and talking about him and what he did, and what happened that day, and what someone who goes through that loss might be thinking. And for me that was the whole point of doing the movie.

Ironically, the person who introduced the film, Doug Coombs, an extreme skier, died soon after at almost exactly the same place that my brother died, falling in a very similar fashion. It was a cruel reminder that this is something that people who live in the mountains go through all the time, and it's something that I hope people think about.

What advice do you have for filmmakers who want to use documentary to tell personal, even painful stories, from their own lives?

That's a good question. My first thing to say is that I think it's a great idea, if that's your medium. But in addition to that I would say, one, to be really honest with yourself and to open up your heart and let your story really come out. For me, that was one of the hardest things, was really letting your defenses down and exposing yourself on camera. The second thing I would say is that it's really easy to be seduced by your own story. It's important to keep a cinematic perspective on it, and to know that maybe nobody will ever see the film. Go ahead anyway, just realize that you're doing this for yourself. If it has a wider audience, that's great, but you have to realize the exhibition limitations that are down the road.

Last question. You work in the rarified world of Hollywood, with big budget fictional features and big stars. To you, what's the appeal of documentaries?

The studio mentality is so careful and so market-driven, that to me, documentaries are a breath of fresh air. For the most part, the stories are small and difficult to market; they're personal and gritty—all the things that generally a studio doesn't want in their big pictures. That's not to say that there aren't documentaries that are commercial or there aren't studio films that are intimate. But the stories that you see in documentary films are so pure, and so authentic—the good ones, that is. They're done out of heart and soul. I'm always going to have one toe in the documentary realm, because it's so passion driven.

25

Onyekachi Wambu

Onyekachi Wambu was born in Nigeria and, following the Nigerian civil war, moved with his family to the United Kingdom. His publications include *A Fuller Picture; Empire Windrush: Fifty Years of Writing about Black Britain* (Ed.); and (forthcoming) *Under the Tree of Talking—Leadership in the African Context* (Ed.). He is a former editor of the *Voice* newspaper. His documentary credits for the BBC, Channel 4, and PBS include *Ain't No Black in the Union Jack, Africa Out of Darkness, Deadly Bliss*, and the series *Hopes on the Horizon*, on which I also briefly worked.

Onyekachi is currently information officer at the African Foundation for Development (AFFORD), which supports the African diaspora in the United Kingdom in its efforts to contribute to wealth and job creation in Africa. We spoke in 2006.

Why don't we start with something you wrote in an e-mail to me. Commenting on the high-caliber work of some of the others interviewed for the book, you noted that the sort of community projects you're involved with may not quite fit, because of their "poorly funded, rough and ready production values—the key thing is getting the message to people." That's perhaps one of the best reasons we should talk—to explore this other kind of documentary.

I think it's really about stories that are not being covered by the general media. And allowing people to develop their own capacity to tell their own stories, as well as allowing them to have an insight and understanding of how important they are, actually, as change-makers. I think those are the two key things.

349

When I say that some stories have been marginalized in the media, I'll give you a context. We've been working with African organizations and Africans outside Africa who make contributions to Africa. At the moment there's a perception, if you watch the general media, that Africans lack agency; they're just supplicants who hold out their hands for aid and aren't really concerned about their own continent or, indeed, doing very much for themselves. When actually the truth of the matter is that if you look at who makes the biggest financial contribution to Africa, it's actually Africans outside Africa who are making these huge contributions. Last year, the IMF [International Monetary Fund] estimated that Africans outside the continent had sent about $32 billion back in. This is way above most foreign financial transfers to Africa, including direct investment and foreign-originated aid going in to Africa. And yet when you watch any of the narratives about Africa and how it's being helped and supported, these Africans outside the continent making these huge contributions are just invisible, and their efforts are not acknowledged. By anybody.

And so the work we've been doing is saying to them, look, individually you're making small contributions. But globally and collectively those contributions add up to quite a lot. You're indeed a kind of invisible social security system in Africa. Many of you are keeping rural communities alive by the money that you're sending. You're paying school fees for young people; you're investing in small and medium-sized businesses; the money that you send to build houses, through the multiplier effect, creates jobs and stimulates the economy. So you're important stakeholders in Africa's development. First of all, you need to recognize that. Secondly, half of the reason that your stories are not being covered is that *you're* silent, as well. And what you need to do is to equip yourselves to release those stories.

How are you helping them to do that?

There are two strategies. One, as an organization, the African Foundation for Development, AFFORD, produces some media around their stories, [which we distribute] through the website, DVDs, and other communication outlets. Two, equipping individuals and groups within these communities to start releasing their own stories. We finished a program recently, called *Aiding and Abetting—Global Image, Local Damage?* And what we did was to work with some African organizations here, some African artists, and the multimedia department of the University of East London, and talked with them to explore different ways of getting out a message through art. One of the artists was an actor, another did fine art installations, another was a poet. And alongside [their collaborations], each artist also did an independent piece of work, their own vision that emerged from these interactions. Some of the organizations built their own websites, and each had a DVD developed around the work that it did. So that was a unique kind of project.

I would imagine that AFFORD has to speak to a range of audiences, those within Africa and Europe as well as the world community at large. How does that affect either the stories or how you tell them?

With the African groups it's much more about getting them to become a player in releasing their own stories and getting across their own narrative about development, about Africa, which is very different from what the mainstream understanding may be. At AFFORD, we're not really interested in poverty reduction, which is the strategy of quite a lot of the so-called "mainstream" NGOs [nongovernmental organizations]. What we're interested in is wealth creation and job creation. We figure that if people are working, then most of the things that the aid agencies are trying to deal with would be solved, because they would have the capacity to deal with those things themselves. Africans who get engaged are very interested in starting small- or medium-sized businesses.

With the broad population, the mainstream, what we're trying to do is to convince them that the only way Africa is going to move forward is if Africans themselves are centrally involved. If you're going to get any kind of sustainable development in Africa, it has to come because Africans are driving it. If Africans are not driving it, it's not going to be sustainable. So this means increasing African agency, African capacity. So that's the central message, the need to support the effort that Africans are already making. One of those, for instance, is a program to see if we can get tax relief for the remittances that are sent. At the moment, if you send a pound to Oxfam to do development work in Africa, you get 28 pence back on your pound. That's 28 percent. But if you send that pound straight to Africa, you get nothing, even though you may be supporting a school, building a well or something that is considered development work. We're arguing that remittances that are going towards productive development—and criteria for defining that would need to be found—then it too should be able to attract tax relief.

How important is media to the work that you do, and what kinds of media?

We use all media. We have to get the stories across, and so you go to anybody who will give you a platform, essentially. In terms of the really effective media that we've been using, what we've found is that the viral platforms, e-mail and web-based platforms, are very important. Obviously they are platforms of choice for many Africans, because they're so cheap and lots of people have congregated around them.

It's been quite interesting. I went to talk to senior officials at the BBC when they were planning their big *Africa 2005* program, which coincided with the G8 summit and also the "Make Poverty History" campaign, out of which grew the *Live 8* concert. When the BBC was first considering *Africa 2005*, they invited lots of different stakeholders to meet, including AFFORD. And I made the point that 10 years earlier, both internally [as a producer] and externally as an independent, I was always badgering senior people at the BBC for more programs on Africa. I used to get really annoyed, because there were so few outlets if you were here, in the U.K., trying to find out what was going on in Africa. But in the last five years I hadn't been contacting the BBC at all, and did they know why? I said, "Because every morning now, I can read every single newspaper from Africa online."

The days when you had to rely on the BBC as your source into Africa has gone. What's been exciting has just been the way that all these African organizations and news media have populated the web; it's a great source of information. You've got the official media and then a lot of blogs as well, and a lot of portals, such as *Ghana Today*. If you're interested in discussions or information from Ghanaians outside or in the country, you just go to that portal.

There's another kind of work you do, which is to bring more popular films about Africa, both documentary and drama, to British audiences— most recently through From Nollywood to Hollywood–Africa Mine, *a 10-part theatrical screening series co-sponsored by AFFORD and Screenstation with support from Film London. According to the website, the series "explores Africa through the eyes of Africans alongside visions of the continent packaged primarily for western viewers."*

The film series grew out of *Aiding and Abetting* and another project that we did with some young Africans here, many of whom have grown up in the U.K. and have never been to Africa. We questioned about 144 of them, between [ages] 18 and 30, and the responses we got back from them about Africa were absolutely amazing. What came through very clearly was that in many cases their own perceptions of Africa were being shaped by the usual sources, the usual suspects—the mainstream media and what the NGOs were putting out. People tend not to recognize that the NGOs have been one of the biggest sources for shaping the image of Africa, certainly in the last 20 years. And their demands for fundraising are driven by what many people would regard as negative images. We can understand *why* that happens: If you show pictures of a well-fed child who's doing well, no one's going to give you money, whereas if you show the negative picture obviously people are moved to send money. But what it ends up doing is putting across a one-dimensional perspective of the continent, and the young Africans here have been picking up on that. Those who have not been to Africa, what they see—which is what their peers see as well—is this strange continent that's full of trauma and tragedy and famine and pestilence and wars. And many of them, quite frankly, have developed—I think an *alienated* relationship with the continent would be too strong, but I would say quite an *ambivalent* kind of connection to the continent. And they desperately wanted different sources of information about Africa.

The other major source of information about what they'd seen about the country was from their parents. And for many of them, Africa was this place that they had escaped from, so they were also looking back with a kind of anger. And when their children misbehaved they would threaten them with sending them back, as punishment! So as far as some of these kids were concerned, Africa was this traumatic space, and if they misbehaved, they'd be sent there.

What we tried to do with *Africa Mine* was to have a space where we could offer a three-dimensional perspective on the continent, and then follow that up with discussions with people from those countries, the filmmakers and people who have some degree of engagement with the culture. Part of the criteria for raising money [for the series] was that we'd show some old classics, films from the 1960s and '70s, and some newer fare. So we got to *Totsi* [a South African film about gang violence], which had just won the Oscar, and also what Nollywood, the Nigerian industry, was doing, looking at their storytelling techniques and the kinds of stories they were putting forward. And then in terms of documentaries, we looked at ones that we felt would engage with issues around identity, the local and the global, migration. It's easier now to talk about yourself being African-British or a black British person, but it's still quite loaded. Even the kids who are now second or third generation here are trying to resolve who they are, still want to be able to talk about that, what it all means.

In your experience, does the storytelling have to follow western narrative conventions in order to appeal to western or westernized viewers? The documentary The Boys of Baraka, *for example, was part of the* Africa Mine *series—it's a strong film, but its narrative style seems very American.*

We've got Ousmane Sembene's film, *Ceddo* [about pre-European colonialization and enslavement of African people], which is unconventional in many ways. It was released in 1977. Part of what people talked about, when we had the discussion afterward, was around how slow it was—and ironically, how much they enjoyed it, being so slow, in terms of the cutting. It allowed you almost to be transported to another world. There was a sense that the times we're in are quite frenetic, and to just stop in that cinema and watch something so slow was wonderful for people, so that was an interesting reaction.

But the American narrative style is now so dominant, that here you watch something like *Totsi* and really, there's no African storytelling in there. What we discovered was that the Nollywood stuff [dramatic fiction] worked fairly well. The discussions were quite intense, about the different ways that people see the world, between Nigerians who are here and Nigerians who are in Nigeria. In terms of accessibility, the documentaries were the most successful.

In an interview I read, you said that in making documentaries, you used skills you'd gained growing up in an Igbo village without a chief. That people would gather information from a range of sources—village elders, their own family, other families, knowing that each group might have its own interests—and then construct the truth for themselves. It reminded me of how we would approach evidence when making documentary series at Blackside (which did Hopes on the Horizon *as well as* Eyes on the Prize*).*

Yes. A lot of what informs what we've been doing here at AFFORD, the watchword is just diverse and multiple images, multiple perspectives. Which is what the world is, really. And we say to people, look you've heard one story. But it's possible to imagine that the typical or the biggest aid donor to Africa is not Bob Geldof, it's the African lady who everybody ignores, who's the office cleaner, and who might send back 20 to 30 percent of her wages every month to relatives in Africa. It might be possible to see *her* as the biggest aid donor to Africa. This isn't an image that anybody would associate with African development aid, but the reality is—she *is*, or at least people like her are. And so the idea is to get people to understand that what is out there is not necessarily the truth all the time. And that the truth itself is a lot more complex.

Do you ever have to consider that line between journalism and advocacy and propaganda and polemic, when putting together media or working with producers?

Part of the problem I always had at the BBC was that I never really understood all of those different lines. I mean, we're advocating on behalf of Africans here, and what they're trying to do in Africa. And in the early days we kept meeting people from the "official" aid industry, the NGOs, and they would say, without any irony, "Oh, but you guys are biased, you aren't neutral." This is somebody who is generally white and middle class working from the U.K. and engaging with a poor third world country, which usually has a historically complex and sometimes torturous relationship with the imperial center, and you have a whole industry dominated by such people, and there's never a sense that they themselves are not neutral. That they're not just another class (or constituency) that's engaged in this process with their own baggage. So I have never really bought that stuff that journalism is what we do, and propaganda or polemic is what the others do.

People bring baggage, perspective, history, bring a whole lot of things to the table when they're mediating the truth. I've never been convinced about those lines being as clear as everybody else seems to think they are. I think you try the best you can to be objective and fair. But in the end you have a perspective. And as a human being that perspective is important and needs to be acknowledged for good or bad.

Let's get back to community work, the films that demand to be made, whether or not there is money or experience or high production values.

That whole thing was really reinforced for me while making *Hopes on the Horizons* [a history of pro-democracy movements in six African nations in the 1990s: Benin, Morocco, Mozambique, Nigeria, Rwanda, and South Africa]. There was this whole experience with people who'd been involved in those struggles in the 1990s in Africa, and when we were trying to get pictures to show these struggles, we just weren't able to do it. I came to a conclusion that as well as *doing* struggle, or official action of any kind, you need somebody there to document it. One of the things I said to the Ford Foundation when I was traveling through Africa was that when they were funding all of these civil society organizations, they should include in the budget a line for media, or for one person to have a digital camera just to capture what was going on. Because in the 1990s, these people had fought huge, incredible battles, and there's no memory of it because nobody bothered to film it! I mean, there is a memory, it's been written about, but that sort of disappears into academia, into political science departments. For popular appreciation of it—perhaps it's there in the popular imagination through music, but visually there just isn't very much of what happened. And it's so critical: some things, as you say, just need to be filmed. So that there is a popular memory of them, in a strange kind of way.

It's still not up there on the agenda. Again, what we were trying to do with all that stuff around *Aiding and Abetting* was to bring that through. To convince these organizations that the reason that nobody knows you're doing this work is because you don't tell it, you're not capturing it, you're not finding inventive ways of sharing it with other people. So what happens is that in another five years' time, nobody knows that you made a contribution to Africa's development that's as big as what anybody else is doing.

You know, there's frustration. Sometimes you would like to paint nice pictures, get the time to do things properly, get a higher budget and a professional staff, not get your friends who are professionals to be doing things for no money. They don't mind doing it, but after a while, it's just gets more and more difficult to call them out, if you're not able to pay them properly.

You've worked as a print journalist and also as a filmmaker. Building on your last answer, why is it important that documentary stories get told, with motion picture and sound?

The role that television used to have, that moment when it was all powerful, I think that moment has kind of gone. There was a time when television dominated the sitting room, and there were so few channels. And now we've got hundreds, and there are so many other different sources [of media]. But there is something about documentary film that's extraordinary. It has to do with a kind of reality that that I don't think print does successfully. I'll give you an example; one of the documentaries I've been proud of making is called *Deadly Bliss*. We were beginning to develop a crack cocaine problem in the U.K. in the early '90s, and what we decided to do was to make a kind of two-sited documentary. We went to the States initially, to try to understand what had happened with this drug as it worked its way through, so that we could bring that back to what was an emerging crisis here. This was about '92, '93; we were in Harlem, the Bronx, East New York. And it was just incredible. These communities were being devastated by the drug. We found out that most of the people in the criminal justice system were there as a result of this drug, and thousands of people had been killed either through taking it or through the criminal networks. We spoke to one expert at a rehab center who [said] that between the rehab, the deaths, people in prisons and everything else, this drug may have destroyed as much as a million people. It was just this incredible phenomenon, and we couldn't find any documentary evidence. We went looking for complex rendering from documentaries or other news footage and there wasn't any. What you got were just the usual images of the young black men with their hands on the police car, the emergency of the shootouts with drug sellers. But just subtle, powerful renderings of what was going on—we couldn't find them.

And so what we had were lots of talking heads and no way of illustrating the story from archive material. The one breakthrough that we had was that, going up and down, up and down, we kept seeing all these murals in Harlem and the Bronx. Graffiti murals. And we were interviewing this person with his back to a mural, and it dawned on me: Of course, the story *had* been documented. But it had been documented by all these street artists. It hadn't been documented in a way that we get our information, which would have been through the 9:00 documentary or some other kind of televisual form. And so that was shocking. And then of course, the other space in which all this stuff had been documented very powerfully was music. I'd been listening to this music in the U.K., but listening to the lyrics again, hearing what people like Public Enemy were saying, I realized that these rap artists had captured, during that period between 1987 and perhaps '92, this whole base culture of crack cocaine. Public Enemy had a track called *Night of the Living Baseheads*, which captured the shocking reality we were witnessing in such a powerful way. And I came to a new respect for the art form, as a result of that.

Are you currently making your own films?

No, I'd like to get back. I'm very interested at the moment in the very quick turnaround of the Nollywood people, two-week films, and what is possible within that framework. I'd like to bring some of the sensibilities that I have to that. So if I'm going to do anything next, it would be going to Nigeria to do something like that, with those guys. Incredibly low budget, no budget; they'll do a drama in that time for £10,000. They'll turn it around.

Part V

ADDITIONAL MATERIAL

Sources and Notes

In most cases, quotations in this book are drawn from interviews conducted by the author during preparation for the first and/or second edition. These include conversations with Michael Ambrosino, Paula Apsell, Steven Ascher, Ronald Blumer, Liane Brandon, Victoria Bruce, Ric Burns, Gail Dolgin, Jon Else, Boyd Estus, Nick Fraser, Susan Froemke, Jim Gilmore, Karin Hayes, Muffie Meyer, Hans Otto Nicolayssen, Sam Pollard, Kenn Rabin, Per Saari, Susanne Simpson, Holly Stadtler, Melanie Wallace, and Onyekachi Wambu. Additional information about films and filmmakers was taken as noted from a range of sources, including information provided by the filmmakers themselves through their official websites and press material and in material included on their DVDs.

Chapter 1: For additional information on current trends in documentary, see, for example, Paul Arthur, "Extreme Makeover: The Changing Face of Documentary" and Pat Aufderheide, "The Changing Documentary Marketplace," both in *Cineaste*, Summer 2005. Definition of documentary, in Erik Barnouw, *Documentary: A History of the Non-Fiction Film* (New York: Oxford University Press, 1974). Documentaries as New Journalism, in Nick Fraser, "In Praise of Documentaries," *Critical Quarterly*, October 2001. Additional information about Witness can be found in Sam Gregory et al., *Video for Change: A Guide for Advocacy and Activism* (London: Pluto Press in association with Witness, 2005).

Chapter 2: Story elements from David Howard and Edward Mabley, *The Tools of Screenwriting* (New York: St. Martin's Press, 1993).

Chapter 3: Gerald Peary's interview with Frederick Wiseman (*Boston Phoenix*, March 1998) can be found at www.geraldpeary.com/interviews/wxyz/wiseman.html. Additional information on Frederick Wiseman can be found at his website, www.zipporah.com. Information on *Sound and Fury* is available at www.nextwavefilms.com/sf/joshnotes.html. Information on *Capturing the Friedmans* is available at www.hbo.com/docs/programs/friedmans/interview.html. Information on *The Sweetest Sound* can be found at www.alanberliner.com. Information about *The Fog of War* is available at www.sonyclassics.com/fogofwar/_media/pdf/pressReleaseFOG.pdf.

Discussion of *Eyes on the Prize* comes in part from my own involvement as a producer. Ken Burns's comments on *The Civil War* in Sean B. Dolan, Ed. *Telling the Story: The Media, The Public and American History* (Boston: New England Foundation for the Humanities, 1994).

Chapter 5: Reference to Robert McKee, *Story* (New York: HarperCollins, 1997). George M. Cohan reference in Wells Root, *Writing the Script* (New York: Holt, Rinehart and Winston, 1987). Reference to Madison Smartt Bell, *Narrative Design* (New York: W. W. Norton & Co., 1997).

Chapter 6: Harlan Jacobson, "Michael & Me," *Film Comment*, November/December 1989.

Chapter 7: Transcripts and additional information about *Daughter from Danang* can be found at the *American Experience* website, www.pbs.org/wgbh/amex/daughter/filmmore/pt.html; also see the film website, www.daughterfromdanang.com. Press material and general information about *Murderball* can be found at www.murderballmovie.com; see also information about Participant Production's "Get into the Game" outreach campaign, http://participate.net/getintothegame. The official website for *Super Size Me* is www.supersizeme.com. Information about documentary box office can be found at http://documentaries.about.com/od/basics/tp/top10gross.htm, which as of July 2006 put *Super Size Me* in seventh place; a second source, www.documentaryfilms.net/index.php/documentary-box-office, also as of July 2006, listed the film in sixth place.

Chapter 8: Jason Silverman's interview with Alan Berliner can be read at www.pbs.org/pov/pov2001/thesweetestsound/thefilm.html; see also www.alanberliner.com. The Jay Rosenblatt press material and other information about the filmmaker can be found at www.jayrosenblattfilms.com. The discussion of *Miss America* comes from my own involvement with the film's development. The U.C. Berkeley Library offers some guidelines for evaluating web pages; see www.lib.berkeley.edu/TeachingLib/Guides/Internet/Evaluate.html.

Chapter 9: *Hoop Dreams* press material is available at http://finelinefeatures.com/hoop.

Chapter 11: Note that these *American Experience* guidelines refer to "films in production or at rough cut." It was never our intent to actually submit program ideas to that series. For a discussion of artistic license with fictionalized drama based on real events, see, for example, Linda Seger, *The Art of Adaptation: Turning Fact and Fiction into Film* (New York: Henry Holt and Co., 1992).

Chapter 12: Information about *Winged Migration* is available at www. sonyclassics.com/wingedmigration/media/presskit/presskit.pdf. Information about *My Architect* is available at www.myarchitectfilm.com and at www.hbo.com/docs/programs/myarchitect/index.html. Additional information for *Betty Tells Her Story* is available through its distributor, New Day Films, www.newday.com/films/Betty_Tells_Her_Story.html. For more information on Errol Morris's *Interrotron*™, see Morris's website, www.errolmorris.com.

Chapter 15: Credit and thanks are due to Steve Fayer and Jon Else, who created earlier versions of this list for the producers at Blackside, Inc., in Boston.

Chapter 16: The filmmakers' website is www.westcityfilms.com.

Chapter 17: The filmmakers' websites are www.urcuninafilms.com and www.pipandzastrow.com. For additional information on *The Kidnapping of Ingrid Betancourt*, see also www.wmm.com/filmcatalog/pages/c625.shtml, and www.cinemax.com/reel/ingrid_betancourt/interview.html.

Chapter 18: Ric Burns's website is www.ricburns.com. Information about *New York* can be found at www.pbs.org/wnet/newyork (*New York*, Episodes 1–7), and www.pbs.org/wgbh/amex/newyork (*New York*, Episode 8). Information and transcripts for many of his films (search by title) can also be found at the *American Experience* website.

Chapter 19: For more information on U.C. Berkeley's "Documentary Cookbook" go to http://journalism.berkeley.edu/program/courses/dv/cookbook.html.

Chapter 20: D. H. Lawrence, "Never trust the artist. Trust the tale." In Lawrence's *Studies in Classic American Literature* (1923), available online. Information about *Storyville* and many of the films discussed can be found at www.bbc.co.uk/bbcfour/documentaries/storyville.

Chapter 21: Information about Maysles Films is available at www.mayslesfilms.com/company_pages/maysles_productions/history.html.

Chapter 22: Information on *When the Levees Broke* is available at www.hbo.com/docs/programs/whentheleveesbroke/index.html. Information on *The Rise and Fall of Jim Crow* is available at www.pbs.org/wnet/jimcrow.

Chapter 23: Kenn Rabin's website is www.fulcrummediaservices.com. In addition to the "Documentary Filmmakers' Statement of Best Practices in Fair Use" (www.centerforsocialmedia.org/fairuse), the website of the Center for Social Media at American University's School of Communication has a variety of resources for filmmakers. For additional information on the archival organizations mentioned, go the websites of the Federation of Commercial Audiovisual Libraries (FOCAL, www.focalint.org); the Fédération Internationale des Archives de Télévision (FIAT, www.fiatifta.org); and the Association of Moving Image Archivists (AMIA, www.amianet.org).

Chapter 25: Information about the African Foundation for Development can be found at www.afford-uk.org.

Films

Many documentaries, including not only recent releases but also classics from previous decades, are now available for purchase through online vendors, such as Amazon and PBS Video. A growing number are also available for rental through online companies, such as Netflix and Intelliflix, which have their counterparts worldwide.

Through the web, viewers may also be able to find information about specific films, including official press kits, teachers' guides, and outreach plans. Transcripts and other material are available online for many documentaries that have been shown on PBS, including *American Experience* (a historical series, www.pbs.org/wgbh/amex), *Nova* (science, www.pbs.org/wgbh/nova), and *Frontline* (current affairs, www.pbs.org/wgbh/pages/frontline).

Balseros: Produced by Loris Omedes; directed by Josep Ma Doménech and Carles Bosch; scripts by David Trueba and Carles Bosch; edited by Ernest Blasi.

Betty Tells Her Story: Produced, directed, and edited by Liane Brandon.

Blue Vinyl: Produced by Daniel B. Gold, Judith Helfand, and Julia D. Parker; directed by Judith Helfand and Daniel B. Gold; edited by Sari Gilman.

Born into Brothels: Produced and directed by Ross Kauffman and Zana Briski; edited by Nancy Baker and Ross Kauffman.

Bowling for Columbine: Produced, directed, and written by Michael Moore; additional producers Kathleen Glynn, Jim Czarnecki, Charles Bishop and Michael Donovan; edited by Kurt Engfehr.

The Boys of Baraka: Produced and directed by Heidi Ewing and Rachel Grady; edited by Enat Sidi.

A Brief History of Time: Produced by David Hickman, Gordon Freedman, and Kory Johnston; directed by Errol Morris; edited by Brad Fuller.

Brother Outsider: The Life of Bayard Rustin: Produced and directed by Bennett Singer and Nancy Kates; edited by Veronica Selver and Rhonda Collins.

Cadillac Desert (series): Episodes 1–3 produced, directed, and written by Jon Else; based on Marc Reisner's book, *Cadillac Desert*; Episode 4 produced and directed by Linda Harrar; based on Sandra Postel's book, *Last Oasis*.

Capturing the Friedmans. Produced by Andrew Jarecki and Marc Smerling; directed by Andrew Jarecki; edited by Richard Hankin.

The Civil War (series): Produced by Ken Burns and Ric Burns; directed by Ken Burns; written by Geoffrey C. Ward and Ric Burns with Ken Burns; edited by Paul Barnes, Bruce Shaw, and Tricia Reidy.

Control Room: Produced by Hani Salama and Rosadel Varela; directed by Jehane Noujaim; edited by Julia Bacha, Lilah Bankier, and Charles Marquardt.

Culloden: Produced, written, and directed by Peter Watkins; edited by Michael Bradsell.

Darwin's Nightmare: Produced by Edouard Maruiat, Antonin Svoboda, Martin Gschlacht, Barbara Albert, Hubert Toint, and Hubert Sauper; directed and written by Hubert Sauper; edited by Denise Vindevogel.

Daughter from Danang: Produced by Gail Dolgin; directed by Gail Dolgin and Vicente Franco; edited by Kim Roberts.

The Day after Trinity: J. Robert Oppenheimer and the Atomic Bomb: Produced and directed by Jon Else; written by David Peoples, Janet Peoples, and Jon Else; edited by David Peoples and Ralph Wikk.

A Decent Factory: Produced by Thomas Balmes and Kaarle Aho; directed and written by Thomas Balmes.

The Donner Party: Produced by Lisa Ades and Ric Burns; directed and written by Ric Burns; edited by Bruce Shaw.

Enron: The Smartest Guys in the Room: Produced by Alex Gibney, Jason Kliot, and Susan Motamed; directed and written by Alex Gibney; edited and coproduced by Alison Ellwood.

Eugene O'Neill: Produced by Marilyn Ness and Steve Rivo with Robin Espinola and Mary Recine; directed by Ric Burns; written by Arthur Gelb & Barbara Gelb and Ric Burns; edited by Li-Shin Yu.

The Execution of Wanda Jean: Produced by Liz Garbus and Rory Kennedy; directed by Liz Garbus.

Eyes on the Prize (series): Episodes 1–6 produced by Orlando Bagwell, Callie Crossley, James A. DeVinney, and Judith Vecchione; edited by Daniel Eisenberg, Jeanne Jordan, and Charles Scott; series writer, Steve Fayer; executive producer, Henry Hampton. Episodes 7–14) produced by Sheila Bernard, Carroll Blue, James A. DeVinney, Madison Davis Lacy, Jr., Louis J. Massiah, Thomas Ott, Samuel Pollard, Terry Kay Rockefeller, Jacqueline Shearer, and Paul Stekler; edited by Lillian Benson, Betty Ciccarelli, Thomas Ott, and Charles Scott; series writer, Steve Fayer; executive producer, Henry Hampton.

Fahrenheit 9/11: Produced by Jim Czarnecki, Kathleen Glynn, and Michael Moore; directed and written by Michael Moore; edited by Kurt Engfehr, Christopher Seward, and T. Woody Richman.

The Fog of War: Produced by Errol Morris, Michael Williams, and Julie Ahlberg; directed by Errol Morris; edited by Karen Schmeer, Doug Abel, and Chyld King.

4 Little Girls: Produced by Spike Lee and Sam Pollard; directed by Spike Lee; edited by Sam Pollard.

Gefilte Fish: Produced and directed by Karen Silverstein.

Gimme Shelter: Directed by Albert Maysles, David Maysles, and Charlotte Zwerin; edited by Ellen Giffard, Robert Farren, Joanne Burke, and Kent McKinney.

Good Night, and Good Luck (dramatic feature): Produced and co-written by Grant Heslov; directed and co-written by George Clooney; edited by Stephen Mirrione.

Grey Gardens: Produced by Albert Maysles and David Maysles; directed by David Maysles, Albert Maysles, Ellen Hovde, and Muffie Meyer; edited by Ellen Hovde, Muffie Meyer, and Susan Froemke.

Grizzly Man: Produced by Erik Nelson; directed and narrated by Werner Herzog; edited by Joe Bini.

Guerrilla: The Taking of Patty Hearst: Produced and directed by Robert Stone; edited by Don Kleszy.

Harlan County, U.S.A.: Produced and directed by Barbara Kopple; edited by Nancy Baker, Mirra Bank, Lora Hays, and Mary Lampson.

A History of Britain by Simon Schama (series): *Dynasty* episode produced and directed by Clare Beavan; written by Simon Schama; edited by Michael Duly.

Hoop Dreams: Produced by Frederick Marx, Steve James, and Peter Gilbert; directed by Steve James; edited by Frederick Marx, Steve James, and Bill Haugse.

Human Remains. Produced, directed, written, and edited by Jay Rosenblatt.

I'll Make Me a World (series): Produced by Betty Ciccarelli, Denise Greene, Sam Pollard, and Tracy Heather Strain; edited by Betty Ciccarelli, David Carnochan, and Eric Handley;

series writer, Sheila Curran Bernard; series producer, Terry Kay Rockefeller; co-executive producer, Sam Pollard; executive producer, Henry Hampton.

An Inconvenient Truth: Produced by Lawrence Bender, Scott A. Burns, and Laurie David; directed by Davis Guggenheim; edited by Jay Lash Cassidy and Dan Swietlik.

Journeys with George: Produced, directed, and written by Alexandra Pelosi; co-directed and edited by Aaron Lubarsky.

The Kidnapping of Ingrid Betancourt: Produced and directed by Victoria Bruce and Karin Hayes; edited by Geof Bartz, Karin Hayes, and Victoria Bruce.

Kurt & Courtney: Produced by Nick Broomfield, Michele d'Acosta, and Tine van den Brande; directed by Nick Broomfield; edited by Mark Atkins.

Lalee's Kin: The Legacy of Cotton: Produced by Susan Froemke; directed by Susan Froemke and Deborah Dickson with Albert Maysles; edited by Deborah Dickson.

The Liberace of Baghdad: Produced and directed by Sean McAllister; edited by Ollie Huddleston.

Liberty! The American Revolution (series): Produced and directed by Ellen Hovde and Muffie Meyer; written by Ronald Blumer; edited by Molly Bernstein, Alison Ellwood, Sharon Sachs, and Joshua Waletzky.

March of the Penguins: Produced by Yves Darondeau, Christophe Lioud, and Emmanuel Priou; directed by Luc Jacquet; narration written by Jordan Roberts; based on the story by Luc Jacquet; based on the screenplay by Luq Jacquet & Michel Fessler; edited by Sabine Emiliani.

A Midwife's Tale: Produced and written by Laurie Kahn-Leavitt; based on a book by Laurel Thatcher Ulrich; directed by Richard P. Rogers; edited by William A. Anderson and Susan Korda.

The Multiple Personality Puzzle: Produced by Holly Barden Stadtler and Eleanor Grant; directed by Holly Barden Stadtler; written by Eleanor Grant; edited by Barr Weissman.

Murder at Harvard: Produced by Eric Stange and Melissa Banta; directed by Eric Stange; written by Eric Stange, Melissa Banta, and Simon Schama; edited by Peter Rhodes.

Murderball: Produced by Jeffrey Mandel and Dana Adam Shapiro; directed by Henry Alex Rubin and Dana Adam Shapiro; edited by Geoffrey Richman.

My Architect: Produced by Susan Rose Behr and Nathaniel Kahn; directed, written, and narrated by Nathaniel Kahn; edited by Sabine Krayenbühl.

New York: A Documentary Film (series): Episodes 1–7 produced by Lisa Ades, Ric Burns, and Steve Rivo; directed by Ric Burns; written by Ric Burns and James Sanders (episode 5 with Ronald Blumer); edited by Li-Shin Yu, Edward Barteski, David Hanser, Nina Schulman, and Juliana Parroni; Episode 8 produced by Marilyn Ness and Ric Burns; directed by Ric Burns; written by James Sanders and Ric Burns; edited by Li-Shin Yu.

Nobody's Business: Produced, directed, and edited by Alan Berliner.

Recording The Producers: *A Musical Romp with Mel Brooks*: Produced by Susan Froemke and Peter Gelb; directed by Susan Froemke; co-directed and edited by Kathy Dougherty.

Roger & Me: Produced, directed, and written by Michael Moore; edited by Wendy Stanzler and Jennifer Beman.

Shelter Dogs: Produced by Heidi Reinberg and Cynthia Wade; directed by Cynthia Wade; edited by Geof Bartz.

Sing Faster: The Stagehands' Ring Cycle: Produced, directed, and written by Jon Else; edited by Deborah Hoffman and Jay Boekelheide.

So Much So Fast: Produced, written, and directed by Steven Ascher and Jeanne Jordan; edited by Jeanne Jordan.

Sound and Fury: Produced by Roger Weisberg; directed by Josh Aronson; edited by Ann Collins.

Southern Comfort: Produced, directed, written, and edited by Kate Davis.

Spellbound: Produced by Sean Welch and Jeffrey Blitz; directed by Jeffrey Blitz; edited by Yana Gorskaya.

Super Size Me: Produced by Morgan Spurlock and The Con; directed and written by Morgan Spurlock; edited by Stela Georgieva and Julie "Bob" Lombardi.

The Sweetest Sound: Produced, directed, and edited by Alan Berliner.

The Thin Blue Line: Produced by Mark Lipson; directed and written by Errol Morris; edited by Paul Barnes.

Troublesome Creek: A Midwestern: Produced, written, and directed by Jeanne Jordan and Steven Ascher; edited by Jeanne Jordan.

Vietnam: A Television History (series): Produced by Judith Vecchione, Elizabeth Deane, Andrew Pearson, Austin Hoyt, Martin Smith, and Bruce Palling; edited by Eric W. Handley, Carol Hayward, Ruth Schell, Eric Neudel, Glen Cardno, Paul Cleary, Mavis Lyons Smull, and Daniel Eisenberg; chief correspondent, Stanley Karnow; executive producer, Richard Ellison.

When the Levees Broke: Produced by Spike Lee and Sam Pollard; directed by Spike Lee; supervising editor Sam Pollard; edited by Sam Pollard, Geeta Gandbhir, and Nancy Novack.

Where Did You Get that Woman?: Directed by Loretta Smith.

Why He Skied: Produced, directed, and edited by Per Saari.

Winged Migration: Produced by Christophe Barratier and Jacques Perrin; directed by Jacques Perrin; written by Stéphane Durand and Jacques Perrin; edited by Marie-Josèphe Yoyotte.

Yosemite: The Fate of Heaven: Produced and directed by Jon Else; written by Michael Chandler and Jon Else; edited by Michael Chandler; executive produced and narrated by Robert Redford.

About the Author

Sheila Curran Bernard is an award-winning filmmaker, writer, and consultant with experience in the creation, development, and production of documentary programming for national broadcast, theatrical release, and museum and classroom use. Her work has been honored with an Emmy Award for writing, the George Foster Peabody Award for Excellence in Broadcast Journalism, and the Eric Barnouw Award from the Organization of American Historians. She has been a fellow at the MacDowell Colony and the Virginia Center for the Creative Arts, and recently served as the Anschutz Distinguished Fellow in American Studies at Princeton University.

Index